"The Cut-Away City" (available as a 25" x 34" poster–see Order Blanks)

the Velvet MonkeyWrench

By

JOHN MUIR

ILLUSTRATED BY
PETER ASCHWANDEN

OCEAN TREE BOOKS
SANTA FE & NEW ORLEANS

OCEAN TREE BOOKS
Post Office Box 1295
Santa Fe, New Mexico 87504
(505) 983-1412 • oceantre@trail.com

ISBN 0-943734-39-8
(supersedes 0-912528-02-8, 0-9662824-0-X)

CONTENTS

Advertisement

WHAT IT'S ABOUT
& SOME HABITS

COMING or going, we must view the new century with an eye toward the possible continuence of our species on this planet and I'd rather be coming.

Our history indicates that solid changes in establishments have been accomplished by the rise and fall of individual, focal point humans. There are so many of us now that a second Messiah, even, probably wouldn't be given equal television time with football or soap operas. If an individual cannot arise to save us from ourselves, our greed and our short-sightedness, maybe books can. Anyway, that's why I wrote this one. Maybe our going is inevitable. Maybe it's time for the next species, like ants, to have their chance to peacefully and profitably populate this lovely green and blue planet. But I think this is a piss poor, paranoid attitude. How about you? Cousteau said we have about fifty years left at our present rate of dumping poisons into the seas, which means that my own sons could die gasping for breath.

This book presents a way for mankind to exist on *this* planet, in balance, sensibly using what Earth has to offer. It explains a way to create a modern governmental structure, which gives the People, finally, the right to choose their present and their future: a blueprint for a consentual society. The structure is cellular, like people are and can expand and contract with the ebb and flow of population tides. A Utopia, a place where people are expected to act in a certain manner to gain a specific living end, has no relationship with reality and is certainly not the aim of this book, so cast it from your mind in front.

As the system we have doesn't wish to be changed—none of them do—the method for changing it is deliberately laid out to use the procedures provided by Their existing rules so change can be made without people being gassed, shot at, maced, ravaged by killer doberman dogs, jailed or having other indignities heaped upon their bodies. Many people are tired of the way the dice are loaded and want, at least, new dice in the game. We need a leaderless, bloodless, riot free change to a People's Establishment and Society: one in which we have something to say and which we have a part in forming. **Complete directions enclosed.**

5

This book is divided into eighteen handholding Segments which make a complete circle. This means the WHOLE thing is one package and if some part is not explained where you are reading, read on with the confidence that your questions will be answered. Be patient: the threads of the net do mesh.

SEMANTICS is the science of Communication of Meaning. We all have semantic habits, especially me, a writer. Here are some of my habits:

Where I use a noncontextual stopper like, *OK?* or *Right?*, I simply mean for you to pause and think about what was just said before dashing on. OK?

I use the word *like* where I give an example knowing there are probably many more. Like, that's the way I talk.

Throughout the book I define words as I go along, words for which I might have different definitions than you. For starters, here's the way I feel about:

KNOWLEDGE is what we take in with our senses.

UNDERSTANDING is the action verb of knowledge, what we *use* of it, what we actually *do* of our knowledge.

WISDOM is what we pass on of the knowledge we *really* understand.

BULLSHIT is passing on knowledge without understanding. (Do as I say, not as I do.)

TEACHING is unfortunately generally bullshit.

LEARNING is taking in knowledge and converting it to understanding.

WRITING is a mixture of bullshit and wisdom with humor as a suppository.

When I speak about *Them* with a capital T, it indicates a Power Group, a bunch of people acting together to program *US* into doing what *THEY* want done.

If you and a friend can read the book aloud to each other, some things may be clearer, as I tend to write the way I talk. If you can see me smiling as I write these pages (generally true) perhaps you can smile a little, too.

The book talks a lot about things like Justice, Money and Business—much more than most people will ever need to know to practice the art of living together. I tried to cover all cases: answer as many *What about if* questions as I could, so you can pick your own degree of involvement.

I feel really good about being able to lay out this structure, the bones of a completely new establishment, leaving the living filling to you. I've thought and consulted with my friends for many years and now I'd like to flush it out, all I know and understand about it, then process the effluent to fertilize my mind's garden.

STAY WITH ME WHILE I REACH UP AND PULL THE CHAIN

IN WHICH WE LEARN NOT TO LEAVE CHANGE TO CHANCE

THERE'S nothing *wrong* with the present establishment that isn't also *wrong* with 14 year olds who are outgrowing their clothes.

Our *child* is about 200 years old and has grown from a population of four million to over 200 million. It's over 50 times as big as the *clothes* cut for it. Everything it has to wear is too small and out of date.

There's nothing in the present establishment that doesn't need changing on one level or another.

We invented the system we have and have been ingeniously stretching it, but the elasticity is gone and it's time to come up with something new.

Do you know about earthquakes? An earthquake is a sudden movement of the earth along a fault line: an adjustment to the slow, steady displacement the two sides of the fault have been making for some time. On one side of a fault line, the land moves in a different direction than the land on the other side. When the two sides adjust to each other suddenly, the jolt shakes the earth violently and topples things. Throughout history, the act of changing establishments has followed the earthquake pattern. Wars, revolutions and bloody purges are ecologically wasteful and costly earth jolting type shakeups. We cannot afford to go that route anymore. Some peaceful solution to our displacement-adjustment problem is necessary so we can use our remaining resources to their continuence. There is a great difference between mankind's needs before Whitney's cotton gin and what they are now. It's time to deliberately change the establishment to fit what we have become. This book presents some deliberate changes to use as grease or other slippery stuff to lubricate the fault line so things will smoothly *slide* to an adjustment with maybe a few minor tremors.

In order that a people change their society, the individual members of that society must be able to change. **CHANGING is applying intelligence to movement. BEING CHANGED is what happens to you when outside events force you to get different.**

We can look at the whole changing scene as a game of chess or checkers. The board is where you are and the piece on the board is you. We want to move ourselves intelligently on the board instead of being moved by that Giant Invisible Hand: by THEM. The game is to be played without any idea of winning or losing. In this struggle for human survival we are all on the same side.

However, just moving doesn't hack it. Take the example of living in New York, hating it, hating yourself, the crowds, the crime, the cold, the heat, the long walk up and the bills you owe; so you decide to move to L.A. That will make a Change, you say. But after a couple of months in L.A. with the eye-burning smog, the crowds, the crime, the absolute need for a car, your New York bills have caught up with you and you now hate L.A. and yourself even more. That is a Demand Change; you move to L.A. and demand that it Change you—L.A. can't, Buddha couldn't. **Changing you is your job and only you can do it.**

Now I didn't say that Changes don't occur out of Demand Change type things; the New Yorker could get picked up for Vag, get sent to the L.A. County Jail and therein get hooked on heroin—that's a Change! When you make a Demand Change, you have no choice of Change and have to accept the Changing given you.

It takes Juice to Change, can you dig it? JUICE OF CHANGE! variously called *Qi, Kundalini, Righteousness, Go Power, Neural Energy,* you name it. I call it *Juice.* Each name implies a different method of raising it; like Yoga, Zen, Chinese Moving Meditation, Worshiping God—they will all work, just pick one.

You have to dig it where you are (you choose the way) long enough to build up some juice of change—then change!

After you decide on a change, rest, think, meditate; give it some time, then, when you're strong and full of Juice, take the action toward change. Hating yourself and wishing you were elsewhere or somebody else only keeps the Juice Barrel empty.

Only you can change yourself. Really. No one else can change you, nor can you change anybody else. Take a good look at some of your changings and you'll find that the real changes you make are those that you can develop (usually quite sneakily) into your own idea—make it something YOU thought of. Like when your Mother tells you that eating sugar will make holes in your teeth, do you stop eating sugar? No, you don't, not until you've had a couple of painful sessions with the dentist. THEN you can make not eating candy bars your own idea.

To make deliberate Changes requires practice, certain delicate communications between the various departments within us and a lot of a thing called *Seeking Agreement*. Here's a personal example to clarify my point: I am a very experienced Smoking Quitter, and I do mean Quitter. Every so often, with the Lung Department screaming at the work load, I can build up enough Juice to actually quit—withdrawal symptoms, nerves like a shattered cat and real true primeval HUNGER—so I suffer and EAT! One month, two, I get on the scale and find the body like 10 kilos up and I hear from the Heart Department, "My God, John! You're carrying a 10 kilo suitcase around full of useless fat just on account of that damn Lung Department," so I diet, which all the departments hate. Pretty soon Wormtongue is cravenly whispering, "Man, if you smoke a little, you won't need to diet so much." On goes the eternal internal argument; soon there's enough support for a plebescite and the Lung Department loses, but not without some qualifications—only the purest pipe tobacco, lovingly rolled into the purest rice paper and only a few a day—then a few more and more until the Lungs are again getting signatures on their petition. As yet, I haven't made the trip to Virginia to find out if my tobacco is organically grown, but I may have to to keep the uneasy peace now existing. All the outside influences in the Universe couldn't make me quit; laws, Nagging Wife, cancer ads. First I gotta work the idea around to where it's my own, then persuade all the departments to agree to make the change. Please note: *changes of this sort need not be considered permanent changes in order to be effective.*

The kind of changes that we People can make are in the direction of harmony, humor, helping and honor among ourselves, which simply means feeling good together. All the changes proposed in this book head in that direction.

Here's a change we can start practicing on to get ready for the bigger changes later: Take war—make it humorous—FUNNY—by laughing at people who are involved in creating situations that allow wars to develop. If all of us can really see War as funny, not serious, that bell ringing over there is the death knell of War. Like: "You're a General? HA HA HA, HO HO HO, HEE HEE HEE," rolling on the floor in the throes of uncontrollable laughter. Or in the draft center: "You want me to be a soldier and go out there angry enough at other people to kill them with one of them M-1's? HA HA HA, HO HO HO," and you roll on the floor some more. Or, "Your job is what? Making things to kill People!" Hee Hee! With this attitude, war is dead.

Here's another change to practice on: We can change our heads about errors. ERRORS ARE NECESSARY. It makes little difference *who* makes them as long as *someone* does, so WE can learn from them.

Another change some of us will have to make is how we feel about machines. Machines and computers are our tools. We cannot dis-invent them, but we can be willing to concede that our life styles are the way they are because of machines. Without them we'd be living a much simpler, day-to-day life, which is a groove, if that's what you choose, but for me it's limiting and foraging for food is impossible for all. For the second straight year in a row the world has not produced enough food to feed its population. In order to get maximum yield, machines are needed. And consider Baggies.

The change needed is to admit we're committed to the machine, then resolve to what degree. If we admit the degree of involvement each of us personally has with machines, we can have something to say about the use of the ones needed to maintain our individual life styles. Not all of US need to know how they work, but some of us do. We are being pushed around by computers because they're in the hands of those who want the pushing around power and admit they are committed to the use of the computer. In order to be in Business, for example, a company needs a computer and admits it.

If we want to use machines and make them OUR slaves, we must first admit we need them, then understand that a machine can only do what the people who run it tell it to. Machines can be made to work for life instead of against life depending on who is telling them what to do. Programming a computer to *compose music*, then asking a group of human musicians to play it, has never been successful. There's a big difference between this and a bunch of cats getting together and using all kinds of electronic machines to create the sound they want.

There's a real communications problem. If we don't speak the same language as our slaves, how are we going to tell them what to do? For instance, *Car* is a language that most of us learn enough of to drive one, but few ever learn enough

Car to be able to fix one. To tell a washer, "Work forever, Idiot," shows you don't understand washerese. It'll work, OK, just as long as you let it (clean corrosive soaps out of its moving parts) and for as long as it was built to work.

To understand machines better, let's examine our bodies as machines. Take pouring. Pour yourself a drink: did you spill...a drop, two drops...a lot? I once watched a kid in a gas station pour gasoline directly into a narrow gas tank neck without losing a drop...he is totally out of my class! I have to use a funnel. Learning to control the machines we live in is a way to learn how machines made by humans are controlled. The same type of circuits humans use are used to make machines do what we want them to do. In order to be efficient, we make many of our physiological controls totally automatic by practice. A machine's controls must be designed, constructed and coordinated with function before the machine is even started up. Being automatic makes control a little hard to control in both humans and machines and very often accuracy must be sacrificed for necessity. Like on a dark night, outta gas, you lug a gallon can from the nearest station with no funnel...you're lucky to get half the gas into the tank, the rest all over the car and yourself. Spilling is not *bad*, only something to wipe up—wasteful. Just so, inaccurate machines are wasteful.

A big difference between us and machines is: the human machine gets better with practice, but the machines we make can only wear out with use.

Something that's hard for us to understand is machine humor; the little tricks and breakdowns when we need them most. When the repairer finally comes, the thing works fine. Often they wear out before they're even paid for. All these things are funny if we speak their language. I can bust a knuckle underneath the car and keep my cool because I know where I am in relation to it and cursing only dims that relationship.

These are just practice Changes, but ones that will give us some idea of the kind of thing we're learning to do. This book is about making some very serious Changes without any of us getting hurt and will require each of us to make some Changes in ourselves. Our learning curve on Changing has to take a sharp break toward decreasing the amount of time it takes us to make a proposed Change our own idea, like one you thought of yourself. We have to have open minds about new ideas and new concepts. The Open Mind and The Open Road and The Open Hand should not be confused with The Open Mouth.

Remember there is nothing really *wrong* with the present Establishment; it just needs to be changed to fit the facts of today's thinking, today's population and today's technology. In order to Change it, we must examine its bases, its roots. A man named Korzybski got to thinking about the differences between us and all the other animals and came up with the observation that the main difference is a thing called TIMEBINDING! Timebinding is the ability to write and then read; the ability to store data to pass on to future generations; the ability to bind time so ALL the data can be used now and in the future for making decisions. Porpoises communicate with each other probably as well as we can with other humans, but if they do store knowledge, it's only from memory to memory, not in books.

From our ability to Timebind, we have pretty good evidence that centuries ago the philosophy of **Might is Everything** was the order of the day. The change in that philosophy came with the Greeks, or at least they timebound the change to the two-valued philosophy of **Right and Wrong**. This *new* thinking, from over two thousand years ago, has been passed on to us virtually untouched by human mind until just recently. Of course, Might is Everything is also still with us.

It is difficult to impress the magnitude of this Change from the single-valued Might is Everything to the two-valued Right and Wrong philosophy on you who have been thoroughly indoctrinated and raised in the two-valued logic of our Civilization, but you gotta see that it changed a lot of things. It presents the idea of a conscience; it keeps people from fooling with other people's things; it makes technology possible. A machine is either *off* or *on*—a thing either works or it doesn't. It leads to the idea that things that are *Right* are *Right* all the time and the same with things that are *Wrong*. Two ways of looking at everything is a lot more complicated than one way and when a trip like that gets sold, it's damn hard to change.

Many people's thinking has now evolved beyond this two-valued logic to a **Multi-Valued** logic which states that there are an infinite number of positions between *Right* and *Wrong, bad* and *good*, even *moral-immoral, legal-illegal.* There are many shades of gray between black and white, many needle positions between *Full* and *Empty*. **Even relativity is relative!**

In his book, *General Semantics*, Korzybski tried mightily to help us learn, step by step, how to become Multi-Valued. Capsulated his ideas are:

THOU SHALT NOT IDENTIFY!

THOU SHALT NOT REACT!

THOU SHALT BE CONSCIOUS OF ABSTRACTING!

With these admonitions properly ground in and practiced, it was guaranteed that your mind would cease and desist the practice of judging everything on a *right-wrong* basis. Because it is important that we all have the same chance to kick this habit, I will define: **IDENTIFICATION: the process of confusing the name with the thing**. The term *apple* is not really an apple but just the word we use, plus adjectives, to describe the actual fruit. It is not the fruit. Is your mind constantly trying to establish a word or a symbol to describe an object, a thought or an idea? Does your mind really think in words? If it does, you've been taught by identification and it takes a hulluva lot of difficult training to stop your automatic mind from identifying the Word with the Thing. I am not even proposing that you try. Just admit that you do. To whom? To yourself. If you **understand** that Western learning has taught you to identify the semantic symbol with the actuality, you are well on the road toward clarifying your communications.

Take the word *Chick.* What immediate picture does it make in your head? Here are some examples from friends: a baby chicken, something yellow, a coward, a woman, a girl, *my* girl, trouble. In the U.S. the word *Chick* is identified with so many different things it's become dangerous to use.

REACTION: an action taken immediately, without thinking, after a stimulus; the absence of thinking; instant decision. If seeing or hearing the word *Chick* or *Boy* causes a flurry in your insides, you are reacting. Do the letters xes cause a flurry? How about sex?

The first about seven years of our lives while we have little or no conscious minds, nor vocabularies to make them work, are spent in a totally reactive condition: hunger-tit-embrace are nice forever. With vocabulary and experience come a certain amount of thinking, but mostly we learn and are taught *habits* and *conditioned reflexes* just like dogs, man, DOGS. That's the way they teach us—learning habits, bathroom habits, table manner habits, you name it habits and if you carry this out to its fullest, like, thinking habits—they actually teach us thinking habits. A habit makes for reaction and a reaction is the absence of thinking, so how in hell do they get on a crazy trip like that? It's the bell or button pushing Power Game. And the more buttons you have available for others to push, the more power you allow them over you.

The mind thinks in similarities and differences, not in reactive *right-wrong* terms. When you think about something you consider it, use your inborn ability to compare it with the other things in your mind to see if some similarity exists, and to what degree. Every event taken in by your senses on which you're expected to act must go through the same long laborious process of comparison to be considered thought. If the process isn't long and laborious; that's *reacting.* Astronauts use a *Moon Flight Simulator* to take thousands of trips to the moon without ever leaving Houston. Each trip is made with varied and varying conditions: there you are in the middle of space without Oxygen—your tail just fell off; what do you do now?—like that. Your Simulator allows you to imagine the end results of certain actions; allows you to take trips without going; that's *thinking.*

Now I never said reacting is *Bad;* there are reactions we want and ones we don't. Athletes and musicians must practice until their movements are automatic—reactive—without thinking, so their minds are free to think about where the ball should go or about how they sound. To think or not to think is a function of the Time involved; when you have time, think and when you don't, reaction is what's left—so enjoy.

Think before you speak is an old admonition, but it doesn't mean think about what you are going to say next. It really means to think about what the other person is saying, then think about what you are going to say in reply. When thinking, you consider every sensual event as brand new—never seen before—then run it through your mental equipment to determine response, which may be the same or different from the times before. An *opinion* is the answer to something you have thought about once and are not willing to think about again, even though the way things are may have since changed. So, an opinion is a kind of reaction.

Thinking is a slower event-response cycle than reacting and if you wish to convince everybody that you are a great thinker, pause after you have seen or heard something—you know, like count to ten or even twenty if you can hold your face straight that long, then reply or remark. If you keep your cool, speak in lower tones and make every word seem somehow to count, plus listen intently to what the others are saying and wait very patiently for your turn, you can build up a helluva reputation as a heavy thinker. That's what I did and it not only works reputationwise, but you actually do start thinking. So the total answer to beating the reaction thing is to pause between event and response and your head will take care of the rest. Check this out by remembering what you would have said had you made an immediate reply, then compare it to what you actually say on the count of twenty and see which is the reply you prefer.

CONSCIOUSNESS OF ABSTRACTING: the realization that others have totally different definitions for words and verbal ideas than ours. Words like *communism, freedom, liberty* are abstractions and make no sense to anybody but us; they are blahs or worse in the listener's head unless we carefully define them as we use them and state clearly just how we are using them—and that's a drag when the wine is flowing. So what we do is just go ahead and use them, fully realizing that we're being semantic boors, and if we get blank looks and misunderstandings, we have to start defining our terms. There's a trick we can learn about being semanticists: put every abstraction in quotes like, "I saw some *hippies* on the street today and they looked like *Communists*." It's just a little raise of the voice which, with practice, gets the point across: "I am using a word which may mean something else to the hearer and definition is available." OK?

The way to instant multi-valuedness is to go ahead and develop the head—be a brain OK—and now add a quality called *Feeling* to our semantic efforts—add feeling to what we are saying and pick up on the feeling being expressed to us—feel about everything. This doesn't mean to feel *bad* or *good* or *right* or *wrong*, in fact, if we FEEL, the minute we feel, we'll find those things have lost all validity. The answer to conversion from our taught, learned, propagandized two-valued value-judgement reactions is to add your feelings to the product of your brain.

Adding feeling to intelligence, then considering the whole event-response cycle as a process of feeling is the path to multi-valued living!

The various parts that are together with me in this entity, in this body, in this symbiosis, must all cooperate to make a life No part has total control over the rest. My lungs are important; my kidneys are important, so I will learn how to care for them by breathing pure air and by eating unpoisoned food. My brain has an important part, but is not the Boss. My interest is in Being—Being whatever all of me is and can be.

Please note: I never said anything about getting emotional about anything. **EMOTION: an insane feeling. INSANE: out of control.** So, emotion is an out of control feeling, one for which we feel no responsibility and which drives our lives instead of our doing the driving—remember, not *bad*. Who likes to ball *sanely*? People (like missionaries and orators) who are trying to create an emotion in us about something are creating a kind of insanity.

Emotions and opinions clanging together in the head create the effect of living in a boiler factory.

"While we have been so completely enchanted with the two-valued thinking, what the hell has happened to the old single-valued, Might is Everything, idea?" you ask. Well, the State has it and uses it. On the State level, even on a crowd, mob or corporate level, the conscience disappears, *Right-Wrong, Moral-Immoral,* even *Legal-Illegal* disappear and in their place rises *Might is Everything for State and Mob.* You can see why they don't want us to gather in groups, Parade and Demonstrate—they are afraid we will revert to the single-valued Might is Everything idea and plunge humanity into a new chaos. Have you ever considered that what you are afraid of, you get?

When you think about it, you'll be totally amazed at the amount of time the single-valued State spends training and propagandizing US into a two-valued philosophy so we can be depended on to REACT whenever THEY push our button, ring the dinner bell, wave the flag and all those other things THEY do when they want us to kill or salivate or BUY CHEVROLET. We have been deliberately conditioned into two-valued thinking, because if we revert to Might is Everything and get out of hand, They will have to kill a bunch of US—*bad* for the *Image*.

Fighting THEM is NOT the answer.

HUMANKIND MUST LEARN TO PROGRESS WITHOUT CONTENTION

THEY cannot see and I really mean CANNOT SEE that WE are not interested in returning or regressing to Might is Everything. WE ARE NOT ON A POWER TRIP but are interested in a more complicated, more efficient, more responsible type of Establishment in which we do not have to do what THEY say, but get to decide for ourselves what we are going to do. So, we are not going to fight them because that is PLAYING THEIR GAME, which they gotta win because they are also the Rules Committee. We're going to start a new game for which People will make their own rules. If enough of US learn to feel and think and live with multi-valued logic, we can create a two-valued *Right-Wrong* Establishment in time to replace the old *Might is Everything* conscienceless State so we're not destroyed when the quake comes. Then we the multi-valued (hopefully all the People) will be able to decide what is *Right* or *Wrong* for the Establishment and our ecology. We'll be in a position to decide questions such as, "Is chewing up the continent what we really want to do?" "What is waste?" "What is pollution?" and put in a little "Consideration for Everybody." **The systems humans set up to govern themselves must be philosophically simpler than the philosophy of the individual humans.**

A while ago I mentioned that MANKIND MUST PROGRESS WITHOUT CONTENTION and I feel some definitions are due, so: **TO PROGRESS: to go forth.** Contention is that human quality exhibited by the two upright husky, exuberant football players who, in an intercollegiate football GAME, deliberately jumped on my left knee when it was already on the ground and destroyed the cruxious ligament. They did this so their TEAM would have a better chance of Winning the Game with me out of it. I certainly was and have had a bum knee ever since. Contention, then, is putting the other fellow *down* or out of the Game, so you can win. The syndrome—Our Team (school, business, town, church, whatever) is *Right* and theirs is *Wrong*, therefore we can put 'em down, step on 'em, kill 'em, or whatever becomes necessary to *Win*—has gotta STOP.

A way to practice stopping is to call the Game by its true name in the first place. If I'd known the name of the game was *Cripple Your Opponent*, I would not have been playing or, at least, I could have played by THEIR rules. The two alternatives to Contention are Competition and Cooperation and all three are admittedly *Higher Order Abstractions.* **CONTENTION, like I said, is jumping on a guy's leg when he's down to get him out of the game so you can win; COMPETITION is helping a guy to his feet so the game can be won by the team with the ability to win; COOPERATION cannot be applied to situations where winning is the thing** but Delattre's *Tales of a Dalai Lama* tells of a Game the Tibetan Monks play in which they all hit the ball to keep it up in the air and feel a little sad when they miss and it touches the ground—that's COOPERA-TION.

We are in the process of learning to eliminate CONTENTION because putting people down to win is outadate, but I feel that COMPETITION is necessary at this time because the basic nature of Mankind is directed toward striving and reaching a little bit further—the desire to win. Winning is something most of us like to do, I guess, but is no *better* than losing. My son came home from school P.E. with a strange notion about tennis. He had been taught how to win and how to keep score, but his mother had to show him how to stroke the ball smoothly and cleanly and straighten out his head about how keeping score usually has your mind on that and your eye somewhere else besides on the ball. In tennis, people and cats, stroking is more important than keeping score. Perhaps when we have evolved a bit more, we can try for: Progress through Cooperation. However, there are many living situations where it is *not* necessary to win, so we can learn to apply cooperation wherever we can.

For example, we can stop teaching our children that everyone is out to *get* them—or even that some people are—stop using bogey men to force them into some action we want. If you're taught that people are out to do you in, you expect it all the time and it colors your relationships with others, at least until you know them well enough to *trust* them. Even when you really *trust* your business or living partner, you're still on the lookout—a little. What can happen if you're completely open and *not on the lookout*? Occasionally you're *had,* but it becomes an isolated event instead of a justification of everything you've been taught. If we help each other protect our things, our living situations and teach our children the same, it will be possible to eliminate the hiring of some of us to guard the rest of us from each other. And who is guarding US from THEM?

In this first Segment, I've been talking about Changing: changing our logic from two-valued to multi-valued: changing our Establishment's logic from Might is Everything to a two-valued one so People can have something to say about their lives. Remember, being two-valued isn't *wrong*, in fact, it is totally necessary for business and technology. But living as if we people were push-aroundable machines is boring, unnecessary, old fashioned and a stone drag.

Over thousands of years, Humans have learned and nurtured many Rights. Since Rights are hard to come by, they are hard to give up. But there are ten of these Rights we no longer need, in fact, need not to have, in order to create the structure of our new establishment. Each of them that we give up makes a part of the overall structure possible. So: In order for Humans to LEARN TO PROGRESS WITHOUT CONTENTION and really have a little CONSIDERATION for everyone, let's agree to give up these Rights:

The Right to let others make decisions for us.

The Right to let others classify us.

The Right to profit financially by Death.

The Right to lay OUR trips on EVERYONE.

The Right to possess the Four Elements.

The Right to lie about what we did or agreed to do.

The Right to count Money.

The Right to Contend.

The Right to limit learning.

The Right to "not wait" for Transportation.

A Segment will cover each of these in detail while laying out the bones of the new Establishment.

HUMANKIND MUST LEARN TO PROGRESS WITHOUT CONTENTION

DECISION, "the *act* of making up one's mind," says Webster and I only feel we can change it to read: the *art* of making up one's own mind. If we start thinking of it as an *art* instead of as an *act*, maybe we'll sit down and really learn it then do it, so we are no longer dependent on other people's decisions.

The Right to make our own decisions has always been an undeniable Right, you say? The hell you say! We haven't been allowed by the present establishment to even make our own simple, "Do I really need a deodorant?" type of decision—we are conditioned to having a choice of *which* but not *if*. We are seduced, blatted at, class conscienced into making the decisions THEY want us to make. Since, as yet anyway, there are no courses taught in school about how to make decisions, like

19

'Decisions 1A,' here's an idea of how to go about learning the art of Do It Your-self decisions.

The nitty-gritty bones of 'Decisions 1A' would say: Decisions and reactions must be considered separately; a reaction is an act which has been conditioned and is done without thought, while a decision just plain requires thinking about. Habits and conditioned reflexes are not decisions; they are reactions.

A decision must be delayed to the last possible moment so that all the available data can be at hand when the decision must actually be made.

The old saw, **A coward dies a thousand deaths, the hero dies but once,** is definitely applicable to decision making. The worrier makes the decision a thousand ways and even after the action has been taken, seldom is deep-down certain while the hero, the person who has learned to make decisions, makes only one decision, at the second it must be made, and is sure about it because that was the action taken.

EVERYTHING THAT IS HAPPENING OR HAS HAPPENED IS EXACTLY RIGHT.

There is a definite *time-gap* relationship between the time the decision is firmed up and ready to act on and the actual action. This *time gap* depends on the portion of our time and our lives the decision is going to affect; like, if the decision you are making will affect one hour of your life, make it instantly; if it will affect a week, wait an hour before acting; if five years is involved, like buying a new car on the *never never* , you might want at least 24 hours after picking our the car as a minimum *decision time gap*, but three days would be surer before signing the contract. If you are thinking about a partnership or any living relationship that may last your lifetime, maybe six weeks should elapse between the time you decide to do it and actually making the scene operational. What this means is simply that after deciding to tie up our lifetimes, let's wait six weeks before doing it, OK?

We must also allow others their right to this *decision time gap*...just get used to doing it.

'Decisions 1A' would include many methods for gathering data using all our senses, then sorting it to use as bases for making decisions so that accurate end result predictions can be made. Here's an example of data gathering: I ask all the writers I meet if they describe their own sexual experiences or if they describe imaginary or vicarious experiences. With one exception, they all (about 50 so far) have admitted that they wrote about imagined experiences. I collected this data from curiosity and it has no basis of need, but look at what we have had timebound for us in the books we read—imaginary sexual experiences. Think about how many other kinds of *bad* data you may be taking in in this way.

DECISIONS MUST BE MADE WITH ALL OF YOU.

Your brain is only the calculator, computer of your mind, and must be kept to the level of its own excellence which is help in obtaining, then sorting, classifying and remembering data. When the brain has done its work, the mind can be assured that it has all the available information on which to base a decision and the mind's end product comes out as a feeling.

In order to feel decisions, that is, allow the way we really feel about something to tell us the way to decide (so we know it's not a false opinion created within us by others), we will need to learn to sort and classify all the available data with our brains, deliberately not making anything even faintly resembling a decision until the actual dive into cold water. Then, when that moment comes, allow our feelings to decide the action. This process must be learned, practiced, memorized, but not talked about. The minute we start to talk about a decision we are going to make, our talking about it allows our brains to have more to say about that decision than they should. It's one thing to gather data and another to talk about the decision, OK? Therefore, committing yourself about decisions by talking about them is bullshit, just feel about them at the exact time they must be made using all the equipment instead of just the egoistic brain.

DECISIONS TO BE REAL MUST BE FELT RATHER THAN HEARD.

'Decisions 1A' would be taught to 11 year olds so by the time they reach 12, kids can be counted on to make their very own feeling decisions—thought about, considered and time gapped—based on their very own needs, desires and abilities to pay their own *dues* for the way they decide.

DUES: what we must do that we don't like to do to get what we do like. To be doctors, for instance, people not only have to spend a lot of years studying but also have to put up with having their movements restricted for their practicing years. For some of us this is heavy dues but others dig to be doctors in spite of the dues. OK on dues? Dues are different for everyone.

And let's not forget to give and take 'Decisions 7A and 7B,' which are remedial courses in decision making for adults. 7A is like 1A and says: Decision, the art of making up one's own mind, which is composed of brain, senses, glands and feelings. The course then gives instructions on how to feel; instructions which children don't need. 7B is a course in the art of *un*-making up one's mind/brain/subconscious about all those already decided opinions.

The brain is a computer, right? OK, now what the hell happens when an adding machine (a simple computer) has one stuck key? All its calculations have the stuck key either added to or subtracted from the answer. 'Decisions 7B' would be limited to the unsticking of the stuck keys we have about people and relationships with people. If we can unstick most of these keys, people can start to make clear uncluttered decisions about other people. Example, please? OK, "Communists want to take over the world and they are evil. Fulano, the Communist, therefore is evil." There's no question about this, is there? The stuck key is the conditioned statement that "Commies are evil." Fulano may be a college professor whose greatest offense is picking his nose in private and thinking that Karl Marx was a great man. If you decided long ago that you can't stand tomatoes, your ability to make cool decisions will probably not be much affected, but if in your head you find any fixed, rooted, already made from a long time ago, conditioned (often parentally) ideas about yourself, other humans or groups of humans, sit up and listen because you haven't made a clearly defined real honest decision about ANYbody, especially about yourself, since those stuck keys were conditioned in you. We have to eliminate prejudicial opinions before having valid thoughts about people is possible. Premade and/or fixed ideas about the way we are going to feel about an individual person or group of people are stuck keys.

OK, so now we all know how to make our own decisions, so now what? It is time in the course of human events for man, woman, MAN, WOMAN to start to take a mite of responsibility for our own actions and here we find ourselves living in an establishment that has been conditioned and has conditioned us into allowing THEM to make OUR decisions. We have to set up an establishment wherein we not only make our own personal decisions, but our community ones as well.

At the present time, we elect other people to make all of our important decisions for us: people we don't know, have never talked to and have maybe seen only on the telly. We have been electing painted, ghost-written images for years expecting them to make competent decisions for us. An ability to stay out of trouble is the main characteristic required for election to a public office, not any ability to work for the people. If we wish to make our own decisions, we must build a new structure to govern ourselves, one in which we get to make all the decisions concerning ourselves then stand ready to pay whatever dues that brings.

I have asked over 100 intelligent people what part of a building an engineer must design first and, again with one exception, they have all flatly stated, "The foundation, of course!" (I didn't ask any engineers.) What do you think? Before the answer? OK? The first thing engineers design is the flagpole and they think about things like is it ever going to be used for a flagpole sitting contest? Or is it ever going to need painting? If so, then it has to be able to hold a person's weight. But right under the flagpole is the ROOF, which is the correct answer. The engineer must know what the roof is going to look like, have on it and weigh before designing the next floor down, which must hold the roof. The next floor can then be designed to hold the floor above plus the roof and finally when all the weights and stresses that will be supported by the foundation and what kind of strength the soil has to resist all these things are known, our engineer can design the foundation which, of course is last. However, it is the first part to be built.

Our forefathers, tenscore minus a few years ago, when they designed our present government's structure didn't know all this nor did they know that all this balling and birthing would occur. While they designed a helluva foundation they forgot about the roof, so what we have now is a tremendous umbrella. This umbrella has been extended to cover all of us from Alaska to Texas and over to Hawaii. You should see the damn thing from a structural engineer's viewpoint. All they've done for years is repair and patch it and if it ever did drop on us, just the stuff they've used to repair it would damage a lot of people, so let's get with it and stop repairing the old and build us something new—like maybe new barns.

OK, Barns. Let's look at governments all over the world as though they were barns and see what that brings. There are straw barns, adobe barns, wooden barns, steel barns, all kinds of barns and the paint they paint them with is the name of the political system. OK, so we have red barns, true blue barns, barns that aren't painted at all because of lack of bread and funny mixed up stripey barns where they can't make up their minds what to call themselves, but beneath all this paint the barns are being run by Bureaus. These Bureaus, non-elective throughout, do all the actual work of government: all the people-pushing, the law enforcement, the tax collecting and spending of the people's money. Bureaus the world around operate under Parkinson's Law which can be stated: *any government supported agency tends to increase in size and expense as time passes with no regard for work load.* A bureau has no responsibility to the people and there's no way for the people to tell any bureau what they want.

Let's see what we can come up with from Webster as a definition for the word *government:* "The exercise of authority; a system of ruling, controlling; a system of political administration for a political division." Here's more Webster:

"*Democracy:* government by the people either directly or through elected representatives; rule by the ruled; majority rule.

"*Republic:* a state or nation in which the supreme power rests in all the citizens entitled to vote (the electorate), and is exercised by representatives elected, directly or indirectly, by them and responsible to them; common interest, the public, (obs).

"*Franchise:* to make free from servitude, the right to vote, suffrage.

"*Enfranchise:* to give liberty to."

What's needed is a rewording and reunderstanding of what these lovely words mean. If we can agree on and stick to some definitions, maybe government by Bureau can slide softly down the drain as it well should. Let's elevate government to the status of a science which allows it to be two-valued instead of the single-valued *Might is Everything.*

GOVERNMENT: the science and the art of finding out what the people want to do and then helping them to do it.

DEMOCRACY: government by the People directly, with elected Representatives whose jobs are to determine what the majority of the People wish to do, then help them do it.

REPUBLIC: a governmental organization in which the supreme power rests with the citizens.

As **FRANCHISE** means to make free from servitude as well as the right to vote, let's combine the two meanings so we're free to vote the way we really feel.

IS GOVERNMENT OF, FOR AND BY THE PEOPLE WHAT WE REALLY WANT? I am assuming that we all have made this decision affirmatively. OK? And in order to make such a government, we have got to get Power Groups totally out of the action.

When our founding fathers created the present governmental system, there was nothing like Big Business or Labor Unions. The power group was made up of land holders in a nation of farmers, traders, trappers, hunters, slaves and Indians, so it is a miracle that the system they created has lasted so long and done so well. The land holders lost out to Big Business in the Civil War; then Labor Unions and other power groups arose to counterbalance Big Business. And instead of any idea of *cooperation*, there is constant *contention* with Big Business generally *winning.* If we are to survive on this planet, we must stop wasting our Ecology for the enrichment of a few. The general idea is to disenfranchise super powerful lobbies as well as Wealth to create a system in which every Citizen will have a vote and that vote will really count as part of the People's Decision. And every single variation and nuance of government will actually be made by voting on it, so the decision of the group is the sum of the decisions of the individuals in the group. In order to be really franchised, we as individuals put our votes into a pot so the decision of the majority is a *conglomerate decision* and not some sort of *average opinion*, which is as close as we get right now.

Because individuals vary, individual decisions vary. Each person's decisions are totally valid from that individual's viewpoint, the place the person is standing while looking at something. City dwellers are concerned about the rising mountains of shit, plastic and metal which threaten to engulf them so they must provide for their removal from their sight and smell. The farmer calmly plows the things that will plow back into the soil and uses the rest as fill material in some arroyo. When we talk to either about the garbage problem, we are dealing with totally differing viewpoints and when we try to make the same laws apply to both, we are being silly.

A BASIC DECISION WE MUST MAKE IS TO SEEK AGREEMENT WITH OTHERS.

We need to change the kinds of Barns we have altogether. Since we don't really know what kind of Barn we need, we have to build flexible Barns that can be changed with time, with the total individual decisions of the People and with the fluctuations of the ecology—and the paint? You choose the color but I'd like to see them left natural with many coats of oil and wax lovingly applied.

These new Barns, to make sense, must be smaller, built to house a certain number of people and built by the people who are going to live there in harmony with the ecological situation that exists where the Barn is built. The old huge Barn we can use as a museum to house all the relics of the way things used to be: policemen's uniforms, pistols, judges' gavels and like that. It will be a great place to spend an idle afternoon. There will be a push-button sound movie explaining how before the Change humans had allowed their government to become a gigantic, inefficient dictatorial agency which told them what to do, instead of them telling IT what to do and everyone will laugh a bit and some of the older people might shed a tear or two. The movie will go on to show how people were so convinced of their impotency that it took them years even after they understood that it had to be changed to make the change.

So we're going to construct a whole new thing based on People and what are you made of? Sugar and spice, puppy dog's tails? Who me? Cells, I guess. And what are cells? They're little things that divide to multiply and crawl around toward food and you can see them under a microscope—we had 'em in school. And if we are made up of cells, what do we have to make up? Cells, I guess. Right! OK, if you were going to construct a cell made of people, how many will it take would you say? Oh, about a thousand, I guess. That's about all the People I could relate to as part of a community. OK, a thousand, but what the hell are you talking about? I'm talking about the fact that any organization made up *by* humans must be organized *like* a human.

Any organization made by humans must be organized like the human organism to make any sense at all.

So if we are going to succeed in governing ourselves, we have to start with cells: self-governing cells of about a thousand souls who get to know each other well enough to be able to live together under the same set of living rules. Let's call these cells Neighborhoods and place some definite limits on them. Cells of less than 500 people have to join their neighboring Neighborhoods and when they grow to over 1500, they have to split into two. These Neighborhoods as living groups get to make all their own rules about living, Rules of Order, that is. This means that each individual has a great effect on the rules under which he or she is expected to live. Thus the dictatorship of the majority in the Neighborhood affects only about 1,000 people.

When young people reach 18, they become Citizens and get to vote on the Rules of Order in their Neighborhoods and get to choose their Representatives and get to vote on everything that is voted upon: the things that affect their lives. We have been talking about making our own decisions, making up our own minds about things, about taking responsibility for our own lives and actions and this is as good a way as any I can see. These Neighborhoods are small enough so it is possible to know the person who represents us in the outer world fairly well and that is important to both of us.

There will be every type of Neighborhood you can imagine and some you would prefer not to. Some Neighborhoods might allow the practice of black magic, some might make us turn the radio off at 9 o'clock and some may make no rules at all.

The principal enforcement methods in the various Neighborhoods will be expulsion with, I suppose, minor types of consequences for minor infractions. That's all up to us who are trying to live in peace with each other. The unusual Rules of Order for each Neighborhood can be posted on the boundaries so they can be read and understood. If we don't like the rules, we can stay the hell out of that Neighborhood; the same would be true if we didn't like the lack of rules, but we get to choose.

OK. Where does our chosen representative go to represent us? What is the next sized group in a cellularly organized state? What kinds of *organs* do we need?

There is a point at which population grouping is most efficient for self support and ecological self regulation. If you think I *know* what it is, you're mistaken, but I am ready to lay one on you that I have thought a lot about and am sure will work for us here in North America. I will call it a Council and perhaps its full name will be The Council of Two Hundred which gives an immediate hint as to its population size. The Council has two hundred Neighborhood Representatives give or take a few and is the government (new definition) for two hundred Neighborhoods or about 200,000 people. The Council (barn) exists between the population limits of 125,000 and 275,000, joining or splitting at these outside points but without splitting Neighborhoods. The principal Council function is to balance the needs of its People with its resources; bring in from other Councils what its People need but cannot produce and send out its excesses in a balanced manner. To do this it holds so much land as long as its population is between the above limits. Councils are totally responsible to the People who populate them for the ecology of their territory. They are the People's Business and will, in many ways, compete with regular Business. Remember we want government two-valued and expect ours to compete in a business way with Business to our profit. The Councils are in the Ecology Business. The Councilors' (Neighborhood Representatives) will elect a Senator from among themselves to represent the Council and its interests in the Central Government.

The major problem of today is misuse of our ecology. So while we're changing everything, let's consider ourselves Ecologists and see what division of the planet Earth would make the most sense ecologically in order to provide a way of life for us and our jillions of descendents. We gotta think big. We must have sufficient land and ocean area which we can learn to farm, not mine. We need plenty of plankton to make oxygen and keep the oceans alive for food; and consider the porpoises who may have something to say when we get the communication problem solved. So let's whack off a chunk that will insure the way of life that we expect to become accustomed to. Start at the North Pole, go around Alaska, South along the International Date Line to the Equator and East along the Equator to just short of the Galapogos. Go East and North through the southern border of Panama, include the Virgin Islands, around Greenland, maybe Iceland, then back North to the Pole to make a big bag called The Republic of North America, the great and livable RNA. Don't get shook at this point about how we are going to get all this done. The steps are laid out later so for now, just assume that it's possible.

In this area there will soon be about 340,000,000 People which makes roughly 1,700 Councils with the same number of Senators to make up the Working Core of the Central Government. The principal tasks of Central, as it is loosely called, will be to deal with the other countries or continents on all matters, patrol our borders and balance out the financial positions of the 1,700 Councils by playing Robin Hood. Central will also help to protect the Right of Challenge which is the way we decide all questions of justice in the RNA and correct injustices. Central is not a government at all by the old definition, only by the new. It is there to do what we tell it to, not to tell us what to do and that's about the same degree of difference as between a venetian blind and a blind Venetian. We are creating an Establishment in a geographical area wherein all animals including humans will be able to survive and exist. The People will make all their own decisions by voting on everything and we are going to have a Society that will seek agreement with itself without Laws and Enforcement.

Let's take an example of how the new thing will work and run it out. Central has the task of balancing the Budget, which is a nice term for stating that it takes enough bread from the fatter Councils to run itself, provide the budgets of the various Sections (like Foreign Contact, Environment, Business, Education, Boundary Patrol) and to pick up the slack in the poorer Councils' Budgets. This slack will probably be called a deficit. Each Council, you see, has to provide for its 200,000 People and if some cannot, Central must subtract from the fat to feed the thin. Each Council will provide Central with its income information and the Central Business Committee will prepare the Budget, which is the amount that each Council will contribute to the above ends or receive, in the case of the deficit Councils. This Budget, prepared annually, must be presented to all the People in the RNA as a Bill which, if passed, is then in effect until a new Bill is passed to supersede the old. This Bill will provide for weekly payments to Central from or to each Council and must be approved by the People.

Central has a responsibility to all the People in the RNA to see that the same minimum standard of living can be experienced in all the Councils, fat or thin. The general idea will be to cooperate, with education and tools, to ultimately make each Council self-sufficient. However, the Ecology may be so bare in some localities and the commercial center Councils may be in the funnel position of commodity handling so that there may, willy-nilly, always be a few extra rich Councils and some extra poor ones. Central balances all this with the Budget Bill. The Committee prepares the Bill and all the Senators have their say as to what their People will do with it when they see it and much sweat and effort is spent in making a Budget Bill that can pass the vote of the People. Fortunately for their sanity, the 1,700 Senators will never have to gather under one roof to do this. They'll use video tapes and other modern communication methods, like the telephone. Remember...government is the science of finding out what the people want and then helping them do it.

When the Bill is finally ready, the Senators make 1,700 copies, each take one and fly on home to their Councils, duplicate the Bill 200 times and explain it at the Council Meeting so that each Councilor knows all its little ins and outs. When they all understand what the score is, the Councilors go home, put on their Representative hats and call the Neighborhood Meetings together. The Bill is again duplicated so each Citizen gets a copy. Every citizen can have a file of every Bill—if that's their bag. If you think this is a lot of paper, you should see the mountains used now. Anyway, the Representative explains the Bill in the Neighborhood Meeting and all the Citizens vote in the voting computer which counts the results instantly and sends them to Central and the Budget Bill is either passed or rejected. If the Bill gets over 50 percent of the existing votes, it's by damn passed.

It doesn't take much to see that there's not a lot of use for politics or politicians as we now know them. It is directly the will of the People—
YOU GET TO, GOT TO, DECIDE.

I've been talking a lot about Ecology and maybe I'd better define it the way I think about it so we can both know what's in my head when you see the word. **ECOLOGY: the relationship between living organisms and their environment; the relationship between People, where they live and what they need to live.** So Ecology is a relationship and let's add the idea of balance to the relationship. The Council wherein you live will have the total responsibility to do exactly what you say to do with your very own Ecology. Therefore, we as Citizens will bear the responsibility for the balance of the Ecology, which in cities might have to do with pollution and in the country with land use.

In our efforts to make an establishment modeled on the human organism, we have to realize that the human organism is a **SYMBIOSIS, the intimate living together of dissimilar organ(-isms, -izations) to their mutual benefit.** The Neighborhoods (cells) make up a Council (organs like liver, heart, bowels, etc.) and the whole is the RNA (the entity)—symbiosis.

If you and I and everybody want to have the say about what goes down in our new Establishment, we should know that it will take some of our time and effort to get our say said. If we go to all this trouble to put in a system where our votes really count for something and our ideas and suggestions can be voted and acted upon, we better damn well be prepared to make suggestions to our Representatives then vote on them. Hopefully, we will soon get used to being an actual part of the governing body. That's US, the governing body. It will make a helluva big difference in our degree of involvement. Our ideas, our votes, our parts in the whole, will become important possessions. All this will involve our time—time to understand what the rules and Bills mean, what their effects will be on us and our families and how much effort we are willing to put out to see they are carried out. If the vote goes for the way you feel, groovy, no problem. But if it goes against the way you feel, it is a requirement of the *democratic way* that you get behind and help carry out what the majority has decided, all the while trying to get another Bill started so your different idea can be tried next time. It's a personal thing, voting is, and we can allow no other influence except the feeling within us to affect our votes. Read me well. This system can work if we understand that the Bills we vote on, which are actually some Citizen's idea in the first place, can be changed practically immediately if they don't work out. All Bills will have a time limit written into them so nothing can hang up either us or future generations.

In North America there no longer is an ignorant, illiterate *mass* of humanity that can be pushed, coerced and controlled. Radio and television are virtually everywhere.

The present generations must look into the future with some vision and a lot of hope that an Establishment can be created in which People make all of the decisions and carry them out, thus giving each of us the way of life we choose. We have to start somewhere. Even if we don't know how to make decisions now, we can decide among ourselves to start to learn how knowing we're going to screw up a lot. We can teach our children to make decisions and give them a lot of practice, so in a generation or two the problems created by this new type of Establishment will be solved. Please note I'm not saying there won't be new problems by then.

Remember, in all this I am presenting to you and you and all of us and everybody a structure only. This is a structural form of government that meets the basic requirements for giving the actual power to the people and while there may be a dozen such, this is the one I think has the best chance of being agreed to by enough People to get it into effect. I really am talking about pure structure, the crust; the filling and meringue are up to you. It is one way to get us all out of the trap we're caught in and the thing I like about it is that it is flexible enough to change to fit all the conditions which might occur in any future I can see. No Utopias, just the right to make our own decisions and have them count for something.

HUMANKIND MUST LEARN TO PROGRESS WITHOUT CONTENTION

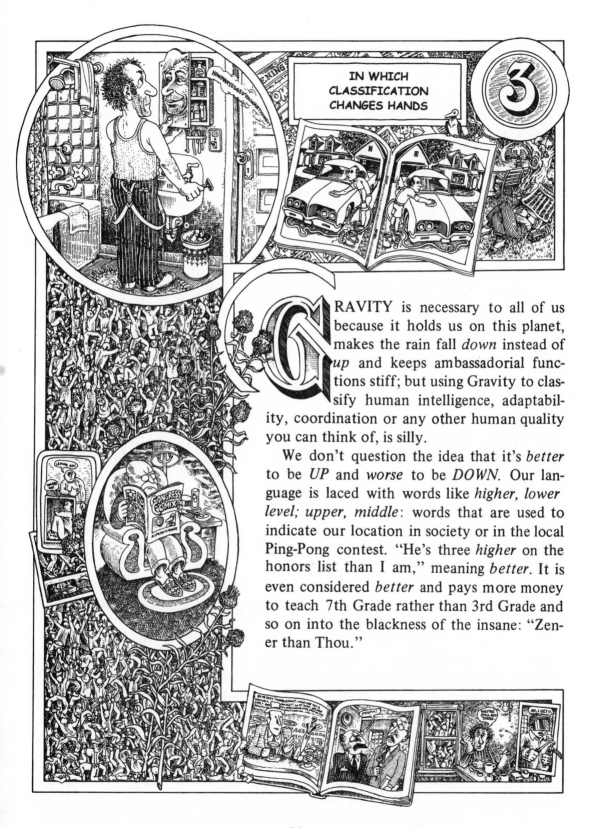

RAVITY is necessary to all of us because it holds us on this planet, makes the rain fall *down* instead of *up* and keeps ambassadorial functions stiff; but using Gravity to classify human intelligence, adaptability, coordination or any other human quality you can think of, is silly.

We don't question the idea that it's *better* to be *UP* and *worse* to be *DOWN*. Our language is laced with words like *higher, lower level; upper, middle*: words that are used to indicate our location in society or in the local Ping-Pong contest. "He's three *higher* on the honors list than I am," meaning *better*. It is even considered *better* and pays more money to teach 7th Grade rather than 3rd Grade and so on into the blackness of the insane: "Zener than Thou."

This Segment deals with the undesirability of others being able to Classify us; deciding whether we are *higher* or *lower* which is, as I said, SILLY. So we give up this Right to let others Classify us and learn to Classify ourselves—OK? Now I didn't say that a computer couldn't classify us into, for example, groups with similar tastes or characteristics like similar fingerprints or whether we dig chop suey and like that, because computers can and do, but we must tell the computers how and what to Classify. The system our present Establishment uses to Classify Humans is not *Wrong*, just totally out of date because it uses GRAV-ITY as the basis for Classification. Looking at humans as being like lightning instead of like rain presents a truer picture. Lightning jumps from cloud to cloud, from the earth to a cloud, between any two points where there is enough difference in electrical potential to cause it to move and so do we.

When Potters or Highway Engineers want to Classify or sort materials like clay, sand or gravel into size of particle, they use a CLASSIFICATION SIEVE which is a stack of screens each with different sized holes. The screen at the top has the largest holes. The clay or sand is dumped into the top screen and the whole assembly is shaken until the smallest particles fall through into a pan at the bottom and every other particle is sitting on top of the screen it can't fall through. Got this picture? In our society we use the same sort of gizmo for peo-ple. We humans have been so used to GRAVITY being all around us that we've let THEM use the same kind of GRAVITY operated SIEVE to classify US. Let's see what happens when you dump a bunch of humans onto the classification SIEVE and shake it. The smallest, poorest, skinniest humans, those which the society deems useless, fall into the pan at the bottom while the people on the top screen are the fattest, with cars, ranches, bank accounts, influence and so on. When the SIEVE stops shaking, being humans and wanting to be at the *TOP*, a lot of people start climbing up to the next level and in order to stay there, they have to get a little fatter. In most of us is some crazy place that keeps us striving to get *UP* onto the screen above. To many it doesn't seem to matter how and lots of People are pushed *down* into the screen below by those step-ping *up*. The fat ones on *TOP* are afraid to have the Sieve shaken—they might fall and be Classified as *lower*.

And we are going to change all this? Right! We are going to turn the damn Classification Sieve over on its side and get Gravity, either kind, totally out of the action. A lot of you might argue, and well, that the whole idea of the sieve should be done away with but that won't work because we need to understand our limits so our children can go beyond them. This is called *The Natural Pro-cess of Selection* and is a necessary part of our Evolvement, but it's not neces-sary to have it operate by Gravity. So, now we have very carefully and posi-tively layed our Sieve over on its side and you can see that we can easily move by just crawling through the holes from screen to screen to find out where each of us naturally fits. We don't have to get fat to stay between any two screens and we can decide for ourselves between which two screens we want to stay at any particular time. If we can borrow a tremendous saw, we can cut the Sieve through the center and lay the two halves out so not only all can live in the sun, as was the former Right of only the *fattest*, but also make room for some of this exploded population.

Now, what will Classification, Do It Yourself Type, do for us that Classification, Gravity Type, didn't? It will allow the Young Humans to wander through the whole Sieve, underfoot of course, so they first get to see it all, then decide just what kind of dues they are willing to pay to be with people they enjoy, with no idea of *Higher* or *Lower* or *Better* or *Worse*—only DIFFERENT! Let's make it possible for a doctor's son to become a carpenter without anyone's thinking he's *worse* or *lower*. You see what I mean.

Of course, there are those who will not fit between any two screens and in the present system they are forced to fit somewhere, usually in the pan at the bottom, but with the sieve cut in half and laid on its side they can wander at will, paying the necessary dues for the length of time they wish to stay between any two screens.

We have to learn to Classify ourselves so we can make the place we are in the sieve our own idea:

If you classify you, you are happy and productive there. If others classify you, you are never sure they have put you where you fit.

The presently used Classification tests produce little but negative data. The IQ tests give you a number which is supposed to show you *your place*; if your number is over 140 or so, you can call yourself a genius and if under 60, an idiot, but between these two points, where most of us fit, it just says that you are of approximately average intelligence, which if you had brain one, you knew before you took the damn thing. So that kind of thing, all those tests I mean, will help in giving us the negative data of what we are not. When they give the same test to a suburban snot-nose and to a slum kid, they always miss by the tremendous differences in their language plus the fact that the test was made up by some College Cat, so where are we then? Nowhere, right? I repeat: the only way to Classify yourself is to go there and find out, preferably when you are young. With a chance to try EVERYTHING, YOU can decide.

One of the bullshit ideas our society lays on us is that you're not supposed to hold your head up tall if you're serving someone. One of the most efficient ways to learn a thing is to serve a person who does it well, thus saving precious time for both of you.

I spent a lot of rainy day time once figuring out one rational (put to numbers) basis for Maturity which I will lay on you for Classification practice. If we assume that one way that Maturity can be gauged, indicated, measured is by the amount of time we spend doing things for others, it can be put to numbers. Take the 24 hours in your average day, subtract the time you spend sleeping and eating—these are neutral things—ten hours, for example. The difference (14) is your base number, the hours you could possibly be doing things for others. OK, now take the number of hours you work, include going to and from (let's say eight), multiply that by the percent of time you work to take care of your own needs (how about 25 percent of your working time?) and subtract that from your base number ($14 - 8 \times .25 = 14 - 2$ which is 12). Now subtract hours of TV, reading, playing games (like 12 - 5) which leaves so many (7) hours to feed and play with the kids, fix things for other people and like that. In the example, 7 hours spent doing things for others out of 14 hours possible, or one half the time, puts the index of maturity at 50 percent by this way of measuring...just another number like IQ.

Now you know, on one kind of scale, how mature you are but if you're a man, don't try to compare with a woman as they are notoriously more mature than men on this basis. The difference being in the environmental conditions under which the work is done; I mean the work for others. But they really are, not only different but more mature, so give it up.

Another basis for measuring maturity, the one that made sense to me for a long time, is the amount of time you are objective. You may be able to figure out the number of hours you are being totally *objective* and the number of hours you are totally *subjective* with some hours in between and come up with some other numerical basis. The advantage you gain by being **OBJECTIVE, the way YOU affect the world**, over being **SUBJECTIVE, the way the world is affecting YOU,** is that in the objective mode your feelings are freer. Outside of this, being objective is no *better* or *worse*, only DIFFERENT! Using this method takes away the advantage women gain in the other way because I've found that women *Don't Like* more things than men *Don't Like* (otherwise we'd probably still be living in caves). Liking or not liking how the world is affecting you is being subjective. OK, so another numerical measure of maturity we can use to classify ourselves is the degree of objectivity we can maintain throughout our day.

The way I measure my maturity now is the amount of time my conscious and subconscious minds talk to each other—so make up one for yourself.

In seeking various ways to classify ourselves we can also look at the time worn methods. For instance, the Pecking Order idea of human relationships. This idea merely states that there is always somebody *above* us who can, and usually does, Peck. It works for chickens but I am suspicious of it for Humans who have that timebinding advantage and, by now, could have learned something different. OK, I will expose you to my own theory of Human Relationships which is different only to a slight degree, but which I feel fits the facts, observed and felt.

THE NEBBISCH THEORY

What's a Nebbisch? A Nebbisch is a person your mother thinks you are *better* than, a Yiddish word meaning *a nothing.*

Everybody is a Nebbisch to someone else for some set of reasons or another-- think about it! I am a Nebbisch! You are a Nebbisch! They are Nebbisches! We are Nebbisches! You see, if that be true, there is no longer a necessity to feel put down by merely being a Nebbisch as it's just as true for all. I feel the important thing here to observe is just who YOU think is a Nebbisch and who thinks YOU are a Nebbisch, because You fit right in between with a lot of friends whom you neither think are Nebbisches, nor do they you! A pecking order indicates that pecking is *in* order and you will surely peck to find out where you stand, especially when young, and pecking is a type of Contention.

So if we can make the Nebbisch Theory our own idea and have enough Juice to Change, we can Change and what a Change that could be: fewer new Impalas, no stupid strivings to be something we ain't, just us and our friends, Nebbisches together walking hand in hand in the wildflowers. No Pecking instead of No Parking?

When I hear or see something stupid, it makes me humble, because I know that I'm *that* stupid about *some*thing.

Here's a beautiful idea to think about. It has to do with *Like* and *Dislike* with reference to other people. I would like to try the idea of *Amount of Time Spent With* and use it to replace *Like-Dislike* so we can truly Love everybody. This idea says that everyone else is OK as far as you are concerned. but that there is a definite amount of time you can be comfortable with each individual. This can be determined by experience. With some people you might be able to spend an infinite amount of time, with others it might be a few days or a few hours or just, "Ciao." And remember it can change. What we do is:

Classify *ourselves* as to the amount of real time we can spend with a certain person comfortably, then limit our contact to that amount of time.

HUMANKIND CAN LEARN TO PROGRESS WITHOUT CONTENTION

Just for fun and perhaps handiness, here are four conversational habits that almost all of us have and can easily lose if we want to.

It is not necessary to deny what someone has said before we add our ideas to the conversation:

This is a way to start to think *positively*. When someone says to you, "Seat belts are a necessity," think a minute, then say, "Yes, and they ought to be sold in accessory shops so everyone has a choice." No need for, "No, you're wrong, they're a stone drag." Try it and see what happens.

Learn to properly use qualifying words:

"Democracy is the *best* form of government."

"Democracy is *a* form of government."

"Democracy is *our* form of government."

Best, a and *our* are qualifying words and the way we use them indicates our degree of Seeking Agreement. We can put whole bunches of different words in the places of the three mentioned and the words we use indicate our opinions: from positive (best), through neutral (a) to negative (worst) and on into possessive. The idea is to pick the qualifying word that exactly expresses an opinion, then feel the same way about it the instant we're saying it—the way we do when we say things like, "Far Out," "Really?" "Ouch!"...like that. This is the place, communicationwise, where we can substitute exactness for bullshit. Of course, we have to THINK.

Stop using the pre-answered question:

Expressions like: "You don't really..., do you?"

"It's..., isn't it?"

"Don't you think that...?"

"Are you really thinking that...?"

are all questions, OK, but they indicate the desired or expected answer whereas, "Do you think...?" is really asking people what they think, instead of making them feel like idiots if they don't agree with you.

Every *should clause* needs an *if clause*; so do clauses containing the words *right* and *wrong*. Like:

"That's right, if..." and "That's wrong, if..."

"You should..., if..." and "You shouldn't..., if..."

IF WHAT?

These four things well learned and practiced will allow you to reclassify yourself semantically and may make you lots of friends as well.

One of the things we gotta realize in Classifying ourselves is that something has changed. It doesn't take much looking around to find out that our kids are **SMARTER (able to pick up concepts quicker)** than we are.

So if you're over 30-35, you better take a look at why. They have been audio-visualized, that's why. And as soon as we can, we will teach everything that way so everybody can be that *smart* with accurate data as well. Kids who have been subjected to TV before they are seven have built in concept pluckers that we old radio babies never had a chance to have. Take a moment or a year to dig what TV really puts out. "My God," you think, "those kids have more various ideas presented to their little heads in one night of television than I had in my whole first six or seven years!"—concepts such as *the world is round*. Sure, my father told me it was round, but he didn't prove it to me. The modern kid has seen an actual moving photograph of it along with many other wonders we didn't learn about until much later. They pick up and make part of their automatic equipment (before they're seven) concepts that none of the Greek Philosophers knew in their whole lives. Some things are not only put to them, but ground in: news, deodorants, aspirin, stomachs, *good* guys, *bad* guys; a lot of inaccurate data because of the bias. They're even told what's *good* or *bad* weather. Now you know more about bias than they do, but they have grasped more concepts than you had at their age and knowledge is a pyramid as all of us old fools know and what a conceptual base they have—a base we can't possibly match.

So, one of the things we have to consider in Classifying ourselves *is* our age group. How about that?

Another thing that separates people from people is *Word Problems*; some people know how to work them almost from birth and some people never really learn. It is a real difference in people. And where do you fit? "The ones who can do them think the ones who can't aren't trying and the ones who can't, think the ones who can are lying."—a poem about *Word Problems*. My wife is both a Beautiful potter and a beautiful Potter, but she cannot work *Word Problems* so every once in a while I find something like this on my desk: "I have a fifty pound bag of clay which I want to become 40 percent of my clay body so if 50 pounds is 40 percent, how much is the total?" To save her life, she couldn't figure that out. So I do things like that for her and dig it. Am I *better* than she is because of my gift? Am I even *better* at Math than she is? I don't think about it that way. My Math head works differently from hers, is all. She mixes up glazes using so much of this plain white material and of that plain white material and when the pot is fired, outasight colors of her choice result which I couldn't even begin to do and that's still basic Math, so what's *Better*? Why not be happy the way you are and just admit—after trying, of course, that you can or can't work *Word Problems* and let it go at that. It's no big deal.
WE MUST ACCEPT AND NURTURE THE IDEA THAT PEOPLE ARE REALLY DIFFERENT ONE FROM ANOTHER, OK?

*　　*　　*　　*　　*　　*　　*　　*

"NO MAN IS AN ISLAND"

Someone said that and it's true. There's part of every human that is Island and part Continent, part Moon and part Sun. What you are trying to do is find out how much "Island" you have in you and how much you have to depend on what kind of people for your happiness and well-being. We are trying to create an Establishment in which living the way we would dig to live can be learned and practiced. You have to decide whether you prefer the calm and quiet and familiar faces of a small town, the bustle-hustle and strangers of the City or a lonely mountain top. Such a decision might depend solely on your physiological ability to withstand the sound level of Megapolis. You might like part and part. Everybody has to have a chance to try a bit of everything, every kind of Being and the new Establishment must thoughtfully provide for this, so each person can determine for themselves how much of their Island, their Sun and their Moon they want to develop.

Going to Church is either a godsend or a drag depending on how YOU feel about it. Wherever *being* is easier for you is where you belong.

no one outside of you can determine this for you

you gotta do it

please

*　　*　　*　　*　　*　　*　　*　　*

Now that you're a Human Being, the best that you can be for you, please cease and desist trying to make the rest of the world feel that where you are is the best place for everybody, that the path you're on is the *only* path. What's good for Bull Moose is NOT necessarily good for the rest of the world.

Timebinding......HOORAY!!!!　　　　　　　Missionaryism......BOO!!!!

A couple of years ago I was stopped in a Sovereign State by a very polite policeman who pointed out that my left taillight was not burning as it really MUST be in that State, especially at night. He dragged out a form, a full page form, and coyly intimated that if I would answer these few questions, a ticket I wouldn't get so I did and WOW! The thoroughness of that questionnaire was unquestionable. When he got through, he knew everything about me that my best friends do. Being experienced with policemen, I calmly and correctly answered his questions, signed the paper and we went our ways. A few miles down the road, I passed him doing it to some other poor unfortunate: the same long form and the same polite smile (as best as I could see by my headlights). A little later when I stopped for the taillight bulb and coffee, he walked in so I asked him, "How come?" He told me that some National Agency or another was paying the State five bucks for every one of these data sheets they returned filled out and also, he said, it was pure profit as they didn't have to split with a judge and that as far as he knew, all the data went into some Computer so THEY would know more about ME—my mind boggled!

What do THEY do with all that information I gave them? They put it into a computer and out comes a bunch of answers not really about people, but about bunches of people, about *segments of the population* so THEY know where to aim their big propaganda machines with different semantic lies for the *southwestern farmer*, the *middle-western businessman* and like that. The more THEY know about us the more they can push US around. I would like to see US put a stop to it. How about you?

While in England I had the opportunity to watch a friend fill in the census form. I say *opportunity* because I had never thought to write "none of your business" beside questions I feel are none of the census bureau's business, but wait until next time. Why do THEY need to know how many indoor and outdoor toilets there are at my house or even how many TV sets?

The present establishment is using the computer to *control* the people. In our new Establishment, the computer must be considered a data tool to increase the decisive capability of the people.

As the new Establishment will have some of the same problems the old one had, let's talk about what we can do to Classify ourselves for Establishment Computers. Remember, that WE are the Establishment and WE decide what WE need to know about each other.

What DO we really need to know about each other? We must know how many there are of us to provide for—instantly and automatically, all computerized—INSTANT CENSUS—not just every ten years like now. We must know what age groups people fit into for education and old age and such and we need to know everybody's address so we can provide them with mail and phone service. We'll need a number which has to do with individual ID so it cannot be duplicated and everybody has a specific number. We'll need a new type of number which describes our degree of participation in society.

We need a numbering system ready so the changeover will be easy; then NEVER NEVER let them know anything more than what we have decided is necessary, making our privacy, if not assured, at least a lot more likely.

Let's get some agreement going on a number. First, all of us were born. When? On some date but what's important to us is month and year. OK, let's use our Astrological Sun sign as the first symbol then the last two digits of the year. The first thing on my number would be the sign for Capricorn (I'll use C on account of this typewriter hasn't been enlightened). OK, so C 18. That's all the number you need to get born with. When Mother registers your birth, she needs only her number plus your sign and the last two digits of your year of birth. THEY won't even know if you're male or female much less a bunch of other crap. The next part of our all purpose number has to do with ID—four digits for the Council you were born in and four digits indicating you. Like if you were the first baby born in that sign, this number would be 0001. For this part of my number I will make up a Council number for what is now called Hunter, North Dakota, like 5408 and I'll figure I was the 1,232nd baby born that Capricorn. So my number thus far is C1854081232, OK?

The next part we'll never forget as these three little digits stand for the next three years we spend serving our new Establishment as Trainees. At 18 you can start to work for Society, if you wish, and it's an exchange that serves everyone: you learn to work and the people get a lot of work done. A few years before you're 18, you can learn enough about the various choices so you can begin to decide what kind of Service you'd like to do then learn enough about your choice or choices so when the time for assignment comes, you know enough to get what you choose.

TO GET YOUR CHOICE ABOUT ANYTHING, ANYWHERE, ANY TIME YOU HAVE TO KNOW ENOUGH ABOUT THAT CHOICE AND THE OTHER CHOICES TO BE ABLE TO CHOOSE.

The kind of Service we do determines this part of our numbers; one number per year for three years. Here are the choices:

0. Acceptable Non-Service, special conditions.
1. Boundary Patrol; protecting our borders.
2. Ecological Service; learning about our environment and helping to put and keep it in balance.
3. Educational Service; assisting children to learn.
4. Medical Service; helping to keep People healthy.
5. Order Service; helping to keep Order.
6. Shop Service; maintenance shops—mechanical, electrical, etc.
7. Computer Service; learning to repair and program OUR computers.
8. Public Service; training required—typists, clerks, drivers, etc.
9. Public Service; no training required—manual labor.

So, if you work three years in the Forestry Service planting trees, fighting fires, preventing fires, measuring logs or whatever for us, all of US, your next three numbers would be 222. If you start out with one year in Forestry and switch to hospital work for two years, they'd be 244...like that. Since I'd probably pick mechanics, my number would be C1854081232666: Birth, ID and Service, which altogether are known as the E number.

The next Number, A for Address Number, is to simply tell some idiot machine where we are physically located on this planet so it can direct communications to us automatically. As we are starting all this, let's take 1 as our Continent Number. Then come four digits which represent the Council and I sincerely hope we never exceed four digits worth of Councils. Next come three digits as a Neighborhood number and finally a three digit phone number—that's it. I'll make up an address number for myself, like 1 6605 613 127: Continent, Council, Neighborhood and Phone. If the last three digits are 000, it means you don't have a personal phone but can receive messages at the Neighborhood Center as 000 at the end means the Neighborhood's phone. The A number, Continent plus 10 digits, has the same number of digits our phone numbers have now, thus saving the phone company a lot of equipment change.

$$C18540811232666 \quad = \quad \text{E number}$$
$$16605613127 \quad\quad = \quad \text{A number}$$

To the computer, this number means me and where I can be reached. This is admittedly a mouthful of number, 25 digits, which we'll all have from the time we're twelve years old with spaces for the Service number until we've done our Service. "But look at the extra work caused by using this great long number," you say. My address now is: John Muir, Box 613, Santa Fe, New Mexico 87501, USA...this is 38 symbols all by itself and does not include my phone, library card, birth certificate, passport or any of the rest. Our new 25 digit number is for EVERYthing. And your Name? That's for friends and changeable at will.

I like to feel that we'll see a return to the old family Bible idea so a family can maintain a personal history of who married whom, who begat whom—a Family History for friends and heirs but not Establishment business.

The less the Establishment knows about us, the less it can push us around.

So let's classify ourselves into beats, hippies, soldiers, cooks, doctors, ranch hands, squares, physicists, computer programmers, church members, pilots, skydivers; into anything that pleasures us, but let's do two things: first, try, investigate, read about, look at, all the other things there are before we choose and remember that we can change if we don't really dig what we started out to be. Second, once we have found our diet, our idea, our occupation, our way of life, let's Understand that it doesn't make us any better than others and we will not waste our time and theirs trying to convince anybody that our way is THE way and that everybody should be like us. Timebinding what we know, however, is more necessary than ever. You can dig that!

People are only different one from everybody else, not better, nor higher, nor further out, nor zen-er, nor -------er.

HUMANKIND MUST LEARN TO PROGRESS WITHOUT CONTENTION

IN WHICH
THE PEOPLE INHERIT

AS INDIVIDUALS, we are giving up the Right to Profit from Death. PROFIT: a financial gain becomes the Right of the Councils when we die.

There's nothing *wrong* with inheritance, it just needs to be understood and brought up to date. When I say we cannot inherit, I mean we cannot inherit Financial Things we didn't earn like money, stock shares, annuities, things like that. We can't inherit anything to do with the Medium of Exchange, including debts.

The symbol ₵ stands for Credit which, in turn, means the balance on the right hand side of a ledger—what you have, in other words—and will be an excellent term to describe our new Medium of Exchange unit. Credits now replace Dollars, Pesos, Quetzals, Lempiras, Cordovas, Balboas and like that. With the change in name comes an entirely new concept or a return to an old one: **THE CREDIT, ₵, is only a Medium of exchange; its value represents a certain proportion, a share, of the net worth of the RNA as a whole; one part of some fixed number of Credits.** Its value is determined by what it can be exchanged for, not by what can be made from it by manipulating it financially. Credit, ₵, is the new name for bread, OK?

A few thoughts about inheritance and what it does to people: If we seek an improvement in our Natural Process of Selection, everyone should have an even financial start in life. Being given a head start financially implies that you need it.

The loss you sustain from the circumstances of inheritance seldom balances the gain.

How many kids are actually *hindered* by their parents' financial wealth? How about the poor *rich* cat whose whole family is sitting around impatient for him to die? Death is a drag and an ecstatic adventure and as far as we know now, inevitable, so when it becomes imminent, why not be able to relax and enjoy it?

Some of our best people are lost to us through worry; worry about having to spend inherited money instead of learning how to make some themselves. The responsibility for spending well the bread that someone else busted his ass to make is more than I can bear. If someone were going to give me something I hadn't earned, I'd like them to be there to enjoy my enjoyment of it. You can give it away while you're still alive and watch the fun.

Immortality is like muscle; it must be earned; it cannot be bought; it cannot be inherited.

What I'm saying is that inheritance is a drag for both the Inheritor and the Inherited from (who is feeling no pain). This Custom of not profitting from Death will make a lot of people happier and the Council richer.

There'll be a lot of action in this book involving CUSTOMS, so here's its definition according to Webster:

CUSTOM: **"noun, a usage or practice common to many. The whole body of usages, practices, or conventions that regulate social life. Adjective, made or performed according to personal order."**

Customs are supposed to have the weight of years of social or other usage before they become customs and they vary from region to region, like the way the table is set, saying "excuse me," where the pencils are kept, when and how to celebrate holidays and all that. Here, I am talking about Customs as a way of agreeing to live together without Laws and their attendant Enforcement—a bunch of made up Customs which have no basis in years of tradition but are simply things that allow us to live together without friction and that don't have to be enforced because they are really agreed upon custom-made Customs. Like "If you'll smile, I'll smile;" "If you have no fear of me, I'll have no fear of you;" "If you'll keep the place in front of your house clean, I'll keep the place in front of my house clean."

CUSTOMS ARE DESIGNED TO ELIMINATE PRESENTLY WRITTEN LAWS.

OK, so now we all agree to make it a custom-made Custom that profitting by someone's death financially is out. The basic idea that your family will starve after you die or that a member of your family won't have the necessary medical help they need for lack of money or that your kids won't get educated has already been made old hat by the present Establishment; at least they're trying! In the new Establishment we're going one step further and give everyone a share of the economy. This share won't be enough for nightclubs and automobiles, but will be enough for the Basics of Life and at the same time eliminate any idea of Welfare.

Along with the Welfare bureaus, Life Insurance Companies had better get ready to head for the hills. Their main selling point has been, "You don't want your family to SUFFER after you die, do you?" and that kind of fear is to disappear along with the people who prey on it. There will be no such thing as Life Insurance—Fear Insurance—as there is no way to insure against fear.

We are going to prevent anyone's starving to death at any time throughout their lives by allotting EVERYONE a fair share of the Economy. Everyone, NO MATTER WHO, will receive their share every week—all done automatically by computer; no waiting in line or being made to feel like shit.

The amounts are determined by an approximation of minimal living level based on today's economy and can be changed. A family with two children under twelve would receive $¢30 + ¢30 + ¢10 + ¢10 = ¢80$ a week on which to live with no additional working income at all. Each Mother will be paid $¢10$ for each child she has under twelve—up to two children. This is both a population control measure and an economic requirement. As children reach twelve, they get their own $¢$'s, then if Mother has had a third child under 12 she can receive the $¢10$ for that child and so on. Two kids under twelve per mother at any one time—OK? Of course, if you have more kids, you can get a job.

Everybody gets this Manna, the People's Share—no worries about if your family is going to survive if you are taken from us—no fears, Right? People who have jobs can share their paycheck Credits with one person of their choice.

Following is a schedule of Council Payments to every human living in that Council, so you can always be assured shelter, food, inexpensive medical care and the like.

Age and Status	¢ per Week
From birth to 12 years	10 Paid to Mother, up to two children
From 12 years to death	15 Paid to you. You become a Citizen of the RNA at 18
After first year as Trainee	20
After completing second year as Trainee	25
After completing third year as Trainee	30 You become a Member of the RNA

Please note: *amounts shown here are play figures only.*

When you reach 18, you can start to serve the new Establishment in whatever way you can best serve. Under special circumstances, you can start to serve earlier than 18, and there's no upper age limit. Everyone can serve; the blind, the halt, the weak and the strong and when they put in a year's work, the Council raises their Share by one third of a Citizen's Share. ¢5 a week isn't much but multiply it by the number of weeks in a lifetime and it's a lot of bread for a year's work—like ¢13,000 in 50 years. After people serve their three years (the most there is), they receive not only their ¢30 a week for the rest of their lives and their three digits but also their second vote. A Citizen has one vote; a Member, two. A Citizen is anyone over 18; a Member has three numbers in the Service Number space.

The Medical care situation is like this:

From birth to twelve your folks take care of you; pay your bills according to their ability to pay.

From twelve to nineteen and as a Trainee your medical care is totally provided by the Council where you live or serve.

Everyone else pays their own, proportional to their income. As all of the hospitals except, perhaps, for a few private ones, are provided by the Councils, Hospital Insurance goes down the drain. Remember, no Fear Insurance! But you can prepay your hospital bill by filling a hospital's everpresent need for labor. When you're well and have nothing special to do, you can take a quick course in bedpan dumping and work three shifts for a voucher which entitles you to a day in the hospital should you become sick. If you never get sick, use the vouchers as trading stamps. After you've earned a day in the hospital, it doesn't matter who uses it. These vouchers are good from Council to Council.

As no one but the Council can profit by a person's death, you will find the mortuary is a naturally efficient part of the hospital complex. I am sure that we as a community can tastefully and beautifully handle all the details concerning whatever particular way you would want to be buried, crypted or cremated. Paying for mortuary services to your own taste is usually done beforehand and hospital vouchers are legal tender. Each Council decides about cemeteries, cemetery parks, high rise crosses, some sort of recycling process or whatever the people in a certain community feel is the best way to fill these needs.

Even though profitting by someone else's death financially is out, movable possessions are still passable on; stamp and coin collections, Grandfather's table, objets d'art, your condominium; all these things can go down from generation to generation.

The problem area I find is what the hell to do about mobile possessions which are registered to the deceased like cars, boats (ocean liners?), and airplanes. I see the Council evaluating possessions of this sort in an individual manner like deciding that a person's mobiles represent a lot of bread and sell them; or that they represent a taxable value and give them to the heir or heirs upon payment of a tax or that they are of small value and can be dealt with like furniture. Let's go and see.

Homesteaded property, the *one* property you have registered as your homestead: your home, your ranch, the property you have spent years in building up: your Castle can be assigned to any one you pick, any Member, that is.

There is an exception to the Custom of not gaining financially from death that might be a gas. Suppose a single human has built up a financial Empire and upon evaluation, the Council finds it would be less profitable to split it up than to keep it whole. If such an Empire Builder lived and died in your Council, you could make up a Bill and everyone could vote whether to split up the empire or keep it together—with opinions flying like geese. If it were decided to keep it intact, the Council could sell raffle tickets at ¢5 each to everyone in the RNA who wanted to take a chance on owning such a fortune. The Council could make as much as ¢500,000,000 less expenses if it sold a raffle ticket to everyone in the RNA. I'd buy a chance, wouldn't you? Any wealthy person's estate could be handled this way—doesn't need to be a Tycoon and what a STATUS SYMBOL, a new type immortality—to get so rich that your Council raffles off your estate instead of selling it piecemeal. Just think of the Publicity!

HUMANKIND MUST LEARN TO PROGRESS WITHOUT CONTENTION

I F YOU HAVE a majority inside of you, then and then only are you prepared to join a majority on the outside. This is the basis of democracy in all its forms. When the inside and the outside present similar aspects, then the whole is one with the Self. Imitating someone else's life style just because they are stronger, richer, *fatter* or *hipper* is a stone drag. Picking our very own life styles is a process of self-classification, experimentation and elimination, not one of copying.

This Segment is about giving up the Right to Lay Our Trips on Everyone. Remember: Timebinding...Hooray!   Missionaryism...Boo! People who live together will be laying the same trip on each other, but what goes down anywhere else is none of their business. We get to help decide how we and the thousand People we live with comport ourselves so that the

49

life styles we choose will be available—somewhere—in some Neighborhood. If our life styles change, we may have to change Neighborhoods.

By Custom, Neighborhoods will decide in a town-meeting type Meeting (probably meetings) just what kind of rules they need to keep peace and love alive within their boundaries. The deciding is done by a show of hands, standing up, voting by machine or whatever, but just because some people have earned more than one vote on Council and Central Bills doesn't mean they have more than one vote in the Neighborhood. It is imperative that the Rules of Order we live by are made on an equal footing. When people stand up tall enough to be seen, like at 18, they'll be counted. There is no difference between Citizen and Member in the Neighborhood.

The Neighborhood is the basic cell unit of the new Establishment wherein all the Rules of Order and the enforcement thereof will be the responsibility of the People who live there.

Neither the Councils nor Central have anything at all to say about behavior in the individual Neighborhoods, unless this behavior starts to interfere with the lives of People in other Neighborhoods or with the Council ecology. The idea is basically that we can live the way we want as long as we don't bug others and I mean actually interfere with their life styles. This here drum I am beating on says:

MIND YOUR BUSINESS WELL; LET OTHERS MIND THEIR OWN!

HUMANKIND MUST LEARN TO PROGRESS WITHOUT CONTENTION

One of the ways we can eliminate contention from our lives is to eliminate policemen and the entire idea of enforcement. If we make all the Rules of Order, the rules by which we live, and enforce them ourselves at the Neighborhood level where the maximum enforcement is expulsion, we won't need police. People who want to be in the policing and guarding business can start up such a business. If someone needs this service, a phone call will get it; like "I need protection immediately," or "On Saturday the 10th starting at 9 P.M. I'll need four Rent-a-Cops." The same with the Fire Department when there's a fire.

The idea of making laws against everything, then paying a whole battery of police, lawyers, judges and jail-keepers to enforce them is insane. The body doesn't keep troops of white blood cells on the alert all the time but only manufactures them in case of infection. Laws are not an agreement. They are a mandate laid down by the group in control and enforced by THEM to make other groups or individuals do what they say is *right* or be shot (or equal).

Furthermore:

Laws are like lies; it takes several to make one stick. It even takes a law to abolish an obsolete one. Take a silly thing like schools and skirts. Girls started to wear mini skirts; schools made rules, "skirts must be longer." Girls started to wear long skirts, Oops, new rules, "skirts must be shorter." Even after schools give up on rules for skirts, they will have to make a rule that says, "no rules about skirts."

A batch of laws we can do without are those books and books filled with divorce laws. These we eliminate by simply all agreeing to a general RNA custom-made CUSTOM which says:

WOMEN CHOOSE WITH WHOM THEY LIVE. This is not a reversal of the old way—women have been the choosers whether men admit it or not—it is only an acceptance of the way things are. Women seem to be genetically equipped to choose and it would be nice if we allowed their sixth sense to operate in this area. We can learn that the man gets to do the searching and chasing and keeps the ultimate decision capability (he doesn't have to go or stay), but it lays the responsibility of choosing well where it belongs and will sure eliminate a lot of contention. So we agree that women get to choose with whom they live. If you gotta have rules about this stuff, make and enforce them in the Neighborhoods.

No matter what kind of living group choices are made, it really concerns only the people involved. They are not *worse* or *better*, only living with *their* choices.

There can be as many TYPES of Neighborhoods as there are Neighborhoods. The only thing we need to decide about a Neighborhood is whether we'd dig it there or not. If, for example, you don't want alcohol drinking in your Neighborhood, make such a rule, post it at the boundaries and eject anyone who tipples... these people can wander off to some Neighborhood where there are bars, probably not even very far away. The same kind of thing for drugs, pot, noise, music, gambling, even maybe kids. A rule could be made that no kids are allowed to let the last dying rays of the sun hit their heels in a Neighborhood made up of Senior Citizens. Some Neighborhoods might be under the domination of a Strongman who does everybody's deciding for them, which would work as long as the majority there dug it. Some Neighborhoods might have no rules at all. If you find yourself with an un-put-up-able majority in your Neighborhood, I suggest you move or relax your views and go along with the majority, if staying there is your thing.

The structure of the Neighborhood is super simple. We get together in a Meeting, a picnic or whatever and pick three people to supervise our local community scene for us: a triangle, which any engineer knows is a stable physical structure and I feel that it works for governmental structures as well as it divides stress and responsibility by three. They are: the **Representative**, the person who faces the outside world for us, becomes our Councilor and takes care of our Council business. When in the Neighborhoods, they are Representatives and when at Council Center, the same people are *Councilors*. Their jobs are to find out what the people want from their Council and try to get it. The second leg of the Neighborhood triangle is made by the *Order Tender* whose job is to enforce the rules we make in the Neighborhood Meeting according to our instructions. This Tender has the right to call a posse or any kind of Citizen support because:

Whatever rules we make we also have to enforce.

The *Education Tender* completes the triangle and is responsible for the mental development and physical well-being of the Neighborhood's children under twelve.

Any one of these three Tenders is empowered to call a Neighborhood Meeting, as can any group of neighbors. These three people are paid by us personally, ¢10 a year from each man, woman and child in the Neighborhood gives them about ¢10,000 a year which should make the job attractive enough financially to find someone who would really dig to do it. We can pay them more if we choose but, by Custom, ¢10 apiece is the minimum. That's ¢30 a year out of our Share of the economy that we pay for representation, protection and education, so far.

These people will need help to do their jobs and this help will be furnished to them by Central in the form of Trainees. The Order Tender will need eight to ten Trainees as the Order Office will be open 24 hours every day; the Representative will need two secretaries in the Neighborhood and help at Council Center as well. The Education Tender will need Trainees in addition to volunteers to help with the children, probably about one Trainee for every 30 to 40 kids or so, plus a secretary or around ten Trainees all told. The Neighborhood boards and rooms these Trainees but their Share of the economy is their pay. In addition, there will always be plenty of volunteer help with Order and Education from among the neighbors and from young people who are getting ready to begin their Service and want to learn what they can. The Classification sorter in Central is set so Trainees cannot be assigned to their own Councils. Thus, these Trainees will come to us from all over the RNA. Of course, we can hire additional professional help if we have the bread.

To house these necessary functions, each Neighborhood has a Center which we provide for ourselves in the style that suits our type of life, but there are minimal things each Center needs: a Meeting Hall, a many purpose, folding chair, dance and gathering place, large enough for everyone to come together. It needs three offices, one for each Tender, and unless the Trainees sleep and eat in private homes, it needs a Trainee dormitory and kitchen. The Order Office needs a bed since it's open 24 hours a day and it also needs 22 pigeon holes for mail, like General Delivery. Mail, Parcel Post and Express go from Council Center to Council Center only and it's up to each Neighborhood to get it together and decide on someone to go to the Council, pick up the Neighborhood mail and bring it to the Neighborhood Center where an Order Trainee sorts it according to the first digit of our phone numbers (9th digit of our A Numbers) or for People without phones into the signs of the Zodiac. We either pick up our mail in the Neighborhood Center or hire someone to bring it to the house. Whether or not a Neighborhood provides parcel post and express service to and from Council Center needs to be voted on. In front of the Order Office will be telephones and the Voting and Exchange computers. These are the basics and we can do anything we want from here on out, like a Coffee shop, craft displays and shops, bowling, whatever we want in Our Community Center. One Neighborhood could, for instance, provide a well-equipped stage and give plays and musicals and become known throughout the land. Another could become a religious Neighborhood with a Church for a Center...like that.

Each Neighborhood will have definite Boundaries—a street, a road, a corridor. In the center of the division, we can put a line, real or imaginary, and on one side of that line one set of Rules of Order apply and on the other, another. Neighborhoods can post their major or unusual Rules of Order on their corners so they can be seen and read by all who intend to enter. People who are not ready to abide by those Rules should not enter that Neighborhood. You might make a Rule that everyone in your Neighborhood must wear a necktie. I live in a different Neighborhood and I don't own a tie so I had better either stay the hell out of your Neighborhood or borrow a tie—my choice. If I did enter your Neighborhood without a tie, I would expect the first Citizen I saw to say to me politely: "You are supposed to wear a tie in this Neighborhood, Sir." Or, "What'sa matter wit you, dope? Can't you read? You gotta have a tie on a-round here." And if I didn't immediately start for the boundary, I would expect him to call the Order Tender or Trainee to eject me. And so it will go. It's not either *good* or *bad*, you know, it's just the way it is THERE.

Each Neighborhood will have a lot of decisions to make such as where to put all the garbage for the Council truck to pick up. My wife asks that I note that it behooves us all to help the Council and the Ecology in any way we can by separating garbage at the kitchen level so everything that can be reused will be, and maybe the Council truck would pick up different kinds of refuse on different days. Now, if everyone cleans up the sidewalk and street in front of their places as well—elimination will be a snap and public constipation at an end.

Another decision will be about stores and small businesses. I think grocery stores, boutiques, nightclubs, bars and all kinds of small businesses would be a groove in my Neighborhood as long as they and their customers abide by the Neighborhood Rules. When a business gets so large that it becomes a bug, a lot of transients and trucks, we would all get together and do something about it. Small shops may have to charge more than the super-doopers, but they insist on quality merchandise and fresh. They're a gas to shop in and you are spending your money with a friend.

France, which has held on to its small shops mostly because of French taste buds, is also well known for the excellent condition of her farm land.

A decision a City Neighborhood might make is to bar cars from its streets, make a community parking lot and convert the existing streets into parks and playgrounds with places for people to walk and bike ride. Maybe even the neighboring Neighborhood would join it and the next and the next...we can all dream. Maybe you're a night-liver and dig a place with nothing but bars and nightclubs and a few shops. Do you like flowers in the streets? Public vegetable gardens? Herein is only the structure, all this filling is up to YOU. How would you like to live?

There is just no limit to the ideas that can be developed, but one thing for sure is that our Neighborhood reflects what we are, as a group of about 1,000 People, as a Community, as a cell in the new Establishment with our individual decisions interlocking into a Neighborhood decision. We people must have the opportunity to live exactly as we wish as long as we don't harm anyone else doing it.

HUMANKIND CAN LEARN TO PROGRESS WITHOUT CONTENTION

THE ELEMENTS: Earth, Air, Fire (energy) and Water are basic to the needs of all living things on the planet Earth. To an extraterrestrial observer it must seem that the intelligent beings on this planet hate life and all living things: mining, spraying, killing and polluting. We used to think that Earth, Air, Fire and Water were inexhaustible but we know more now; land *does* stop producing if you always take out and never put back (*mine* instead of *farm*). Lake Erie *did* die, there *are* rivers that catch on fire, there *is* an energy crisis, the air over LA and Mexico City *is* virtually unbreathable, the oceans *are* polluted to the extent that plankton are endangered. Remember, Cousteau estimates we have fifty years left on this planet and without plankton to produce oxygen to burn the fuel to make the smog which we can't breathe anyway—

well, we gotta admit, we've been careless and unnecessarily destructive and as yet our technology hasn't come up with another planet we can move to and start over.

None of this has been *wrong*, just thoughtless. I suppose you have to reach the brink to see the abyss, but it's time to Change. It's time to take the elements out of the hands of individual greedy Humans and appoint Guardians of the Four Elements; Guardians of the Ecology. These Guardians are the Councils in the new Establishment. They cannot own any of the elements—no one can—they are not ownable. They belong to the planet, to life, and we are only a part of this whole.

THE COUNCILS ARE THE GUARDIANS OF THE FOUR ELEMENTS—OF THE ECOLOGY—OF THE THINGS THAT SUPPORT LIFE.

The land and continental shelf areas of the North American continent will be divided into Councils that contain about 200,000 people. Councils come in six main types: City, Suburban, Farm, Ranch, Waterfront and Transportation, like organs in our symbiosis. There are also mixed Councils (combinations of the main types) and Central Lease Councils.

City Councils are bounded by an encircling highway, an arbitrary division made by the people who will do the dividing into Councils. City Councils are inside while **Suburban Councils** and other types are outside of this highway. Councils that make up one City or Megapolis cooperate with each other to operate and maintain the necessary communal services to make the area happily habitable by all the people who live there. Like in the Greater New York area there could be a total of 70 Councils: maybe 40 City types, six Waterfront, four Transportation and 20 Suburban Councils which cooperate to provide water, sewage disposal, electricity and other community services for the 14 million inhabitants.

Farm, Country and Town Councils watch over and farm the land that provides us with most of our food—200,000 or so people whose business is farming and agricultural marketing. **Ranch, Forest and Wilderness Councils** are the largest in area and include forests, deserts, mountains, jungles, scenic areas and like that. Their interests are lumber, cattle, sheep, mining and probably tourists. **Waterfront and Shore Councils** are in the business of taking care of our water resources and water transportation facilities. They include all or parts of islands and main shipping waterways and are centered on port Towns and Cities along the sea and lake coasts of North America. Each has a specific area of the continental shelf to care for and fish making possible unpoisoned fish for all. The land areas of a Waterfront Council may be scattered along the coast including fishing and port towns, but its continental shelf area is in one piece. The shore line between ports may be parts of other types of Councils for which the water is pleasure, not business. Waterfront Councils will pick up the ultimate responsibility for sewage and perhaps garbage disposal making sure pollutants don't reach the lakes and oceans. They charge the other Councils for this service. Wouldn't it be fun to see garbage scows going *up* the Hudson River to spread their wares onto the land?

Transportation Councils operate and maintain the major land transportation arteries and airways of the RNA. They stretch out along the land expressways until 200,000 people are included—people whose main source of revenue is from moving people and things. Their borders are the highway fence or service roads and areas, widening out to include towns and small cities that are a part of this ecology and narrowing to the fence again as they pass through City or Suburban Councils.

Central Lease Councils are not Councils in the sense the others are. They are areas leased by Central from Councils for various purposes and do not have the requirement to include 200,000 people. Central will lease areas where people will go who do not wish to or cannot live in our society: the socially unadaptable. The present Establishment puts these and many others into jails, mental institutions, penitentiaries, somewhere confined behind the strongest steel. In the RNA social unadaptability is redefined because of the wide variety of Neighborhoods and there will be fewer of these people to care for.

THERE'S A PLACE FOR ALL HUMANS TO LIVE OUTSIDE OF CAGES.

Central leases its own site from some Council and also leases, administers and maintains our *Continental Treasures* which formerly were National Parks, Monuments, Wilderness areas, archeological sites and like that. Central can lease and staff new Treasures as people vote for them. Another type of Central Lease is the land provided for the Boundary Patrol units, which will be gathered into Councils just like the rest of us. Central also leases pieces of land to use for environmental investigations like sites for large telescopes, weather stations, maybe star ship launching sites and who knows what else.

If you have the idea that every square inch of the continent is part of one Council or another, you've got it straight. This division allows each Council to become expert in and attract experts interested in its unique ecology. Also, Councils with similar conditions can learn from each other. Like Waterfront Councils cooperate in marine life management. Councils which include headwaters of rivers and watershed areas will attract and train experts in that; the same with Councils that have dams, wildlife protection areas, crops that must be picked immediately or rot or intra-urban transportation conditions. Certain Councils, especially Waterfront and Wilderness types, would become experts in extracting bread from Tourists Who Come. Transportation Councils would really find out what people travelling along the main routes need and want; how best to move people and things...like that.

The basis for dividing the RNA into Councils will be by type of ecology.

The Councils will be administered by the 200 Neighborhood Representatives, the Councilors, who have to have a head for business since they have to make a nut of about ₡5,000,000 per week to pay the People's shares, etc., from land leases, land lease fees, taxes, the mortuary business, banking, risk insurance and other types of revenue which are peculiar to each type of Council. Taxes, banking and insurance are explained later on. Here I will talk about land leases and fees.

When thinking about land ownership, I want you to make a deliberate semantic change. If we cannot own any of the four Elements, who owns the land? Nobody! Well, how about MY land? I own it, paid good money for it and now you are going to take it away from me and my family? Calm yourselves! Nothing as drastic as all that; we're just going to make a simple semantic change. Substitute:

> *Land Lease* for *Deed*
> *Land Lease Fees* for *Property Taxes*
> *Land Lease Lien* for *Mortgage*

Councils will assign specific numbers to every cohesive piece of land in their area. The Lease of this number then becomes the possession, the thing you own, not the land, which you cannot 'own' anyway. You can't even move it. "Why the hell the Change if it's the same thing?" The answer is: to get ecological guardianship of the land.

Land Lease Fees are a portion of the income of the Council and are based, by Custom, on what the land is used for. Farm land used as farm land has a low land lease fee. Farm land used for industry tends to get expensive while land useless for farming can be cheap for industry. If someone is **MISUSING: misuse of land means different things in different Councils. Each Council will have to decide what *misuse* means for its ecology, but here we can include any action that heads toward death rather than life: building on rich bottom land, overgrazing, mining farm soil, destroying watersheds, like that.** OK, so if someone is misusing leased land, that lease can either be very expensive or cancelled if the treatment of the land isn't changed. Here the Change loses its semantic character and becomes real. We, the People in the Council, can actually be assured that the land is being used to its capability and, further, we can insist on it.

A Lease can become a permanent possession and be willed to anyone we choose by Homesteading it. Every Member can Homestead one piece of property by applying to the Council to add an H in front of the Lease number, then indicating to whom it is to be leased upon death, which the Council will do automatically unless the land is being misused. If the lease has no H in its number, it reverts to the Council upon the Leaseholder's death. This Homestead provision is made to allow ranches, orchards, farms and even apartment houses (if the land the apartment is on is leased to the person) to be passed on down the line of the family to maximize their care. It takes a long time to build a true jewel and it's imperative for someone who is spending all that love and energy to know that it will continue to be loved and cared for. We can increase the sizes of our Homesteads by persuading the Council Bank and Lease Committee to assign one number instead of several to adjoining pieces of land. Empire Builders, pay attention! Conversely, a Council can break up parcels of land into separate Lease numbers.

Councils will also lease land to industry and these leases can be cancelled upon evidence of pollution. Industry, however, cannot own leases. Purifying and recycling the air and water used by any industry is just another process for them, but it's life for us.

THE ONLY WAY TO HANDLE POLLUTION IS ABSOLUTELY.

When talking about Land Leases, we have to also consider subleases, sub-subleases and like that. All of this is completely possible and necessary and the Council only has to deal with the original lessee. It will become a logical development for a member of a Company or Corporation to lease an entire Industrial Complex from the Council, then sublease to individual manufacturers. The leasing company could provide the sublessees with the Elements and recycling processes needed plus guards, fire protection, bus service and parking lots; provide everything needed by sublessees and charge them for it. The original lessee will then be responsible to the Council for any pollution that might occur. There would be no one living in these Industrial Complexes, so the Rules of Order and their enforcement would become the task of the Company.

On the other end of this stick, land which is not cultivatable can be used for living. This means that wilderness land not set aside for public use can be leased at a very low lease fee by People who want to live there. People from the city who wish to lease mountain and desert land might have to take a course in fire prevention and survival type living, but there are millions of square miles of unused land which could be lived on very well when People have enough bread for their survival needs. OK on Land Leases and fees?

The Councils will need definite boundaries. As the Neighborhoods use a street, a road or a corridor in a large high-rise, so the Councils in a city will need a boulevard, preferably with a park communally maintained between the two traffic lanes. In the country a highway or any all weather road would make a good boundary. The point is that the boundaries between Councils must be an accessible traffic movement place, not some mountain top, so there is never any doubt in anyone's mind where one Council ends and the other begins. OK?

Every Council has to provide certain facilities, one of which is the Council Center: the financial, commercial and administrative center of the Council which has offices and committee rooms for the Councilors and the POB (the Post Office, Bank and Insurance business). The POB needs a Computer Security Room, a Business Room, a Possession Room, an ID Room with a closet for video tape storage and a Tax Office in addition to the Post Office and Banking facilities. These Council Centers are not a part of any Neighborhood.

The PO part of the POB is engaged in the Business of sorting incoming mail into bags or bins for the various Neighborhoods in the Council. Outgoing mail is sorted here too, put on Council busses and taken to the Transcontinental Hi-way drop-off points (Way Stations) for long distances or is immediately delivered to nearby Councils—whichever makes more sense. In addition to the Council Center each Council will provide Council Shops which include a hospital with mortuary attached, a Library, the shops and studios, Labs, two TV stations, Council Houses, athletic fields plus things like power, water and garbage and sewage disposal.

The Energy from the atomic reactions in our Sun has been converted and stored by plants and other living organisms which were themselves then stored in the earth as oil and coal; this process happened on a geologic time scale of millions of years. You say, "elemental" and I reply that the process which created all this available Fire (fuel for power) has stopped, quit. We now have all that kind of fire we're ever going to have. It's time to get into atomics with both feet and with all our engineering and scientific talent so we can stop using our stored energy to brush our teeth. Even after we're using atomics, we'll still need oil to overcome the friction of our machines and a lot of our plastics use petroleum too, so let's save some.

Atomic power plants need not be tremendous in size to be efficient, nor do they have to be dangerous to life. There already are experimental models of reactors that will provide power for small loads and would meet our requirements. With these smaller units, Councils can have their own small reactors to provide their own people with power. For sure, several City Councils could provide for themselves the power they need. The present trend toward monstrous units capable of handling an entire state's power requirements (*bigger is better?*) has got to be stopped and development of handy dandy units, similar to an atomic submarine's power plant, begun. This is a sensible approach to getting free power to the people. These small power plants are unnecessarily expensive now but mass produced could be made more cheaply for sale and distribution throughout the RNA. Thus, the People would supply their own power and industry would supply theirs.

A Council with water will sell to another Council that has none. For example, Transportation Councils would probably not provide water works for their residents but would buy water from neighboring Councils along their routes. Each Council must make sure that no water containing sewage leaves its boundaries. If a Council cannot or doesn't want to provide sewage disposal, it can pipe it to the next Council that has a disposal plant and will take care of it—for a fee, of course. Councils with sewage disposal plants can sell the fertilizer to farmers but will put only sweet drinkable water back into streams, rivers, lakes and oceans, for our lives' sakes.

With garbage sorted, first at the kitchen, then at the Neighborhood levels, Councils need trucks which will go to the Neighborhoods and pick up different kinds on different days and take it to places where it can be sold for recycling. They can charge the Neighborhoods the difference between what it's sold for and what it costs to haul it around. Tin, aluminum, paper and plastic can all be used again for something and glass bottles can be refilled.

To do all these things we will use one of the most important ecological assets and resources we have to our best advantage—LABOR. We must learn to help each other even if Credits change hands during the helping.

WE MUST HELP EACH OTHER EVEN FOR MONEY.

For example, you could pay your water bill by working in the Council Water Works, maybe digging ditches, welding, doing what you can do. A Neighborhood could supply the labor to drive the garbage trucks around to pay its bill. Farm Councils could provide housing or trailer outlets and camping facilities to take care of the labor that would come to help during the heavy work load times—planting and harvesting. Those providing the prettiest places would draw the most labor...like that. **Working together, we can work it all out.**

Our other chief asset is Young People, the ones for whom we're doing all this. The Neighborhoods care for their own until they become 12, when the Councils get them. The Council will feed, care for medically, physically, athletically and educationally—fully found, as they say, for all young humans from ages 12 to 19. When kids reach 12, you give them a party, a knapsack, a sleeping bag, a mess kit and a big kiss. The Council gives them their ₡15 a week and the right to live in the Council Houses all over the RNA. They'll come home for needed privacy, visits and to store acquired possessions. If you want to keep your kid around the house, that's between the two of you but the other kids, the all night noise, the ideas, the shouting and the urges will all be in the Council Houses. They will be free to wander where they will.

Council Houses will be miniature Neighborhoods wherein the Rules of Order will be made by the kids who live there so they can practice decision making. Each Council will need, let's say, 300 Council Houses which will hold from 50 to 150 kids each. This is on a one tenth scale to the regular Neighborhood. They will cost less than we're spending now on high schools, juvenile delinquency and all that crap.

Council Houses can be of different shapes, like a long barracks or on top of each other in a high-rise, situated near the Library and the Athletic Field with the Council Shops not too far off. At one end of the Council House is the bathroom with showers, toilets and washbowls and a MedTrainee's room dutch-doored to keep the EYE on the mayhem. The Trainee passes out soap, vitamins, bandaids, birth-control pills and like that as well as watching the kids for more serious things for which a doctor or hospital may be needed. Two of the requirements for this job are a very loud voice and a pulse of steel. At the other end of the long barracks is the galley with long wooden tables, several refrigerators full of milk, wholesome bread, peanut butter, catsup, pickles, onions and lettuce and carrots and fruit in season. There are juice squeezers and extractors and stoves where the kids can cook the hamburgers and frozen fish from the freezer, and in general have *just like home* conditions. They all have their mess kits and utensils—and don't forget the Bircher-Muesli (granola) and enriched corn flakes. However well a Council feeds the kids so shall it be known. Another dutch door, another Trainee who sees they don't waste food and that the stocks are kept up and like that. There is a Council House Manager to oversee the whole schmutz, the only adult allowed in the Council House. Between the two ends lies the bunkhouse with maybe 75 double decker nylon, indestructible but comfortable cots. I figure that if each Council House has enough lower bunks for the regulars, the uppers will take care of the overflow. At the two ends of the rows of bunks are study areas with TV sets for kids who want to study—FOR THOSE WHO WANT. Councils where the skiing and surfing are attractive would have large seasonal overflows and would need extra Council Houses. Now can you think of a better place for kids? I can't.

The Council Houses are for kids only but the shops, studios and Labs are for everyone. In the Labs we can learn what has been discovered about our environment by setting up and watching experiments. Given the information known, it's fun to dream about the things we may discover. The shops and studios are equipped to work in wood, steel, tin, leather, autos, you name it and there's a shop to learn it in; pottery, sewing, theatre, painting (both kinds), sculpture; rooms with typewriters, rooms with computers, rooms with machines—all set up to let those who want to learn, learn, and those who don't can stay the hell out. The shops and studios will provide not only for hand work but for whatever type of maintenance work a Council needs: auto shops (where, for example, garbage trucks and Council busses are repaired), boat shops, surfboard shops, farm machinery shops, horse shoeing, sheet metal, welding, bookbinding, plumbing, sewer, electrical, computer, glass, janitor, whatever kind of shop a Council needs, it provides. If your Council doesn't have a lab, let's say to learn to develop film, pack your pack and go to a Council that does.

These shops will be supervised by hired professionals with Trainees helping out. Everybody gets that weekly share from the Councils and must stretch it into the best standard of living possible by doing things for themselves with the help of others. For example, if your car needs work, you can take it to the Council auto shop and trade your labor or Credits to someone who is waiting for someone like you to show up. This mechanic can use the Council shop and equipment and that's groovy with everybody but he or she must clean the tools, put them back and pay the tool crib Trainee for broken ones. The Trainee can also sell oil and grease...like that. The same kind of thing would be true of boats in a Shore Council. Don't worry about running out of Trainees. There are about 16,000,000 at a time.

The Councils will become the main organizers and supporters of competitive athletics, fat cattle, speed boats, roses, Chess, Go; you name it and there will be competition between Councils for it. We are not going to drive the territorial, group, tribe pride out of mankind by any means I can see, so we will provide means for its expression on a Council level with the winning teams, cattle, whatever, competing for the Central Championship. With Councils at a similar level numerically and economically, it will be a tough contest all the way. Councils will have about the same basic economic situation, the same number of People, so the teams will start from similar bases and no handicapping will be necessary. Some Councils will be Soccer Councils, some American Football Councils, some Hockey Councils, like that, but all in all the Sport and Competitive situation will be a gas.

How do Councils work? How are they organized? Remember the 200 or so Neighborhood Representatives become Councilors in Council Center. These Councilors are the Government (find out what the people want and help them do it). They divide themselves into 10 Committees and these Committees hire, fire (if necessary) and pay the expert professional Tenders needed to do the work. In effect, the Committee hires someone to run the department, then acts as liaison between the Head Tender and the people. Whatever a Council has voted to do, it's up to the Committee of Councilors and the professional Tenders to see it's done: like provide tractor lanes in Farm Councils, bike and pedestrian paths in City Councils...whatever. OK? The people have the ideas, the Councilors and Tenders figure out how to do it, then tell the people (Council Bill) and how much it'll cost and the people vote to approve it or not.

Here's a chart:

COUNCIL ORGANIZATION

COUNCIL CENTER:

Senator
Senator's Committee
Deputy Senators
Trainees

Head Bank Tender	Head Tax Tender	Head Justice Tender
Bank and Lease Committee	Tax Committee	Justice Committee
Bank Tenders	Tax Tenders	Fact Finder Operators
Trainees	Trainees	Trainees

COUNCIL SHOPS AREA:

Head Medical Tender	Head Maintenance Tender	Head Education Tender
Medical Committee	Maintenance Committee	Education Committee
Doctors, Nurses, Morticians, Veterinarians	Tenders: Sewer, Water, Road, Shop	Education and Television Tenders
Trainees	Trainees	Trainees

COUNCIL FIELD AREAS:

Head Electrical Tender	(other) Head Tender	(other) Head Tender
Electrical Committee	Committee	Committee
Tenders: Power Plant and Distribution	Tenders	Tenders
Trainees	Trainees	Trainees

The nine Council Head Tenders are well trained, highly paid professionals of equal rank. They hire the Tenders they require and ask Central for needed Trainees.

The Senator is chosen by the Councilors from among themselves and represents the Council at Central. If the Representative from your Neighborhood is chosen as Senator, you'll have to choose another Rep. The Council pays the Senator. The Senator's Committee collects the information the Senator needs to prepare Bills at Central and Senators choose deputies from this Committee to chair Council Meetings and explain Central Bills in their absence.

You'll get to know more about the triangle of Tenders at Council Center later on, the triangle that takes care of our banking, leases, taxes, computers and justice. The triangle in charge of the Council Shop area includes: the Medical Tenders who are in charge of health in the Council Houses, public health problems like epidemics, preventative medicine like Well Baby Clinic and TB trailers, deal with animal health and supervise and run the Hospital and Mortuary; the Maintenance Tenders who are in charge of the workings of the Council...the maintenance of the water supply, the sewers and vehicles, maybe the roads and streets and run the shops; and Education Tenders who supervise Council Houses, studios, Labs, the library, two TV stations and athletics. Medical Tenders get vehicles from Maintenance Tenders and a lot of customers from Education Tenders...like that.

The Field Tender triangle includes the Electrical Tenders who have the responsibility for the Council's power generating and distribution system. The other two groups of Tenders are different for different Councils. Like, a Farm Council might have a Road Tender, a Marketing Tender or a Land and Agriculture Use Tender; a Waterfront Council, a Port Tender and maybe a Water Safety or Fisheries Tender...or a Disposal Tender...like that.

If a Council forms part of a city, the Councilors choose one from among their number as a City Administrator who represents that Council on the City Board. Again, the Neighborhood whose Representative was chosen for the City Board will need to elect another Representative. The City Board is a Committee, really, whose membership consists of these City Administrators and they hire and fire the professionals needed to coordinate communal city services and to present a budget to the people so the expenses of the city would be paid by the Councils involved. Like the New York City Board would consist of 70 Administrators, one from each Council making up the City. A smaller city would have fewer Administrators making up the board.

Any kind of structure—a building, a bridge or a dam—can be designed and built as an indeterminant structure or as a determinant one. In the determinant structure, the load bearing capability of each member is calculable, while in the indeterminate structure, it is impossible to figure out which member is resisting what kind of stress. Our present governmental structure is an indeterminate one and we cannot tell just what further loads it can take. In this proposed new Establishment, let's make each portion of the structure as simple, as stable and as flexible as we can, so we know what loads each member is to support. We can construct our new Establishment of stable modules and by varying the number of modules, we can prevent an unstable, unfigureable situation from developing. **Let's build a life wherein the help and support we can give each other becomes a force.**

HUMANKIND MUST LEARN TO PROGRESS WITHOUT CONTENTION

TRUTH: the quality of being in accordance with experience, facts or reality.

LIE: a statement not in accordance with experience, facts or reality made with *intent* to deceive.

JUSTICE: the art of discovering which is which in any dispute so the Principals or the People can decide what action to take.

The actual experience of being totally truthful to yourself and others is mind blowing and if we wish to become telepathic, we humans will have to learn to be truthful. A telepath can sense all those falsehoods people tell themselves.

Imagine a gauge like the upper half of a clock. When the hand is at 9:00 o'clock, it indicates 100% lies and when the hand is at 3:00 o'clock, it indicates 100% truth with 12:00 o'clock being half and half. Any statement can be from 100% lie to 100% truth depending on intent and qualifying words. The degree of intent determines where our statements fit on the scale. We can say, "I always intend to tell the truth," and make the needle swing to 50% lie (10:30), because we used the word *always* which is usually lie in front. If we say, "I never intend to lie," we're still on the lie side by the very quality of the word *never*, so the semantics of our statements become important in determining whether they fit on the Truth or on the Lie side. We can clean up a lot of our lying lives by merely being careful with semantics. Then there's the time and place factor. I say, "I weigh 200 pounds," but that's only the truth now before dinner and on this planet. As we blibbity blab our way through life, our statements and actions are usually somewhere between 100% lies and 100% truths. Understanding this goes a long way toward understanding what being multivalued means.

In this Segment, we are agreeing to give up the Right to Lie, but only the Right to tell 100% lies. The rest of the scale is our own business. "I will take my vitamins today," is the truth if I do, a lie if I don't. "I'll try to remember to take my vitamins today," is the truth if I really try. "I took my vitamins today," is either 100% lie or 100% truth, depending on whether I did or not. "I promise you I'll take my vitamins today," is something I agree to do and is 100% lie if I don't. These 100% lies are the ones we agree to give up; the lies about what we actually *did*, what we actually *agreed* to.

Once we give up these 100% lies, we won't need laws, law making and all that enforcement shit. Think about this: today's legal system was set up to find out who lied about what and who did what to whom but courts seem to have become places where, instead of finding the truth of a matter, they find out which side is the cleverer, has done the most research, has the most influence and can tell the most convincing, undetectable lies.

We are taught to lie from the day we break our first sugar bowl and from that day forward our entire social, business, legal and private lives are tremendously affected by our ability to lie and get away with it. People who tell the truth in our present culture are at a distinct disadvantage. Lying has become both a science and an art. For example, count the number of lies you tell yourself in the average day, like, "it's not really hurting me to smoke this cigarette, eat this piece of marshmallow pie," "Sure, I'm an honest, upright person, but *this* is business,"...like that.

Since we're conditioned to lie, we're going to need a way to determine (in the existing generations anyway) if someone is telling a 100% lie.

What the new Establishment needs is a Machine, a machine that will tell us when people lie about what they **did or agreed to**; a Slave **without bias** which will very simply determine from physiological reactions if a person is telling a lie he or she *knows* is a lie. **BIAS is a pressure which causes something to deviate from a straight line. A MACHINE is a device designed and constructed by humans to do work; a tool used by humans to do something they don't want to or cannot do directly.** Machines are definitively two valued. They are either *right* or *wrong*, on or off, within specifications or 'out of spec.' People who run machines must realize this while running them. **A COMPUTER makes the automatic machine possible.** Look at washing machines. The first ones did the scrubbing but you had to wring...then they attached the wringer but you still had to put in the water. Finally came a timer, a small computer, that told the machine when to let water in, when to wash, rinse and wring. Now the human attention still necessary involves sorting and to sort clothes takes certain multi-valued judgements a machine cannot make without some human supplying the bias of what's the right way to sort and what's wrong—different with everyone. If a washing machine is allowed to operate in a straight line, like washing white dress shirts with dark blue jeans, the shirts come out streaky. Washing machines don't care about streaky shirts, but some humans do. Humans sort clothes so white dress shirts are washed together and dark things are washed together and that's bias.

The machine we need to stop existing generations from telling 100% lies, lies we KNOW are lies, is the Fact Finder or FF for short. It can be designed and built using knowledge and technology we already have. It will measure variations in brain wave patterns, blood pressure, pulse rate, respiration rate, perspiration rate, voice vibratory patterns and anything else we forget about or can't control when we start to tell 100% lies. The FF would only light up, buzz and jangle when we tell a lie we *know* is a lie and would not need to sort out the other types or even be told that lies are *bad*. It certainly would NOT concern itself with ideas or ideals, only actions.

We, the People as Councils, will own the FF's and I see them trailer mounted, two units back to back in one trailer, each unit with its own entrance. These trailers will generally be parked in the Council Centers but can be pulled to any area where use is heavy. They can be plugged in but are self-powered as well, when necessary. Councils will have enough FF's for their own work load but can rent them from each other as needed. They are all alike.

In order to eliminate the entire crime-punishment-law-court-jail system we now have crumbing up our lives, would you allow yourself to be forced to tell the truth about what you did or contracted to do by some Idiot Machine? I would! I would agree to use the FF if I knew for sure it would be the same for everybody, rich or poor, green or pink.

With this machine, Crime and Punishment can be changed to Action and Consequence and it's not just a semantic change either, as you will see. **CRIME is** the breaking of some law and PUNISHMENT is what They do to people because they were caught. Punishment as a deterrent to Crime does work to the extent that a padlock on a glass door works. A Criminal merely throws a brick through the glass and walks in, but if the glass door has been mistakenly left unlocked and the mildly dishonest or curious walks in, takes something and gets caught, the only thing the Punishment does is create another Criminal. Our prisons create more criminals than they *cure* (if a criminal can be *cured* or even punished) because: guess what most people think and feel about while in jail and guess what it takes to be accepted in jail by the other inmates? Putting someone in a cage for merely being stupid, especially when young, has gotta be changed. There are two separate types of errors: a more or less unthinking or youthful mistake which hurts others and that committed by the pro, the person who hurts others deliberately for excitement, for a better standard of living or whatever and there's a big difference between the two. Under the present system there is little difference made in how they are treated except that the pro usually gets preferential treatment which comes with knowing the rules of this particular game. **ACTION is an act or non-act (it may actually be inaction) for which or because of which some individual in the RNA feels another should be Challenged. CONSEQUENCE is what happens to people, not so much for what they did but for what they are or more correctly, for what they were when they made the Action and for the possibility of their becoming that again.**

The present legal system of trials (and errors?) uses witnesses on top of witnesses to try to find out what really happened and the stories can be as varied as imagination allows. In many trials today, lawyers never even call the principals in a case. This we gotta stop! Witnesses have to disappear along with their biased and often lying testimony. They're a stone drag! With the FF's we will deal with the principals only (if still with us) and if the principals are required to tell the truth to each other and to us, the dispute is soon settled—and exactly truthfully.

In this new system we will seat the two principals, the Challenger and Challengee, in two identical comfortable chairs, have them don identical natty Crowns while they grasp the two Brass Balls on the chair arms. Central and the Councils cooperate to make certain that a Challengee meets the Challenger. The only way to avoid a Challenge is to split from the RNA. There is someone there in the trailer to set up the Fact Finder, see that the balls are firmly clasped, ask the questions, act as referee and follow the case to its conclusion. This person, *the Fact Finder Operator, can ask questions only about what people did or agreed to do:*

"Farmer Smith, did you agree to milk Farmer Jones' cows while he went to the City?"

"Yes, I did, but the juice cut off right in the middle..."

"But you did agree to milk the cows?"

"That's right, but nobody can milk 50 cows by hand."

Jones breaks in:

"That's a lie, I've done it many a time. When a light pole breaks or something, you gotta!"

"Mr. Smith, do I understand that you cannot milk 50 cows by hand and have never done so?"

"That's right..." The bells go off and the lights flash.

"Well, I could when I was young but I don't think I could anymore." The machine quiets down.

The Operator asks, "Your failure to milk the cows caused some of them to go dry, is that right?"

"Yes, that's right; I admit it."

"Then why don't we get together and see how we can settle this with some sort of equitable solution. How many cows?..." and so on until the dispute is settled with the Fact Finder Operator as the mediator in an already established breach of contract. The Operator uses the tool, the Fact Finder, to establish the truth, then the Principals settle the case if they can.

If they cannot, who is watching the painful scene? Just Everybody who wants to, that's all. There's a video tape camera mounted high up, behind the FFOperator's seat which makes a tape of everything that goes down from the instant the machine is snapped on until it is shut off. If the two dairymen agree on some settlement, the tape is erased as soon as the bill is paid but if they cannot settle the dispute with the FFOperator's help, the content of the tape is advertised in the papers, then played on one of the Council TV stations. Tapes that aren't erased are stored in the storage closet in the Post Office Bank (POB). Anybody in the Council who is interested can watch the show and the next morning can help decide, by a kind of voting, how much the Challenger should get from the Challengee per dry cow.

THE PEOPLE ARE THE JURY. THERE IS NO JUDGE. The Fact Finder Operator is a referee, not a judge.

The Right of Challenge or **THE CHALLENGE** is all the Rights we have ever had and some we've never had, all rolled up into one BIG RIGHT.

THE CHALLENGE IS A PEOPLE'S RIGHT. IT CANNOT BE USED BY GROUPS BECAUSE THERE ARE ONLY TWO CHAIRS.

People can Challenge People and can Challenge any kind of Groups of People and force the Group to choose someone to represent it and sit in the other Chair. But Groups do not have this Right. Anyone who Challenges you does it as an individual, even though a part of some Group. Do you dig it? The Government cannot Challenge; the Council cannot; the Boundary Patrol cannot, pigs even. But you can Challenge THEM, like:

"Do you guys put old dirty nasty weevils in the snuff I buy from you?"

"Oh, yes indeed, sir, one day seven years ago we got weevils in the snuff due to some unfortunate accident and found that weevils add a taste that tripled the sales of our Snuffle and Sniff Snuff. We have continued to add a certain proportion of weevil to that brand ever since and now you must realize, sir, that the weevils we use have been especially cultivated, organically, and are the purest weevils ever known and if our snuff is objectionable to you because it has weevil in it, you have no choice but to choose another brand, but if you like that particular metallic taste in your snuff, you have to change your head around to sniffing weevil along with your tobacco."

For sure, the Challenge will change advertising. Imagine: "Old Grandfather Straight Whiskey can make you feel like the Prince pictured on the left—also like this skid row bum."

Fact Finder Operators become important members of the new society, highly trained and respected professionals well paid by the Councils. They represent the Council, the People, and try to get the participants to settle their difficulty between themselves. This is their main job. Their areas of judgement are whether to play a tape on TV or not. If there has been no agreement or if there is a possibility of future harm to other people, the Operator is bound to play the tape to the People, by Custom. Operators decide who is to pay for the FFTest and are, also by Custom, to give the Media all the information they request on any tape scheduled on TV. There will be no publicity AT ALL before a Fact Finder Test but the Media are entitled to drum up as much interest as they care to after an unerased FFTest.

If during a Test the Operator thinks or is convinced that the Challengee is doped to the eyebrows, the Principal can be checked by a doctor and the Test postponed until the effect of the drug or whatever is gone..This could be expensive for dopees as they pay for the Challenger's fee twice. On the other hand, if Operators are confronted with a lot of I don't knows or I don't remembers or feel that a person is trying to beat the machine, they can call a doctor who could use chemicals to unlock the Principal's mind from wherever it has been sent, like under hypnosis. "Get Challenged, forget and get high," could become a byword.

FFOperators administer Consequences and won't be crooked, either, because they too are Challengeable, so if you feel your FFOperator was biased, all you need do is Challenge. You also have the right to insist to a hearing on TV. If the Operator is bent on settling the matter in the trailer, you can shout, "I won't settle, I won't settle. I want it on TV. I want the People to hear," and, by Custom, so it will be.

The Head Justice Tender hires and fires FFOperators, applies for needed Trainees, makes sure the FF units are in repair, schedules Fact Finder Tests— and is generally in charge of Justice. The aim of Justice in the RNA is to settle disputes so both Principals come out smiling. The Justice function of the Council works to this end.

A new breed will probably evolve in this system, the Advisor. The Advisor is a person who can be present at the Test to advise a Principal what questions to ask, but not how to answer the questions put. It could become a profession or just a thing a best friend would do for loving support.

There are two types of Challenges: **The Challenge** which always requires an FFOperator and may be played on TV for the People's judgement, and the **Minor Challenge** which is run by an Operator Trainee whose only area of judgement is *who pays*. Unless you're an exhibitionist, you try to get the Challenger to make it a Minor Challenge which can't be played on TV. We'll learn to stay out of the People's Eye in this system. Minor Challenges can be used, for example, to find out if the guy really did shoot 71 elephants while on safari in Africa.

Sure...cranks, bugs, assholes, freaks...just anybody can Challenge us and make up a list of questions for the FFOperator or Trainee to ask but we get to bat their heads around as well and it will quiet down to business as soon as we all realize that we really *cannot* lie about what we did without taking the chance of having our perfidy exposed on TV to the People of the Council or of the whole RNA.

By Custom, there is a standard rate paid to the FFOperator for use of the FF, like maybe ¢60 per hour figured in quarter of an hour increments so 15 minutes or under would cost ¢15. If the Challenge is proven, the Challengee pays the machine time plus a ¢15 Principal fee to the Challenger. If, however, the Challenge is not proven, it's the other way around. Of course, the Principals can decide they should share the cost. Compare this to the cost of Justice today.

A guy speeding his car through a Neighborhood full of kids gets Challenged by Irate Citizen; if he keeps the Test down to 15 minutes, it costs him ¢15.00 for the Machine and ¢15.00 to Irate Citizen, who doesn't mind making the bread for the trouble. ¢30.00 plus the bother, for speeding. If it comes out in the Test that he has been often Challenged for unsafe driving; in a Minor Challenge the Trainee would say, "I'm not competent to decide this...I'll have to call an Operator." It might be obvious to the Trainee that the guy's a menace on wheels but Trainees cannot decide to show a Test on TV. The status of the case changes from Minor Challenge to Challenge and the FFOperator could decide to play this habitually unsafe driver's Test on TV for the People's judgement. This system without laws really will work! When you bug someone, you get Challenged so eventually people will learn to stop being bugs. The way to eliminate cops is to keep ourselves in Order.

I remember walking in the park with my father and watching several small boys my age dodging through strolling people carrying off a drinking fountain. Who else noticed? My father, a lawyer, and he called the Man in Blue to chase after the "gang" down an alley to their clubhouse, no doubt. I was hoping they wouldn't be caught. That fountain belonged to the Establishment—nothing to do with ME. Right? In the new system I will know the fountain belongs to Me, not to Them, and both my father and I would act differently. He would ask the kids for their Neighborhood numbers so he could Challenge but I probably would try to stop them from carrying off My drinking fountain. Remember, Neighborhoods are *responsible* for their children under 12.

Ripping off seems to have developed a double standard: when a complaint is made by a store or any business, the police get right on it and try but when People are robbed, they're handed a form and told, "Come back in the morning and see the Lieutenant." So you laugh a little shakily; after all, the guy did have a gun. And the only capital you can make out of the experience is that you have a tale to tell at the next party—only to be capped by another's horror story. If ripping off becomes an act against a People, instead of against the Law, amateurs will dig the bad Kharma and get out of the action. For those whose Kharma it is to steal, Laws are only a challenge.

Our new Challenge is a direct thing and the more harm offered, the tougher the People's Consequences are likely to be. If a man beats a woman and she rushes down to the Neighborhood Order Office to fill out a Challenge-Consequence card, it doesn't mean he's been Challenged. In the morning, the Order Tender would get in touch with her to find out whether she still wants to Challenge or she has already forgotten about it. The Tender would do the same if a neighbor complained of noise or a kid complained of being beaten, like that. Part of a Neighborhood Tender's job is to try to settle all matters of Order in the Neighborhood. In this case, if the woman is sick and tired of getting beat up, first, all she does is tell the man to leave if it's her house (women choose with whom they live) and if he won't leave, she has the Order Tender help him move. If it's his house and she really doesn't like to be beaten, she'd move. No longer is she dependent on his pay check, remember. OK, let's say he's already been helped out of the house, got drunk, returned and beat her up again. This time she is for sure going to Challenge, so she fills out a Challenge-Consequence card and the Order Tender makes an appointment with the Justice Office for an FFTest.

CHALLENGE-CONSEQUENCE CARD

FRONT

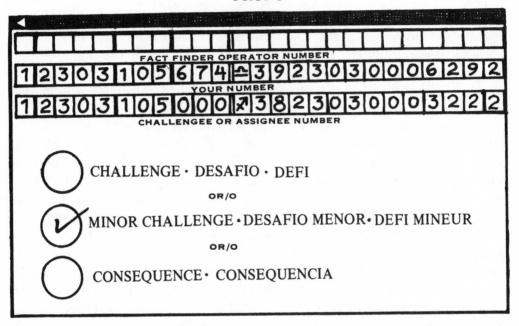

CHALLENGE · DESAFIO · DEFI

OR/O

✓ MINOR CHALLENGE · DESAFIO MENOR · DEFI MINEUR

OR/O

CONSEQUENCE · CONSEQUENCIA

BACK

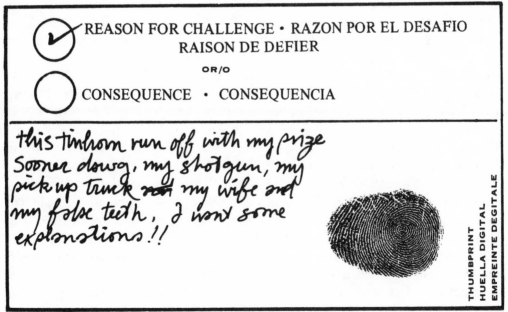

✓ REASON FOR CHALLENGE · RAZON POR EL DESAFIO
RAISON DE DEFIER

OR/O

CONSEQUENCE · CONSEQUENCIA

this tinhorn run off with my prize
Sooner dawg, my shotgun, my
pick up truck and my wife and
my false teeth, I want some
explanations!!

THUMBPRINT
HUELLA DIGITAL
EMPREINTE DEGITALE

After the FFTest proved that he returned to beat the woman and that she needed protection, the first Consequence would be that he'd pay the fees, not because he beat her, but because he's a bug: he insists on doing bodily harm to one of our people who doesn't like it. The night his Test is played, the people in the Council where the action happened can watch while the woman describes how the cat got drunk and beat her and how often. Those who are interested pick up a Challenge-Consequence card at their Order Office, fill in the blanks, put their thumb prints on the card and mail it to the FFOperator who ran the Test. One card per Council citizen.

The Fact Finder Operator would wait about a week to collect all the cards, then tally them to find out what the people in the Council thought should be the guy's Consequence. They have several choices: 1) Loss of Member status for three months, six months, a year or up to the whole 3 years he sweated out doing his Service. 2) a Psychiatric Care Center for three months, six months or a year, but without losing his Membership status. 3) Coventry for three years. That's the lot, the total gamut of Consequences the people can assign him plus damages. Like he may have to pay the dentist if he broke a couple of her teeth.

The cards come in and the FFOperator tallies them to find the people's will. There have to be at least 12 cards with the same Consequence or the case is re-played. In a week the beater receives a post card saying that his Consequence is Loss of Membership for 3 months and to report to the same FFOperator on such and such a date for an Assignment. ¢5.00 are taken out of his Share every week and to get them back, he must do three months of Service...the sooner the fastest from here on out. If he doesn't care about having his Membership back, he needn't do anything, but the last number of his Service number will be a dash (-) until he does.

If you've crossed swords with the Justice system and lost, the scar is the dash on your Number. Remember your E number? The last three digits of it are blank...just blank, no dashes, no nothing...until you Serve as a Trainee for a year. For each year of Service you give the people you get a number and when all three blanks are numbers, you are a Member, OK? If you are assigned Loss of Membership, you'd get a dash for each year (or part of year) you are so assigned.

If you are Challenged when you're under 18 and have messed up enough for the People to assign you a Consequence, they can assign you to a Psychiatric Care Center (PCC), Coventry or just a dash for a certain amount of time. This dash means that you would have to stay out of the Council Houses thus losing free board, room and medical care until you work off the time of the dash. It will be between you and your FFOperator to decide how.

The system is simple. There's no IMPRISONMENT involved and no loss of Citizenship. An assignment to regain Membership means to go to the same

FFOperator who can arrange an assignment in your Council doing something the Council needs done, within your capabilities, thus being able to keep your job if you have one. Or the Operator can have you take a Classification Test for Central Service which means work outside of your home Council. If you feel the Operator is unfair—remember, you can Challenge.

If someone is Challenged for an Action which indicates that he or she is bugging or harming other people because of some sort of mental problem, the People can and probably would assign this individual to a PCC for some period of time.

The PCC, Psychiatric Care Center, is situated on a large hunk of unpopulated desert or mountain land—like about 100 square kilometers. It's leased from the Council by the Central and its fenced boundaries and one large gate are guarded and patrolled by the Central Boundary Patrol. Central, by Custom, builds and patrols all PCC's. Each PCC has a Hospital and Psychiatric Clinic at its logical center with housing for the staff and Trainees.

PCC's are society's buffer zones for people who are disturbed by or can't hack living in society or just want to get out of the swim for awhile. The idea is to let everyone there have lots of room and really *scrambling for survival* conditions. People don't need to be assigned and their families, friends, pets can go with them. The only thing is, if they are assigned, they cannot go out the gate whereas the people who went voluntarily can go in and out at will. Assigned or not, people can still be Challenged in a PCC as they are part of the RNA. Order problems, because of the special nature of the place, will be taken care of on some sort of minimum basis to keep people from bothering other people. I would guess that alcohol, drinking type, would be tough to get in a PCC or even take in. Drugs would be sold at the Clinic on an as needed basis. Hospital and Clinic are run on the same profit structure as in the Councils; that is, you pay according to your ability to pay. People can take their campers, tents, trailers or build some sort of minimal shelter. Food can be brought, grown, gathered or bought at the store. The Clinic is there to help people get their heads straight. I recomment deserts to walk in and mountains to climb. People who have been assigned for a year or more than once might have to convince the doctors at the Clinic of their ability to cope before they could leave, but all that will work itself out. Being assigned to a PCC in no way changes Service numbers: no dashes. There'd need to be a special unit for those who are too helpless to even feed themselves or for those who are homicidal. Different PCC's could become known for handling different types of problems. Remember to make special PCC's for kids under 18 with trees and a swimming hole.

It is difficult to determine in the here what actions will be considered asocial in the there. The whole new system is so different that its parts will be. Take blasphemy: five centuries ago, people's tongues were pulled out with burning tongs for it; my mouth was washed out with 99.44% pure Ivory for it and today you can hardly talk without it. Murder, arson and rape will probably still go on and will be handled by the Challenge, but if we take the profit out of violence a lot of it will stop. Murder will have to involve a non Principal: a member of the family, a friend, a witness, an Order Tender will have to do the Challenging. If no one Challenges, there is no investigation. The following story probably couldn't, wouldn't happen in the new society, but bear with me while I use an example from the old and transport it through time to the new, OK?

Your sister lives in a neighboring Neighborhood and you've tried to call her for several days without success. You get worried, go over to her apartment, have the janitor let you in and find her dead from a head wound in the detective story tradition. What do you do in this new system?

First, you call the local Order Office and tell them where what happened. The Order Tender arrives, decides death was not accidental and calls a detective. With no governmental enforcement agencies, detectives are in business for themselves, like Sherlock Holmes, and bill the person they've been hired to find. If unsuccessful, they make no money so I imagine their fees will be fairly high.

You fill out a Challenge-Consequence card leaving the Challengee's Number blank until it is detected. Let's say the detective, using his training in Actionology, discovers clues that point to the local bartender and writes his Number on the card. The appointment for the FF is set up and the Test goes something like:

Operator: "Did you kill anybody?"

Bartender: "Well...yes, but it was self-defense."

No red lights, no bells. No 100% lies.

It's established, after more questions, that the victim was your sister.

"Did you kill her deliberately?"

"I've already answered that. It was self-defense. She came at me with a pair of scissors so I picked up the poker and clobbered her with it, but I didn't mean to kill her—self-defense I tell you."

"Did you attack her sexually?"

"No..." The light comes on flooding the trailer with a red glare, clashing with the sound of the bell.

The Operator asks again, "Did you attack her sexually?"

"Well, maybe I roughed her up a bit, but you know how women are." Bells and red light again! The Detective who is there as your advisor whispers in your ear. You write down the question and pass the slip to the Operator who then asks:

"Did you have sexual relations with her before or after you hit her with the poker?"

"After, but I didn't know she was dead, I thought she was just unconscious."
No bells, no red lights.

The Detective whispers again and you say, "I have no more questions."

The Operator turns to the Bartender and asks, "Do you have any questions to
ask of this Challenger?"

"No, sir."

"This test will be presented to the People for Judgement so I must ask you
more questions to put them completely in the picture. Do you understand?"

"Yes, sir."

"I see by the dash on your ID that you've lost your Membership. How?"

"Yes, sir. I got assigned six months loss of Membership for fighting in my
home Council and I have been working as a number nine Trainee on 'A' shift
and bartending on 'D' shift for the last two months here in your Council, sir."

"Six months for fighting—that's pretty heavy, how come?"

"I hit a guy with a bike chain...sir."

"Have you ever been assigned before?"

"Yes, sir, six months PCC; got it for molesting a girl."

"Rape?"

"Yes, sir."

"How did you spend your Central Service?"

"Two years Forestry and one year number nine, sir."

"Were you busted out of Forestry?"

"Yes, sir, for fighting."

If you're wondering what the hell all the "sirs" are about, the bartender was
advised that it'd *look good* on TV.

"Will you agree to pay the detective fee? The FF fee? The Challenger's fee?
Autopsy and burial fees?"

"How much are they?"

There's some scrambling around and the Operator turns to you and asks, "Do
you have any bills for the Challengee?"

"Just what the detective will charge me for advising."

The detective waves his hand to indicate, "Nothing" and gives his other bills
to the Operator.

"That's fifteen Credits for the Challenger, thirty for the FF, 100 for the mortuary and the bill for detection comes to three hundred. Can you pay them?"

"OK, I've got that much."

"I will get this on the TV schedule as quickly as possible. In the meantime,
you (indicating the bartender) will be limited to expenditures within this Council and will stay here until the People's Consequence is known. Do you under-

stand?"

"Yeah."

"Now step over here to pay your bill."

That's the end of the Fact Finder Test—half an hour. The Operator sets up the showing of the Test and notifies the media who whoop it up about the murder, interview you, the bartender...all that stuff.

This Test is shown on one of the two Council TV stations and, since it's a murder, a lot of people watch it. It starts out with the facts of the case: pictures of your sister, some taken by the detective, pictures of the apartment and like that to clue the audience. Then it shows the Operator, back to the camera, adjusting the dials to yours and the bartender's characteristics. This part is important in case the Operator is ever Challenged about the way the dials were set. The TV gives the bartender's Number, the Operator's Number and the Council number. Yours and your sister's Numbers are given, but your sister's name is the only one mentioned.

A week later, the FFOperator tallies the Challenge-Consequence cards, finds that more say Coventry than anything else, notifies the bartender and the media of the Consequence and asks the bartender if he'd like to go North or South, gives him a week to straighten out his affairs and arranges his transportation. The bartender must go as he can spend Credits no where else but Coventry once the week is up. His new ID has three dashes—in place of 22- as a Service number. If the Bartender hadn't been able to pay his bill at the time of the FFTest, one of the *affairs* he would be attending to is getting a loan.

COVENTRY: a state of exclusion, a sanctuary, the last stronghold of *Might is Everything*. Coventry is a gigantic PCC, maybe 20,000 square kilometers instead of a hundred. They can be located in the frozen North and in the Southern swamps and jungles, wherever Central can lease large tracts of land from the local Council(s) and patrol every foot of the boundary. The Boundary Patrol will see that no one enters or leaves except by the Main Gate. Transfers between Coventries can be arranged if you have the bread. Like every summer and winter?

There will, of course, be a hospital and clinic, stores and wholesale commodity warehouses but instead of being scattered around, everything will be grouped around the Gate as that is the only place there is any Order at all. Inside, the only rules will be what happens.

Anyone can live there, anyone can go there voluntarily and keep the same Service status with which they entered. When a person like the bartender is assigned, however, he loses all Service status and gets three dashes (---). After being there one year, he gets 0-- and a ¢5 raise in his Share which, if he had to borrow money would go to pay the loan. After three years, he would leave Coventry with 000 (acceptable non-Service). **No one can lose Citizen status and Share.** First assignments to Coventry are for three years and second assignments are from three years to life. One way to gain Membership status is to go to Coventry and make it there for three years.

Coventry is not considered part of the RNA and no one in Coventry can be Challenged. If someone goes there or otherwise leaves the RNA to get out of a Challenge, it would have to be faced upon return if the Challenger is still into it.

Coventries will be exciting places. TV crews will go there to film events; young people will have a place to run away to; people will carry rifles, ride horses, drive dog sleds, build forts instead of houses and possess what they can protect. There are no paved roads, no motorized vehicles, no electricity or telephones except at the main gate and there is a type of freedom available no where else.

I am not in favor of losing the genes of the asocial types by eliminating them, but I am in favor of giving them a society of their own where they can operate freely and have their need for violence taken care of. These people are a naturally occuring part of the species, therefore must be needed for some kind of balance, but whether we need to live with or around them is another question.

If a problem cannot be worked out at the Neighborhood level with the Order Tender, the Council tries to get the two principals involved to agree through the FF (Fact Finder) and the FFOperator. Breach of contract or other money differences go the same route of Neighborhood to Council to the People, but I feel that after a few TV fiascos about money, Challengers and Challengees will be very happy to work out their differences with either the Order Tender's or FFOperator's advice and counselling. If any matter isn't smoothed out at the time of the Test, it must go to the People in whose Council the action happened. If it involves a far flung company, it can be played on TV in every Council in the RNA as information, but not for judgement. Matters of injustice caused by the system are handled first by a Council Justice Tender, then, if they involve more than one Council, by the Central Justice Section.

No one is going to force anybody to do anything in the new Establishment, except to appear if Challenged, tell the truth about disputed events and fulfill certain assigned Consequences. Service and Membership are privileges and one is done with elan to earn the other. With no laws, there is no precedent for anything so each event can be judged on its own merits (or demerits). The advantage to having the People make the judgements instead of some judge or jury is that the People can be as lenient or as tough as they feel, using the facts presented on TV and their own experiences, without having to use precedents that must be followed.

We can indeed have a society without laws if we'll learn to tell the truth or agree to be forced to stop telling those 100% lies.

HUMANKIND MUST LEARN TO PROGRESS WITHOUT CONTENTION

IN THIS SEGMENT we are giving the Right to count Money to past generations. Let us also consider changing the idea that money counts. Of course it still will, but let's start a process of de-emphasizing the power that money gives the possessor over other humans. Money's a gas, not a trip. People with a lot of money are just People who have concentrated on making money instead of something else. They are not *worse* or *better*, *higher* or *lower* than others.

MONEY: a medium of exchange and a measure of value. It is used so someone who makes artificial limbs can buy milk. From the Cow? No. From the Farmer? Occasionally. From the Dairy? Often, if they deliver, but mostly from stores. We need some unit of exchange...money...to be able to exchange labor for goods and services, but with computers, money does not need to be a tangible item, a thing we can finger.

Tangible money has become a thing in itself and more important than our Ecology. It must be de-importanized; it must be disenfranchised and returned to being a medium of exchange. If enfranchised means to give liberty to and we disenfranchise money, we are going to enslave it and make it do our bidding rather than our bowing or curtseying to it. If disenfranchise also means to take away the right to vote, we'll do that to money too by collecting our own data and making decisions and voting by how we feel about something instead of by money impressed influence. What is really best for us, for our Neighborhoods, for the Ecology will be the criteria for voting and we will make our own decisions by ourselves and for ourselves. We will be our own lobby.

How do we make money nontangible? Remember our Number...the only ID needed for anything? Our Number will be embedded in a card; triple layered, tough, uncomeapartable plastic; 9 centimeters x 6 centimeters (about the size of a credit card). All the information on the Card will be in the center section, protected by the two outside layers. Here's a picture:

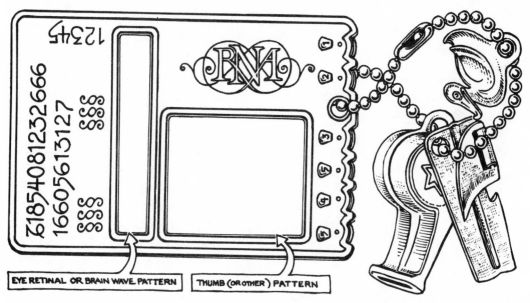

The E (Birth, ID and Service) Numbers will be on the top edge with the A (Address and Phone) Numbers underneath. Under these is room for two C Numbers (children under 12) and on the right hand edge is room for a 5 digit B (Business) Number at 90 degrees to the other Numbers. Under the spaces for children is a space that looks blank, but isn't. Here, a record of our brain wave and eye retinal patterns is encased, which makes positive identification possible. Below this space comes room for a thumbprint—or other, if both thumbs are gone. If a person has no fingers, they'd use a personally engraved symbol. Herein I will use *thumb*. . Under this thumbprint space are six little windows in which the digits from 0 to 9 can be changed manually by turning six dials, cogged so they don't slip. All we have to do is keep it clean so the machines can match their data with the data on the Card.

This Card becomes our money, our checkbooks and bank books, our card to do business, all our credit cards, our passport to the entire world. It is our driver's license, pilot's license, library card, boy scout card, ID card, our *you name it* card. It can become our door keys, car keys, file keys, safe keys. It is our key to the new society. It will revolutionize clothing: one thin, button-down, handy pocket holds everything, except what we smoke. It has a hole in it so it can hang around your neck or waist on a thong or ribbon, if you like. It will save untold hours of fumbling for keys, ID and money and will simplify life, not complicate it.

I have already used a card instead of a key to get through security doors and the system needs some improvement but with total use and mass production, the bugs will disappear and the cost will be something we can afford.

The Card will be easily obtainable from the Trainee in the ID Room at Council Center, 24 hour service...7 days a week...new ones ₡5.00, duplicates ₡3.00 and Cards for children under twelve, ₡2.00. You can have as many as you're willing to pay for and take care of, but you will need a new one every time you change your service status, your address, your Business Number or maybe your finger.

Money becomes Electrical Impulses, stored in machines (computers) and our Cards become the keys which activate the computers to exchange these electrical impulses among us. Wherever we are, our Cards can instantly activate our accounts to either subtract from or add to our Credits in less time than it takes to make change now. This is a change that, once made, will not only save many pine forests, a lot of lost bread and annoying monthly bills, but will also keep us from getting ripped off. Losing or having your Card stolen is a hassle so you will learn to take care of it, but you can imagine: "Stick 'em up! Gimme your Card! Now gimme your thumb!" Silly. We'll get used to putting lost Cards in the mail so they can be returned to their owners...post free.

Computers are counting and figuring machines which can only count what we tell them to. There are two main types plus a third which is a combination of the other two: Analog Computers are used to figure out design problems, do complicated mathematics, direct machines, check up on machines and like that, not the thing we're trying to do. **DIGITAL COMPUTERS are what we will use to count and take care of our bread.** They work with digits and can store tremendous amounts of counting type data in a small space. They use a numbers language which has only two digits instead of our ten. With these two digits, like 0 and 1, they can make up all the numbers there are. **DIGITS are the symbols 0 through 9 and a NUMBER consists of one or more digits.**

Computers are fairly new but here to stay. Let's learn to use their super abilities to count and thus increase the number of hours we have to do our own thing, whatever that is. Of course, if your thing is counting money...

In computer language, the word **CONFIGURATION means a computer system—usually the physical machines of the system.** In the RNA there will be five configurations in general use. They are E for Exchange configuration, P for Possession, N for Numbers of people and votes, S for Small Business and B for Business. These letters are merely code letters to indicate the configuration. Each of these systems consists of a Master computer, a large central machine which stores and processes data and of one or more types of Slaves, which are smaller and are connected to the Master by wire or radio to tell it what data to store and what to process. The Slaves are the machines into which we actually put our Cards. Some will resemble cash registers sizewise; others will be smaller.

The Council computer configurations allow us to exchange money every which way, even over the telephone.plus they figure and collect our taxes and give us our weekly Shares automatically. They store financial possessions like corporation stocks, savings and land leases, copyrights and patents. They ensure the Right of Challenge, take our votes without fuss and count the results immediately so we can really all vote on everything. The Numbers configuration counts us so we can know instantly how many there are to provide for. It also does the vehicle registration trip. The only thing we need to carry anywhere in the world is our Card. The rest of this Segment goes into details to explain, "How? Really?" If, while reading it, your head begins to boggle, skip on to Segment IX, but fold the corner down where you left off and come back when you feel to.

ALL YOU REALLY NEED TO KNOW IS HOW TO USE YOUR CARD.

The Exchange and Small Business configurations work together to provide our means of exchange. The E system holds our spendable bread and when we spend it in a store, it goes into the S configuration which holds Business' spendable money. E accounts will hold up to ¢9,999.99 so if you try to put more than 10 G's into your E account, the extra Credits will be lost forever; they just fly off into the ozone. Put your extra Credits into savings in the Possession configuration, or into convertible Bank Shares.

The five configurations are Council owned and each Council keeps their E, P, N and S Master computers together in a locked room, the Computer Security Room at Council Center. The Business Master is in the Business Room.

The only people ever allowed alone in the Computer Security Room are the Tax Tenders who have special Cards to enter the Master computers. They can bring Trainees in with them to help with their work, repair a machine or whatever, but no one is ever to be in this room unless personally supervised by a Tax Tender. Even a Tax Tender, however, cannot transfer money out of your accounts without your Card and thumb. No one can. Twelve year olds are given a visit tour to the room on the occasion of receiving their first Card so they can see the actual place where their Credits are kept.

Tax Tenders are computer programmer-operator experts, Challengeable like anyone else. They can work *word problems*. Each Council will need several Tax Tenders under the supervision of the Head Tax Tender and part of their jobs will be to correct errors (heaven forbid), change all Numbers which need changing, add new accounts and subtract dead ones.

Tax Tenders are empowered to put a *hold* on anybody's E account when requested to do so by a Justice Tender. Remember the murdering bartender was told by the FFOperator not to leave the Council until his Consequence was known? It was the Tax Tender who actually set the bartender's account so he couldn't spend money outside of the Council and later, outside of Coventry. There are two types of *holds:* no out of Council transactions and no transactions at all...like closed. *Hold* can also be used to locate people in emergencies and to notify them they have been Challenged, if they can't be found simply. Like if you need to get in touch with your mother but don't know where in the world she is, you'd call your local Order Tender who would call the Head Justice Tender who would then request the Tax Tender to put a *hold* on her account and the next time she goes to spend anything...well, there she is with a bag full of groceries ready to pay and instead of her balance a red light flashes on. Grump! So she phones her *home* Council Tax Office..."What gives...?" The Tender tells her to call you and **immediately** takes the *hold* off her account. If your mother were being notified of a Challenge, the Tax Tender would transfer her call to the Justice Office and as soon as she agreed to meet the Challenge would take the *hold* off her account. Tax Tenders will always accept collect calls—just dial 0.

Remember, a Credit is one part of some total number of Credits. The actual number of Credits in circulation will become the subject of a Central Bill. To change the fixed amount will take a vote of the entire RNA. However, with a great many people living on $C15 to $C30 a week, I feel it would be difficult to lower the value of the Credit by creating more of them. It would be nice to go the other way...have the Credit increase its value with time so the People's Share becomes worth more, thus increasing our standards of living.

To insure that no one has slipped unreal, unpaid for, false Credits into our economy, we are going to make a weekly Credit census. On Sunday mornings at 0615 Central Standard Time (0115 in Honolulu, Hawaii), Tax Tenders will switch their E, S, P and B Master computers to make no exchanges; that is, no money can change accounts so these machines can add their total Credits. Each Council's four totals are transmitted to the Central Business Tender's computer at Central where all the Credits in the RNA are totalled. If there is a difference of around a million Credits (plus or minus) from the original total, it's called an Anomoly and must be found. The Masters are switched back on—can't stop spending, can we?—but the witch hunt for the missing or excess Credits starts. The first Masters to be checked are in the Business configuration, then the Small Business and Possession configurations. For example, an S account may have had ₵99,999,999.50 added to it instead of ₵00,000,000.50—like that.

During this weekly chore time, the Exchange Masters not only add their total Credits, but also figure out everyone's tax percentage for the week and give People their Shares as determined by their E Numbers automatically—like I said in front: no waiting in line!

ALL TAXES ARE COLLECTED AT THE CONSUMER LEVEL! They are charged on Credits spent out of your E account. There are no other taxes anywhere. ALL TAXES ARE PAID TO YOUR HOME COUNCIL, no matter where you are. Your *home Council* is the one which has your E account in its E Master computer and your E and A Numbers in its N Master.

When you buy something you right then and there pay the tax on it, figured out by the computer, the rate dependent upon your income for the past 50 weeks. Sunday mornings, the Exchange Master computer subtracts your income made 50 weeks ago and adds the latest week's income, averages your income for the past 50 weeks and comes up with your tax rate for that week, so:

Average Income for Fifty Weeks	Tax Rate in %
₵15 to 20 per week	1
20 to 25	2
25 to 30	3
30 to 50	5
50 to 100	9
100 to 200	15
200 to 300	20
300 to 500	25
500 to 1000	30

1000 to 2000	35
2000 to 3000	40
3000 to 4000	45
4000 and over	50%, the everlovin' limit

You pay tax according to your calculated rate every time you buy something using your Exchange account unless you're using special computer slaves made for under ₵1.00 sales which charge a flat 10%; the 10% rate is also used for telephone calls. There's an exception to the tax rate calculation: if you have saved for bunches of years and are ready to buy your dream house, a Tax Tender can set the computer so this glomp of money isn't added to your account as income and thus make your tax rate higher. The machine is set so it won't *remember* the transaction. This is called a *One Time Exchange* which may be done more than once but not often. If your tax rate is already 50 percent, you wouldn't bother with *One Time Exchanges*.

Our tax rates determine the amount we pay for medical and hospital expenses provided by the Council. We pay what our individual tax rate indicates we are able to pay.

This taxation at the consumer level only leaves a tax hole through which you could drive a semi-trailer full of Credits daily—a lot of electrical impulses. So, by Custom, it is the responsibility of the vendor to see that the Council gets its taxes on any purchase not directly connected with the buyer's business or for resale. Like, I wrote a book about fixing your own Volkswagen and have a small publishing company, so I would have a Small Business (S) account. If I were to go into a Volkswagen dealer to buy a new model to bring my book up to date, I'd expect to be able to use my B Number to pay for it but if I walked into the Cadillac agency, I would expect this dealer to insist that I use my Exchange (E) account. I could buy my Cadillac wholesale if we both agreed, but not without paying taxes on the purchase price. If I used my S account for the Cadillac and bragged about it, just anyone could Challenge the dealer and make ₵15.00. This Custom won't stop all the tax evasion but it will make people think and, at least, keep their mouths shut about it. Remember, I never said Utopia.

Wholesale......HOORAY!   Tax Free......BOO!

You've just had explained every nuance of the entire tax structure of the RNA, which took less time to write than to fill out the first page of my personal income tax report. You see, in the RNA businesses pay no taxes. What? BUSINESS PAYS NO TAXES! Taxes paid by business are passed on in higher prices to the consumer, anyway. I once chased down all the taxes, taxes on taxes, profit on taxes and cost of paying taxes on a $2,000 Volkswagen and found it could be transported across the Atlantic and sold for under $1,200 if all the taxes were removed. In the new system, even at the 50 percent rate, this makes that same VW only ¢1800 and to pay 50%, you gotta be well off. This savings has nothing to do with the cost of collecting taxes. Just the tax collecting bureaus this simple system eliminates will pay for Council Shops and it's all done without your having to add or subtract or figure anything—even without paper. Of course, it's possible to minimize your taxes by spending little when your tax rate is high and spending big when it's low, by splitting your income with a friend or by making a lot of trips through the under ¢1.00 line, if your rate is more than 10%.

Let's see how a Card, magic key, all-purpose little jewel works from the beginning. Soon after you're born, Mother takes you down to the ID Room at Council Center to have your ID registered and recorded into the Numbers Master. The Trainee does this by taking your eye retinal pattern and your fingerprints for the machine and makes Mother a new Card with your Birth data (your C Number) on it so she can start to collect the ¢10 a week that go with having you. You are being counted! If you are Mother's first or second child, you're a standard case—OK? But what if the baby is an orphan or a third child under twelve? At whose doorstep do we lay little motherless waifs? We have two Customs to take care of these problems: 1) The Neighborhood is responsible for children under twelve. 2) Women are the only ones who can bear children and on their Cards only can they be registered. So, the doorstep we need is the Neighborhood Education Tender's who will help find foster homes and deal with all exceptional cases. Father can raise children but they cannot be on his Card.

The first Card you might have is the Child's Card and it depends on Mother at what age you get one or even if you have one. Your Child's Card has Mother's E and A Numbers and your C Number on it, is the same size as hers with room for your fingerprint and the six little dials. To keep a record of your allowance? It's a different color than adult Cards and the places for brain wave and eye retinal patterns are truly blank. It can only be used to make less than one Credit expenditures, like the phone or local busses and can be the key to your home, but it subtracts everything you spend from your loving Mother's account and can probably get you in trouble if you get expansive and treat the whole gang to a soda. You'll just have to work it out together. It's there and reasonably priced, too.

The big Card event in your life happens when you reach 12 when you go to the ID Room in your home Council for your own Card and Exchange account. You can go with or without Mother but she'll need a new Card, too, one without your C number on it. Occasionally it can happen that a child demonstrates to the three Tenders in the Neighborhood an ability to handle responsibility at an earlier age than 12 and, with their approval, gets a Card but no one ever gets more than ¢10 a week until their 12th birthday. At 12, for sure, you get your own Card and ¢15.00 per week which cannot be taken from you and you can not sign away. OK?

In the ID Room the Trainee records your brain wave and eye retinal patterns and fingerprints, compares the data with your original registration and if they match, drops the old ones and registers your new ID. All your Numbers, your thumbprint and ID are put into the Card making machine and out pops your first very own Card. The Trainee directs you to the Tax Office where you'll be given an E account which will be activated by the E and A Numbers on your Card, one Exchange account per person. This way we make sure you only get one People's Share on Sunday mornings.

A Trainee in the Tax Office punches your Numbers onto a computer card, gives it to you and a Tax Tender arrives to escort you on your personally conducted tour through the locked Security Room where you hear the four Master computers hum and click as their tape recorders turn. You see the E Master... the only one there with a thing that looks like a typewriter connected to it (the actual entrance to the computer). The Tender takes the computer card from your awed fingers, checks the Numbers on it against the ones on your new Card, then types something and inserts the computer card into the Master. This puts your new account into the machine's memory. The computer card bounces back out and is thrown away...its job done. The Tender has you put your new Card into the slot in the Master whose window instantly blinks on with numbers that say, "001500"–your first ¢15.00 share. Now you have to match your thumbprint with the one on your Card to make sure your Card has a workable, true copy. As you put your thumb in the thumbhole, wriggle it around and press a little, a bright green light goes on. The Tender thumbs the plastic dials on your Card to read 001500, hands it to you and says, "That's your key to our world, care for it well!" and you mumble like, "Thanks," and head out of there. There is no charge for E accounts nor for your first Card.

"Money to spend! A chocolate sundae would slip down smoothly," you think so you look for the nearest one. Your first transaction with your new Card at the drugstore is a let down as it's the same old routine you've used all along with your kid's Card. You put your shiny Card into the slot in the small machine on the counter and the green light goes on. The soda jerk says, "That's ¢.25," so you punch "25" on the buttons, match prints and the "25" disappears. You know that this slave machine has wiped a quarter of a Credit from your account plus ¢.03 in taxes so you turn the dials on your Card to read "001472," your new balance. To really break in your new account, you wander around looking for something to buy that costs more than one Credit. A groovy stationary display catches your consciousness. You'll be needing some to write letters home so you choose a folder full, walk to the bigger computer slave at the checkout stand and hand the folder to the clerk who says, "One fifty, please." You put your Card into the slot and the Balance window on the slave lights up with "001472," the Tax Rate window with "01." You're thinking you could have saved ¢.03 if you'd bought your sundae on this machine and the clerk repeats, "That'll be one fifty," so you stop regretting and punch the buttons under the Amount window. The first digit on the right already is at zero so you don't touch the button under it but you punch the second button five times and the third one once. If you goof, punch the *clear* button and start again. *Note: this button punching will stop all that 2.99 shit.* The digits in the Amount window now say "000150." The right-hand digit in the Tax window turns and stops at 2, making the Tax window read "000002." The clerk says, "OK," you match thumbprints, the slave goes "click" and the digits in the Amount and Tax windows move to zero while those in the Balance window move to "001320." You start to pull your Card out but the clerk says, "Your balance...?" "Oh!" You remember and turn the little dials on your Card to match what the machine says, "001320," remove your Card, pick up your package and split feeling kinda initiated.

At 12, you can use your Card as a key to enter and live in any Council House free of charge. You can do most things adults can do except vote, but you need the bread. You can't overdraw your account in the RNA. Let's say you have ¢.15 in your account in the Exchange Master and try to spend ¢.50. The machine will subtract the ¢.15 from the ¢.50, make the light next to the Balance window blink red which means 0 balance—and there you'll be, owing the store ¢.35 with no way to pay. You'll just have to work it out with the clerk. From here on out the light will blink red every time you put your Card into a machine until you become solvent again.

All the uses to which a Card can be put are not yet known but the two transactions above describe what you'll need to know about how to use your Card in the computer slaves until you have a business, become old enough to vote or become a Member with possessions to store.

Anyone can go into business in the RNA. In fact, the system is designed so anyone who wants to pay the dues can get rich. From the time you're twelve, you can start any sort of business you choose. They'll be really happy to see you at the Bank in the POB and will lean over backwards to help you. In the Business Room next to the Bank sits a computer slave (the SBDT) that can tell a Banker from information stored in the Library Central computer what the odds are of a certain business succeeding in that Council, like: how many successful restaurants are there of each type? Who needs something I can make, build or do? Where can I get the materials? Depending on the odds of your proposed business succeeding, the Banker will make you a business loan. Whether you need a loan or not, the Banker will help you get started.

You'd probably start your Business using slaves in the Neighborhood Center (EDV's) or by leasing a small portable slave (E¢R) connected by radio to the Exchange configuration only, which you can rent either at the Council Bank for ¢6.00 per week or from your local Order Tender—¢2.00 for 24 hours.

Let's take a look at some of the computer slaves we'll use to receive and spend Credits and to vote:

Type E¢R, Exchange-Credit-Radio, is for portable businesses that sell things for less than a Credit—balloons, newspapers, shoe shines, also tips or a night of street singing. Local busses would have them. If you've rented one, make sure the buyer's Card makes the green light go on before you "Push the button, Max." No thumbprint needed...a good reason not to lose your Card. Rental of this slave means you have a *personal business.* Since it doesn't connect to the S system, you'd get no B Number and you'll have to pay taxes on everything you buy, whether it's for your business or not.

To be classified as *Small Business*, you need an account in the S configuration, which you get by going to the

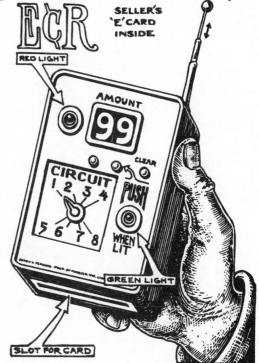

Bank part of the POB and leasing a different type of computer slave. You'll have a choice of three, so pick out the one in the display that'll do your job. The lease of a slave is your permit to do business and the number stamped on it becomes your B Number. You walk over to the ID Room where the Trainee makes you a Card with your B Number on it (or Cards if you've leased more than one slave), then return to the Bank, new Card in hand, and the Bank Tender will open your account in the S Master. S accounts are activated by B and A Numbers and you can have as many accounts in as many Councils as you wish but they cost. The cost is the lease rate for your computer slave or one tenth of 1% of the balance in your S account per week, whichever is greater naturally. The slaves owned by the Council will be installed and serviced by them and kept in peak condition and, by Custom, the lessee is responsible for the slave, meaning it shouldn't be left out where it can be tinkered with or vandalized.

Type ESD, Exchange-Small Business-Direct. Direct means connected by wire. The telephone company will be happy to provide both the wire and the connections. Lease fee: ₡ 20.00 per week or one tenth of one percent. This is the general slave we'll use for everything but voting. The 12 year old just used one to

pay for the stationary. It makes a magnetic tape recording of all transactions, if the lessee remembers to change the tape in the back. "Cassette type," I would answer if you asked. Permanently located businesses that make many transactions over one Credit would lease ESD's; like grocery stores, markets and department stores...super stores would have several, giving them several S accounts. Factories and big businesses will have ESD's to pay employees and local bills; the Council will put them in the Post Office Bank (POB) and at the Council Shops. Out of the RNA, Speaker's Offices will provide them for travellers.

ESD's transfer Credits:

1) from a buyer's E account to a seller's S account.
2) from a business' S account to a supplier's S account. No tax.
3) from an S account to two E accounts. This feature would be used to pay employees and the reason for the spaces for two E cards is that income can be split between two people to reduce the employee's tax rate. Both Card owners needn't be there, just the extra card.
4) from an E account to another E account. Stores provide this service so their customers can exchange money. If you've overbought, you can borrow from a friend using this feature. To let the slave know which kind of transaction to make, punch the correct *function* button.

There are two types of slaves owned and leased by the telephone company: **Type EST**, Exchange-Small Business-Telephone. The phone company keeps a magnetic tape of all transactions. They are used to transfer Credits by telephone, like wiring money or paying by check used to be, only easier. There'll be one or more in every Neighborhood Center, several at Council Center, in Speakers'

Offices and wherever else demand indicates and they won't be vandalized. You could lease one for your home and business. We'll use them to pay bills, mail order purchases, magazine subscriptions, donations and things like that. Businesses, too, can pay their bills by phone and use EST's for tax-free business calls.

Types EĢT, Exchange-Credit Telephone, are found on every phone. They only register the maximum of ₵.99 plus 10% tax at a time, which makes long distance calls a series of ₵.99 transactions as the time is used.

EĢT

Type ESR, Exchange-Small Business-Radio. (₵15 per week or one tenth of one percent). This slave is connected to both E and S masters by two way radio like walkie-talkies and is a fairly small portable with a shoulder strap to

be used by businesses that move and sell things for more than a Credit like airlines, long distance busses, the Jewel Tea *man*, the Avon *lady* and others... no magnetic tape.

Type ES₵, Exchange-Small Business-Credit. ₵10 a week or one tenth of 1% lease fee. This slave will be found in real *small businesses* that don't move about like tobacco shops, fruit stands, gift shops and small restaurants. Stores

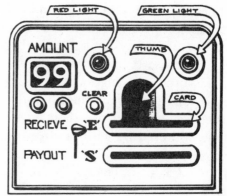

will have them for quick customers like a liter of milk or a sundae. They make less than one Credit transactions or a series of them plus 10% tax. In open markets, they will plug in kinda like telephone jacks and are the ones that will be adapted for use on vending machines charging a fixed amount.

All the computer slaves, except for E₵R's, need a thumbprint to subtract Credits from an account, but not to receive them. If you have a manager or other person who needs access to the funds in your Small Business account, you can have your B Number put on your manager's Card at the ID Room. To get this person out of your account, you might have to ask a Bank Tender to exchange your computer slave and thus change your B Number.

OK, so when someone pays you some money in your new business, it goes into your S account if you have one and when you want to spend this money on personal things, you'd put it into your Exchange (E) account before spending it. Right?

At eighteen you become eligible to vote, for which you'll use a computer slave called: **Type EDV**, Exchange Direct Voting. Every Neighborhood Center will have three EDV's furnished free by the Council. There'll also be some at Council Center and at least one in every Speaker's Office. EDV's have two iden-

tical sides and are used for personal exchanges between people: exchanges between two E accounts. This is the slave you'd use to borrow, lend or give Credits or to buy or sell personal things like a cow, a piece of handcraft, a service, whatever. Taxes are paid at the buyer's, lender's or giver's rate.

The Type EDV is the one we'll use to vote and any one of the three Neighborhood Tenders can call the ID Room to request the machines to be switched to voting. Since they have two identical sides, six voters can use three machines at once and three EDV's can handle 400 voters (more or less, you know) an hour. To vote, put your Card in the slot and when the Bill number shows in the Bill number window, match thumbprints. This matching causes the *Number of Votes* window to light up with a 1 or 2. Now move your thumb to the right for a *yes* vote and to the left for *no*. By covering your voting hand no one can see which way it moves. If you're a Member, vote twice on Council and Central Bills—a real Middle-of-the-Road Member can, of course, vote yes *and* no. If there's more than one Bill scheduled to be voted on, the Bill number in the window changes and you can vote on it. The Master computer sees to it that people cannot vote more than their share. On Neighborhood matters, EDV slaves may or may not be used—depends on that Neighborhood, which may just decide to count standees or YEAH's, but using an EDV is how we'll vote on Council and Central Bills—just our Card—no registering, no pre-registering, no paper work. On Council Bills, you can vote in any Neighborhood in your home Council if you get there at the right time or at the Post Office Bank (POB). On Central Bills you can vote in any Neighborhood, at any POB or at any Speaker's Office out of the RNA. On Neighborhood matters you'll have to be there to vote.

The only other computer slave you'll need to know how to run has to do with Possessions, but to have an account in the P configuration, you'll be a Member as only Cards with three complete Service digits will activate Possession Master computers. You can have as many accounts (portfolios) in as many Councils as you wish but you'll need a different Card with a different A Number on it for each Council. E and A Numbers activate P accounts. The first portfolio in any Council is free but more cost.

The things you'd keep in a portfolio in a P account are savings and Registered Possessions. Savings are stored Credits which collect no interest. You can transfer Credits from your account in the Exchange Master to your P portfolio tax free. No tax on saving money but you cannot put Credits from a Small Business (S) account into a Possessions Master (PM) at all. No tie-in between the S and P configurations. Your savings account in the PM is not an Exchange account; that is, it has no spendable money in it. For most transactions, the money must first be transferred to an E account. For example, if you didn't have enough Credits in your Exchange account to pay for that new coat you'd just picked out, you'd have to move Credits from P savings to your E account, then pay for the coat and pay taxes on it at last week's rate. The money transferred to your E account gets averaged in on Sunday morning as income and might increase your tax percentage unless you can talk the Tax Tender into making the coat a *One Time Exchange*—not likely.

Registered Possessions are the following:

Two kinds of **Council Life Annuities, high and low paying.** These annuities are nontransferable which means they cannot be sold and they revert to the Council upon death. You can borrow against them, however. The high paying annuities, bought with Credits, become part of the Council's capital to pay for public projects such as Shops, buildings, parks, water works, statues, museums and public housing and the low paying annuities are issued to pay pre-RNA public debts. Annuities pay their holders a fixed amount once a week and are a safe, sure way to invest your money and guarantee yourself a weekly income for life. A man could buy annuities for his wife, thus assuring her of an income if he should die, but not for his young children since they wouldn't be Members.

Council Bank Shares can be sold back to the Bank; they are immediately convertible. To hold Bank Shares you needn't be a Member as they can be held for you by the Bank Tender in your home Council. You can buy them for your kids. The Council is in business, the People's business, and is required to make a profit and if run as an efficient two-valued business, there's no reason why it can not. We're used to the idea of government costing us a lot of money but this isn't necessary. The way the Councils get their Credits to lend and to be insurers is by selling shares in themselves and paying weekly dividends. Shares don't guarantee an income; your money becomes a part of what you have a share in and if you buy Council Bank Shares, your fortunes will rise and fall with the Council Bank's financial prowess. When a Council pays a dividend, a Bank Tender puts it into a Member's savings in the same portfolio in which the shares are registered. Citizens must come to the Bank to receive their dividends into their E accounts. If they don't come in for them, a Bank Tender automatically increases the Credit value of their Bank Shares.

Stock Shares are shares in private companies, just like now. The differences are that when a Corporation starts up, it is allowed to make available as many shares as its net worth indicates to a Central Business Tender and these shares can only be owned by individuals. No group can hold shares as they must all be contained in someone's portfolio in some Possession Master. The other difference is that the stock market will be completely computerized. Possession Masters will have tie-ins with the Market Central computer, the computer at Central which becomes the stock market. When the shares you own pay dividends, these will appear like magic in your Possessions Master savings account...no tax until you put the Credits in your Exchange account and spend the money.

Land Leases, Homesteaded Land Leases and Land Lease Liens. If you own a Land Lease out of your home Council, you'll need a Possession account in that Council. You can own leases on as much land as you wish, but you can only have one Homesteaded Land Lease in the RNA.

OK, so if you, as a Member, have any of the above items, you'd need to have a Possession account to keep it in (except Bank Shares). The slaves you'd use are in the Possession Room, in the Bank (POB) or in Speakers' Offices.

The Possession Room will look like the movie version of a wheeler-dealer room filled with people playing the market—some gloating over their possessions, some super high on gains made, some super low on losses. There'll probably be a snack and drink bar at one end and the Big Board Stock Market viewing screen at the other. The screen will operate the 20 hours a day, six days a week the stock market is open with Trainees there during these hours to help you. There'll be computer slaves, comfortable chairs and ashtrays scattered throughout the room for Members' convenience. Members of the RNA are also members of the stock exchange whether they ever buy a share or not. Members can bid, buy and sell at market, sell short...do anything people can do in the present stock exchange, but they will be able to do it by computer. When you buy shares in a private corporation, the money will be transferred directly out of your P savings, through the Market Central computer to the seller's P savings; no tax involved. You'd type out what you want on the slave and the computers match bids with sell orders and vice versa. When the transaction has been completed, it shows up in your specified portfolio with the money in savings in that portfolio increased or decreased. Simple, eh?

Types PD, Possession-Direct computer slaves, work like typewriters and to run one you need to use the limited computer code printed right on the machine. When you sit on the stool in front of one of these slaves, you first put your

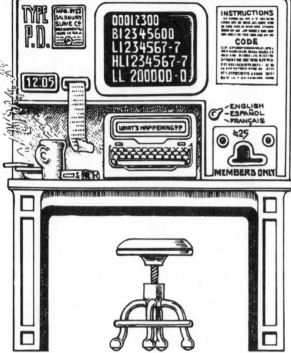

Card into the slot and the machine immediately deducts ¢.25. This slave only works if your Card has three Service digits on it and if you have at least ¢.25 in savings. OK, so now you set the dial on the machine for English, Spanish or French, then type what you want it to do. For example, you might want to see a list of everything stored in your portfolio A, so you'd type something like "list A." You match your thumbprint with the one on your Card, the machine gives a click and a list of your portfolio A appears in glorious black and white on the video screen, while the typewriter types out a list on the paper roll. As soon as the machine has finished typing, it turns itself off, disengaging your Card. You tear the paper off the roller and that's it. The piece of paper could read:

00012300	means ¢123.00 in savings
B12345600	means ¢123,456.00 worth of Bank Shares
L1234567-7	is a Land Lease number – the -7 means you pay ¢7.00 per week Land Lease Fee out of your savings
HL1234567-7	means it's Homesteaded. Followed by an E Number indicates the Member to whom you will the Homestead.
LL1200000-06	means you have a Lease Lien for the amount of ¢12,000.00 and pay 6% interest yearly. You can pay this Lien either by going into the Bank part of the POB and using savings in

this portfolio, thus making the payment tax free or you can pay by phone using an EST but this will cost you tax. The amount of the Lien shown above is decreased by the Bank Tender as you pay on it. If you don't make a payment, the amount of the Lien increases by the amount of the unpaid interest. If you never pay and the interest accumulates to the original value of the Lien, a Bank Tender neatly subtracts the Lease from your account.

100 sh Snuffle Snuff Prod	means you have 100 shares in the weevily snuff corporation.
CA60	means you have Council Annuities which pay you ¢60.00 a week. This payment shows up in savings in this portfolio automatically.

If you mess up in some way as to lose Membership, any savings and registered possessions you have would become inaccessible to you...safe, but unreachable until you regain Membership. When you die, you enrich the entire Council by whatever you had in your Possession portfolios, except for your Homesteaded Lease.

EXCHANGES AND STOCK TRANSACTIONS ARE NOT REGULATED BY LAWS WHICH NEED ENFORCEMENT. THE LIMITATIONS ARE DESIGNED AND BUILT INTO THE COMPUTER SYSTEMS THEMSELVES.

The fourth configuration, N, has nothing to do with Credits. Whenever you need a Card, need to register and crossfile a vehicle or a Lease, find out that day's Census or voting information, find a vehicle owner or a Land Lease owner, register a creative product of your own mind or wish to consult the Library Central, you'll go to the ID Room in the POB where there'll be a Trainee 24 hours a day, seven days a week to do these things for you.

When you want to register a book, a play, a piece of music or an invention or process, anything you want to copyright or patent, you go to Council Center, find an FF that's not busy and tell the Trainee there that you want to register your whatever. You'll be set up holding the brass balls while you describe and demonstrate your thing—sing your song, read a part of your book, show how your model works—all under the watchful *eye* of the video tape. After paying your bill, you take this tape to the ID Room where the Trainee registers it for a small fee and if you wish, sends a copy to Library Central so people will know it's available. The tape itself will be stored under your E Number in the Storage Closet for video tapes in the POB. Now you can feel secure that your brain child is protected and that whoever uses it will pay you 10% of gross, by Custom, or you Challenge. When you die, it becomes public property.

Council Numbers Masters relay their population numbers and votes on Central Bills to the Numbers Central, **Type NC**, located at Central. The information NC's hold on vehicles and patents and copyrights is transmitted to the **Type LC**, Library Central, the data bank for the entire RNA located at Central. The LC contains every item of information there is down to: "Number such and such will have 3,000 turkeys ready for market on November 15th," or "What's today's sugar price in Japan?" The NC can tell you how many people there are today in the RNA, but not how many there were last week; the LC can. The LC is a total Almanac. It has every vehicle, every need, every environmental consideration, every piece of data fed into it ready to spout at the instant it receives a request for information. It can be reached by anyone through the ID Room, through a Bank Tender or with an S or B account through an SBDT slave. If you ask the LC a question and it doesn't know the answer, the Trainee at the LC will type: "Don't know, but ask again tomorrow." Imagine being able to have answers to: "Is this book in print?", "What's been published about this?", "What's the average rainfall in Santiago, Chile, in December?", "What's the estimated world elephant population?" Far out! The LC is our modern miracle, working for the People.

We hear a lot and make a lot of jokes about computer errors but errors actually made by computers are virtually nonexistent. Errors made by people who program and use computers are another thing and WE, the People, will see to it that they don't happen and can make our computers not only error-free but self repairing as well.

All the Masters will be powered three ways to insure their constant operation: a power line connection, an emergency generator plus their own battery power packs. They can switch from one power source to another automatically and instantly.

The Exchange and Small Business Masters will have two identical sides arranged in parallel. This is a safeguard so that if one side malfunctions, the other side takes over. Also one side is constantly, except in cases of malfunction, running a check on the other side.

Transactions in the E, S and P systems are recorded magnetically at the time the transaction is completed. The recording facilities must be able to handle peak load times of maybe 100 transactions at one time. The speed will be arranged so the tapes will last for a week, running constantly. These tapes not only indicate the day and the hour but will have a time tone every fifteen minutes with one minute beeps for help in locating transactions timewise. The recordings will show, in computer language, just which account paid how much to which other account and what the taxes were, if any. A sample bit might be: C1854081232666/000450/000090/23456. This says that an E account, the first long number, paid ₡4.50 to S account No. 23456, with ₡.90 to the Council. OK? Credit transfers are recorded under the paying Number. If you've made a mistake or think the computer has, go to Council Center the beginning of the next week after the tapes are changed and have a Trainee help you find the transaction. The tapes are kept for four weeks before they're erased and reused. Follow the Tender's or Trainee's directions. The error will be found and computer errors fixed. Our computer experts will see to it. If the error was yours, you'll have to handle it.

The four Masters of each Council will not be connected to those of other Councils directly but will use relay nets: wire, microwave, radio and/or cable. If you are spending money in your home Council, the relay nets don't get into the action at all, but if your home Council is somewhere in Panama and you're spending in Nome, Alaska, the signal will go from the computer slave your Card is in to the Exchange Master in the Council Nome is in. This EM senses *out of Council* because of your A Number and immediately transfers the signal to your home Council by use of the relay net. This all happens in microseconds and allows you to buy or sell anywhere.

Out of the RNA, you'd go to a Speaker's Office. There'll be one of these Offices in every major non-RNA city open 24 hours a day, seven days a week with computer slaves you can use to change electric Credits into whatever currency you need, instantly, or as long as it takes to count that old fashioned coin and paper. If you're going to climb Mt. Everest, buy enough Rupees in Delhi to last...you know, plan ahead.

When you put your Card in and activate a slave, the Balance window might flash a red light. This could mean that your mother has become worried about your absence, wishes to speak to you and has talked her Order Tender into requesting a *hold* put on your account. It could mean that you've been Challenged and the Justice Tender cannot locate you. It could also mean you're broke. Overdrawn you can't get in the RNA...there's no way to have minus Credits on your Card.

In the case of the first two possibilities, you'd phone your home Tax Office to find out, "How come?" and in the case of the third, you'd wait until Sunday for your Share, find a job, borrow from a friend, sell something or ride the free bus down to Council Center for a loan.

The Post Office Bank (POB) is open 24 hours a day, seven days a week and you can borrow a tider-over from a machine. Being a machine, it will only loan on sure things, like against your Share of the economy or your Council Annuities, but it will not let you jeopardize your ₡15 Citizen's Share—ever. As a Member, you can borrow on your share from the loan machine until your weekly payments are anywhere from ¢ 1.00 to ¢ 15 including interest and up to the amount of your Annuities. The amount of payment would then be deducted automatically from your Exchange account or your portfolio every week, but the Exchange Master won't *remember* the addition to your income caused by the loan and add to your tax rate, nor will you pay taxes on the payments. When you leave the loan machine, you'll have more of a balance but less of your Member's Share or Council Annuities payments until you've paid the loan.

The Insurance Business is machinated and computerized as well. Next to the Loan machines are four Insurance computers and vendors. They will sell any kind of risk Insurance you can imagine, for a price...no Fear Insurance, remember, just risk. The fine print on all policies says, "Payoff is subject to an FFTest." One machine sells Lease Insurance and one policy will cover you in case of fire, earthquake, hooliganism, storm, et al., anything to do with your Lease and the buildings on it. You'll need a separate policy for each Lease you want to insure. The second machine sells Vehicle Insurance. By punching the right buttons you can buy any kind of coverage on any vehicle you can describe to the machine. The third machine sells Card Insurance. It can insure you against any Credit losses you might sustain due to Card loss or theft. *If your Card is lost or stolen, go to the nearest Tax Office and do as you're told.* The fourth machine will sell miscellaneous Risk Insurance such as crop, cargo, carrier and all that ilk.

When buying insurance, you put your Card into the slot, punch the keys for the amount of what kind of coverage you want for how long.Then the actuarial monster figures out the deal and tells you how much so you decide if it's worth it to insure...your crop against sexy grasshoppers (locusts), for example. If you like the odds, close the deal with your thumb; tax to the Council. Take your Card out of the pay slot and put it in the policy read-out slot, match thumbprints and your policy(ies) number and conditions are printed out for you on a roll tape for only a quarter. Policies are stored in the machine for the length of time you've paid for, then they disappear.

The Post Office part of the POB, too, will do every operation it can by machine. There are three types of things you can mail in the RNA: **mail** includes letters or post cards, **parcel post** is a package one person can carry that fits in the package machine and **express** covers small shipments one or two people can carry that won't fit into the package machine. Envelopes and post cards printed or accepted in the mail have a black stripe along one edge and look like the illustration.

If the person to whom you've written has no telephone, you'll need to fill in the E Number space or use a mark or name the receiver can recognize. After putting your Card and the letter you're mailing into the vertical slot provided, punch *airmail* or not as you wish and your letter disappears into the first sorter and you're a few cents poorer. By Custom, letters are inserted into the slot black edge down, head of arrow first.

If the receiver has moved and has left a forwarding address in the Neighborhood Order Office, a Trainee pastes the new address which is on a piece of gummed tape over the receiver's Number. If, however, there has been no forwarding address left, the Trainee cuts the black edge off and the letter returns to the sender because the sender's address is now in position to be *read* by the sorters. Using standardized envelopes that idiot machines can handle will make mail service so fast and accurate it'll blow your mind.

Parcel post and express labels come double—an original and a copy. To mail a package parcel post, you put it on the scale in the ED package machine, your Card in the slot. Now punch the address buttons...all eleven digits...and, if you want, punch the amount of insurance and the *airmail* button. The machine weighs the package, senses your address from your Card and the receiving address you just punched in so it can calculate the amount of postage. OK, punch the amount the machine shows and match thumbprints. Your label comes bouncing out with your Number, the receiver's Number and the postage stamped on it. Paste the label on the package. Now push the other button and hear the machine give a rumble as two arms reach out, open the door and pull the package onto the conveyor belt. Got all that?

Trainees supervised by a few professional Mail Tenders help sort and hand handle special services like Registered and Certified mail, mail from overseas in old fashioned envelopes and express until someone comes up with ingenious machines to do these things.

Types ED, Exchange-Direct computer slaves, have many shapes and forms and are used in POB's, ID Rooms, FF's...anywhere that Credits go directly to the Council. They subtract no tax, cannot be leased and are found in Council facilities only.

For any financial help you might need, just step into the friendly Bank, the B part of the POB. Bank Tenders (Spender Tenders? Lender Tenders?) are there to advise you, if you need, on investments but are not there to hold your hand if you lose your ass. The Head Bank Tender is hired by the Council Bank and Lease Committee and is our highly-paid financial expert. Challengeable? Of course. Bank Tenders will buy and sell Council Bank Shares and store them for non-Members. To buy or sell a Lease you'd see a Bank Tender who would have to consult the Bank and Lease Committee if you were going to change the use of the land. If you change land use without this Committee's approval, you stand a good chance of losing the Lease, by Custom. If the Council still owns the Lease, you'll need this Committee's approval to buy or lease the Lease.

Councils handle their own *Futures* and bread to be made from this device of paying for something before it is fat or grown or mined or produced will be made with gusto by the Council's Banking and Marketing Tenders for the Council.

OUR COUNCIL IS OUR BUSINESS AND MAKE A PROFIT IT WILL.

Bank Tenders also sell Council Annuities, keep track of Leases and Liens, pay off on Insurance Policies, lease computer slaves, run the Post Office and lend Credits as Liens or as personal or business loans. They help you start a new business, expand an old one or incorporate.

The Council will charge interest. The Council is the only agency that can perform this usurious operation on us People. In this way, if Jesus turns out to have been right and charging interest and going to hell are connected in any way, we'll all go together.

It has only been a few years since people could sell themselves into indentured servitude or be captured and sold into lifetime servitude. Today, these practices have become *immoral*, but it's an accepted practice to sell yourself into credit servitude for as long as 20 years before you're free—to quit the job, sass the boss or even move to where there's breathable air—on account of all those payments you have to make. Isn't this just a new definition of *slavery*?

I don't imagine that we will be able to arrange our affairs in such a way as to eliminate *installment buying* but I do say that no one but the Council can charge interest. So if we must buy something for which we don't have the money, we can borrow from the Council Bank and pay interest—that's one way. The other way is to pay the store, the dealer, whomever, monthly payments which add up to more than the cash price of the article; not *Interest*, just more money for the seller's time and service—another semantic change.

Let's take a look at some sample price tags:

WASHING MACHINE

¢125.00 Cash

20 weeks at ¢10/wk.,
including service

50 weeks at ¢5/wk.,
including service

CAR

¢1,200.00 Cash

50 weeks at ¢35/wk.,
including Fleet service
and all insurance.

100 weeks at ¢25/wk.,
including Fleet service
and all insurance.

Sellers will service what they sell because:

NOTHING CAN BE *OWNED* UNTIL IT IS PAID FOR!

Look what happens because of this Custom:

Sellers will not be able to stretch out the payment period until the whatever is worn out. When the damn thing no longer works, the buyer will quit paying.

Sellers will provide excellent service—maybe like Fleet Maintenance on vehicles and service contracts on other machines.

Sellers will be careful to whom they sell.

Sellers will be more interested in having the whatever paid for than ever before because they own it until it is.

Sellers can use the Right of Challenge if their merchandise has been mistreated and will give thorough *use* directions.

If all this sounds like a bunch of rules about time payments, look again. The above things happen because of the simple Custom which says that sellers own what they sell until it's paid for.

The buying of individual articles on Time Payments thus remains a valid part of Business, which brings us to the next subject wherein

BUSINESS
BLOSSOMS
WITHOUT
CONTENTION

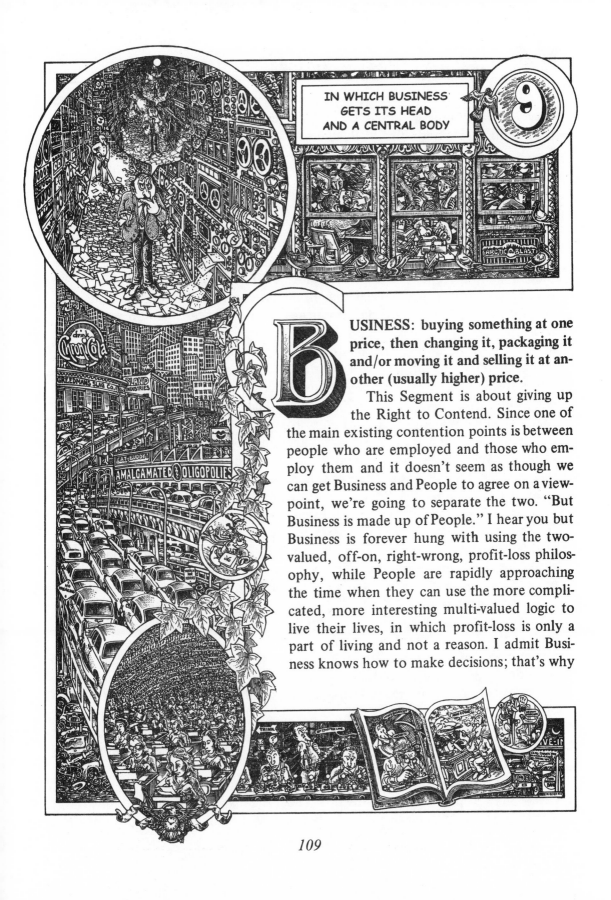

BUSINESS: buying something at one price, then changing it, packaging it and/or moving it and selling it at another (usually higher) price.

This Segment is about giving up the Right to Contend. Since one of the main existing contention points is between people who are employed and those who employ them and it doesn't seem as though we can get Business and People to agree on a viewpoint, we're going to separate the two. "But Business is made up of People." I hear you but Business is forever hung with using the two-valued, off-on, right-wrong, profit-loss philosophy, while People are rapidly approaching the time when they can use the more complicated, more interesting multi-valued logic to live their lives, in which profit-loss is only a part of living and not a reason. I admit Business knows how to make decisions; that's why

they run everything including the government but they've had only one purpose in mind—making a profit. Business will have to learn to make a profit without despoiling the rest of the planet and we'll have to learn, in our Councils, to
make profit making decisions along similar lines. I would like to get the idea of
serving humankind out of the recipe stage.

The first point of separation between People and Business is Power. There are
two things we must learn to handle with more sense than we have been if we are
to survive on this planet. One is the Ecology, the other is Power, and they meet
at the point where one is being wasted to provide the other. Since we are, as
they say, "on the threshold of the ATOMIC AGE," we might as well prepare for
it because if THEY are allowed to continue to control the new atomic thing as
a threat to the rest of the world, as a means of total and terrible destruction, we
will surely go down the drain. Imagine saying to another group of humans, "We
have more Atom bombs than you do and with our toys can totally destroy your
whole Country and inflict upon your People, the ones who survive, the same
political system we have which allows us to make the previous statement." Now
what kind of a statement is that? If an individual were found to have these sentiments...into the booby hatch. Insane! Right? How come whole countries get
to make this threat without being considered insane as well? They cannot. Ideo-
logically painted governments tend to develop collective insanity in the People
they rule. Having power over people is insane.

By using the atom FOR THE PEOPLE we will, through the Councils...our
Business...supply ourselves free power and without those expensive and ugly
transmission systems either which waste almost 20% of the power generated
just transmitting. 220 volt, 60 cycle, small load house, apartment, farm and
ranch electrical service is so easy you wouldn't believe with small atomic power
units. We can hide the cables and wires underground where they won't bug our
eyes, then plant trees for the birds to perch on. To assure the security of the
people, deep wells can be dug underneath the atomic reactors. These wells will
not only provide the tremendous amounts of water needed to cool the reactors
but will also provide a place to dump one if it reaches critical mass by retro-
rocketing it 300 meters into the bowels of the earth where either the water and
pressure will cool it or it will cause a very small earth-type-quake that might
break a few windows. There's really no need for the reaction to get out of hand
except through carelessness. So we, through the Councils, will furnish our own
power and Business will furnish theirs and not by tearing up the remaining natural resources, either.

The next point of separation is just that...separation. With no laws, they will
need fences to protect their own stuff. They, the manufacturers and industries,
will have to provide their own guards, rent-a-cops, fire prevention and the equip-

ment to do it with. We provide ours. When we, as workers, go through the Business gates, we live by their rules and when we all come home, we live by our Neighborhood Rules of Order.

The third point of separation is excrement. There will be NONE. Businesses, industries and manufacturers can haul all the stuff they want up to their front doors but everything that comes out is neatly packaged for sale. They will reprocess their water, recycle their air and we'll let them have a sewer connection for their human excrement, but that's all. There will be no, NO, discharge of any type from a plant in the RNA. If it piles up and covers them...still none of it will ever get out the gate. The Councils will protect the elements using the Land Lease to back them up.

THE ONLY WAY TO DEAL WITH POLLUTION IS ABSOLUTELY!

Inside its walls Business can set up its own government...it can even have the one we have now if it wants it. If an unwanted monopoly develops, it's not the People's business. Business will solve its own problems, of which it should have fewer. Businesses pay no taxes!! Nor do they have to keep tax records. Furthermore: BUSINESS HAS NO GOVERNMENTAL SUPERVISION! It can spend the money saved on bookkeeping and tax accounting to deal with its excrement. The People's main protection against the *robber baron* types is the Challenge which we'll use to guarantee claims in advertising and even, to some measure, the prices we pay for things. There's a Custom which says that over a 20% net profit on things sold to the People is excessive. If we suspect we're being gouged, we'll challenge and if proven and the price isn't lowered, that Business can lose its Lease. How about making Business disgorge its profits over 20% to Universities? We are interested in buying the best quality merchandise which wastes our Ecology the least for prices we can afford and all that consumer stuff. Businesses will learn to put out accurate specifications, wear factors and operation blurbs or they will find themselves grabbing those Brass Balls a lot.

On the other hand, Business is entitled to stabilize its topsy-turvy world by paying for labor according to units completed. The way we are doing things now is silly, stupid even: to go to the job to do as little as we can is wasteful of one of our most important assets—labor. We even laugh about it and that's sick. Here's the Custom: Production labor in the RNA will be paid by the acceptable unit completed method, wherever possible. All other jobs will be let by Contract. The idea of payment by the hour must go. To expand on this, I'll tell you about the shifts.

We will align our new job lives to the machine's best schedule; make this concession to it. The maximal use factor of most machines is about 120 hours a week. While the argument about this is raging, I give you the shifts.

A Shift	from 0600 to 1600 hours, Monday, Tuesday and Wednesday
B Shift	from 0600 to 1600 hours, Thursday, Friday and Saturday
C Shift	from 1600 to 0200 hours, Monday, Tuesday and Wednesday
D Shift	from 1600 to 0200 hours, Thursday, Friday and Saturday
E Shift	from 0200 to 0600 hours, Monday through Saturday
SA Shift	from 0600 to 1600 hours, on Sundays
SC Shift	from 1600 to 0200 hours, on Sundays
SE Shift	from 0200 to 0600 hours, on Sundays
	(0600 hours is 6:00 a.m.)

There are four production shifts: A, B, C and D and one maintenance shift, E. Each regular shift is 30 hours a week with 24 hours for the maintenance people. These shifts fix one thing that our lives turn on: the hours we work at a job. For people in production or maintenance, any time worked over their regular shift times will be considered overtime. Government employees will have to co-operate to cover all the shifts as government (Neighborhood, Council and Central) is a 24 hour, seven day a week operation. Trainees working extra shifts will shorten their time in Service. Company executives, office personnel, stores and restaurants will have to work out their own shifts.

IN THE MACHINE AGE WHEREIN MACHINES ARE THE WILLING, IF OILED, SLAVES OF HUMANS, WE WILL ADAPT OUR HOURS TO THE MACHINE'S OPTIMUM HOURS OR WE'RE BOTH WASTED.

Now, when you contract for a job you agree to work. For example, A Shift and make whatevers at so much per...this way if you make more things than another person, you're paid more bread...Natural Selection at work. Or you will contract to work on C Shift for so many months, weeks, or even days, for so much. Each job is a Contract between the employer and the employee. The Labor Contract is not necessarily a written one. It can be a simple handshake between Boss and Worker but each time you shake hands, you gotta mean it. If you cannot be there, YOU get someone with the necessary training to take your place. We should learn to split jobs between two or three of us if we don't want to work all the time. No personnel department needed, just a sharp receptionist.

The idea of paying people more because they have worked at a job longer than someone else disappears along with unemployment insurance, paid vacations, retirement funds, hospitalization and other *fringe* benefits. Pay us well while we work and we'll take care of the rest. When we want a vacation, we will find someone to take our job for the length of time we'll be gone. People who contract by the year will undoubtedly get time off as part of their contract.

Free People don't need supervision to oversee that they do their work but Quality Control will still be needed. I suppose QC jobs will pay by the actual number handled as bad ones take just as long (or longer) as good ones.

These are the things we agree to do for Business: keep their machines busy, do the job we contracted to do and be responsible for it. We'll file through their gates, past their guards and do their work the way they want it done. Inside those gates they are *right*, right?

We'll furnish the labor, with love if we have any sense, and make all the bread we can so we don't need to work at a job any longer than we have to to maintain our chosen standards of living. And the first suggestion box they put up will get torn down and stomped on. We'll do it their way, OK, but if we come up with a more efficient way to do it, we'll go the Bank, get a loan and compete...of course, they can pay us if they'd rather for our thinking and inventive ability.

The things they'll do for us are to supply a decent working space or we won't work, pay a decent wage or we won't work, supply us with safe tools or we won't work. We don't have to have jobs anymore to eat. Right? Let them automate everything and make fewer jobs. HOORAY!

Now please don't confuse *job* with *work*. There's a helluva difference and I'll explain.

WORK: The product of force and distance; the idea of moving anything by applying a force through some distance (no matter how much force you apply to it you haven't done any work until you've moved it). So work is related to what it is you are trying to do. Like, the work of punching these typewriter keys is actual; the Work of thinking up the words to punch out is valid work but until you have heard these words and have been moved by them, no Work has been done in the way I am thinking of work as I write this. Work is one of the most *multi-valued* of our human ideas and usually has to be defined for every operation that's done. Pushing the car to get it started is a lot of Work but the Work idea in your head is to start the engine, right? So no matter how much Work you do, you have done none until the engine starts when it will do the Work of moving the car for you. You see what I mean!

A JOB, or employment, is doing somebody else's idea of work for them, in the way they define it, for some reward that is agreed upon between you. A job is two-valued; the Boss is right. The reward can be a smile, bread, giving pleasure, whatever, but no one does a job without some reward.

WORK IS MOVING SOMETHING BY APPLYING A FORCE THROUGH A DISTANCE, AND A JOB IS DOING WORK FOR A REWARD.

WORK AND PLAY ARE ONE!

In the early 50's in San Francisco, I met a man from Japan who was a Zen Master with a small state-paid income which allowed him a generous living in Japan but was peanuts in the U.S. He picked me and two other men (three people from different backgrounds and with different interests) and sat with us three or four evenings a week while we asked him questions which he promptly answered with tougher questions. While we were learning that answers to our questions were tougher questions, he was learning English. After a year of this he wanted to make his tour of the country and go on back. He had taught us much, without any reward beyond the language, so when he mentioned his desire we proceeded to provide the means. One fellow had a car that could be fixed up to make the trip, so we went to work (we were all poor) and gave him waxed transportation ready for 10,000 trouble-free miles but he still lacked cash and sought the first job in his life, after 15 years of Work. Our lessons were suspended but not over. He became a presser in a cleaning shop where he could be seen through an open window, hot weather, wet weather, ventilation fan going so loud that no other sound could be heard; the sweat ran off him. He was totally involved. I became so entranced I stayed to watch him instead of going to my own job and learned about Work from Hari. His face was concentrated Beauty as he laid someone else's pants on the board, sponged a spot, lowered the top of the presser down, gave it a shot of steam with his foot, pushed down a little harder to finish, lifted the top, then pressed the other leg. I could run one of those machines today from the memory of watching him during those Enlightening hours. He was the best presser in the world. You felt it, knew it, felt him feeling it. I can't go on because I'm all choked up with it still after twenty years. So you learn it:

A JOB CAN BE A DRAG OR YOUR DESTINY—WORK AND PLAY ARE ONE!

The new way is to make as much as you can for the Boss, waste as little as you can for the Ecology while making as much bread as you can for yourself. All people who work at jobs will have substantial increases in their standards of living.

IF EVERYONE IS FOR MAXIMUM PRODUCTION, WHO THE HELL LOSES?

We want to automate everything we can because for a Republic to be successful, it needs a large leisure class (bums?)—a large creative group who think and create and, in this case, automation is creation. We will start right out in the RNA with the idea that only those who want jobs can get them and those who don't won't need them.

One of the products of the Industrial Revolution is a thing called the *Job Ethic* which says, "It is right to have a job, moral to have a job, legal to have a job. It is wrong and immoral to not have a job and illegal as well if we catch you wandering around being vagrant."

With new production methods the need for all this cheap labor has disappeared. The people who are against automation are those who fear that they and their families will go hungry because of it. With everybody having a People's Share, this is no longer valid. With total automation, furthermore, the craftsmen who are free from having to work at jobs can work at home making beautiful, made-with-love articles and increase their standards of living by selling these products. For instance, fine boots that really fit each individual foot cannot be mass produced by machine.

The avowed goal of the new Establishment is:

MAXIMUM UNEMPLOYMENT

"Won't we have a lot of trouble with people who have nothing to do?" "Hell, no." People give trouble when they don't have enough to eat, a place to sleep or anything to learn, not because they don't have a job. Besides there's plenty of work, like making our Neighborhoods beautiful and healthy by growing flowers and vegetables, keeping the sidewalks and streets in front of our houses clean, spending time making the parks nice. When the whole world is beautiful again, maybe we can rest. We can go to the Council Shops to work on our cars, make our own coffee mugs, build our own furniture or learn an art or a craft. It takes a lot of hours just to live well, like six hours for good spaghetti sauce. THROW AWAY YOUR CAN OPENER AND LIVE! We've been crowded into a life that gives us ulcers, shortens our time on this planet and makes us cranky and mean. Smile! Make some wine and laugh. Play Bingo, play the piano, the guitar; not for money—for kicks. Take time to visit Uncle Ed in the country and help espalier his peaches and when they're ripe, preserve some. How many times have you said to yourself, "If I had a little more time..." Well, now we're going to get it. That's the name of our new game, *Living Time!*

So unemployment doesn't mean that people don't Work, only that fewer of them have Jobs. Look, if cotton is grown and cloth is woven totally by automatic machinery, there'll be labor involved in sales and distribution but the major cost is making clothes. We'll have time to make our own if we want to.

As there are several types of Business in the RNA, I will do some defining; rather, let the computers do it for me. You have a Card. Right? You can run a steam bath or roller but if you manage to use only your E account, you are not *in Business. You are personal.* To be in Business, you must lease a computer slave, connected to the Small Business (S) Master in the Council or Councils of your choice. The computer slave you lease gives you a B Number, your permit to do any kind of Business, even monkey. The S Master computer has a tie-in with the **Type BM**, Business Master, through a **Type SBDT** slave, Small Business-Business-Direct-Telephone. With your B Number, you can get an account in the BM from the Bank Tender. These accounts are for Businesses which make transactions in more than one Council like large Corporations which pay dividends, Clearing Houses, chains with far flung outlets and for the People's Businesses—the Council and Central. BM's store operating capital.

Because we have a limited, not small, mind you, but limited number of Credits in circulation, I envision large and extensive Corporations and Companies doing transactions among themselves using Commodity or Business type Credits...kinda like pieces of paper that keep track of who owes whom for what—something new like checks. This is up to them and not our business. It is the business of Business to make and supervise its own system of barter and trade. They can use our People's Credits, if they wish, but I think they will use checks and clearing houses. This means that Business will need a meeting point with our Credits. They deposit into the Business Master and use the SBDT slave to transfer Credits into their Small Business accounts so they can pay employees, local bills and such. They are paid for products into their S accounts then can transfer this money to the BM. OK? All the workings of B accounts cannot be predicted as they will be set up by Business.

An account in a Business Master costs its holder one tenth of one percent of the balance in the account weekly, deducted automatically every Sunday—no bookkeeping needed. B transactions and account balances are a secret for your protection, just like Swiss Banks. No one, not even a Tax Tender, can find out your balance. Tax Tenders only have access to BM accounts, when the holder is present, to correct an error or if an Anomoly is suspected in that account.

The SBDT slaves are used for transfers from B accounts to S accounts and vice versa. To make B to B transfers, **Types BDT**, Business-Direct-Telephone, are used. These two types of slaves plus the Business Master itself live in the Business Room at the POB. This room is entered through the Bank and only by those with B Numbers on their Cards. It is a quiet, heavily carpeted place with SBDT's arranged along one wall while the BM and its two, three or four entries, the BDT's, take up most of the other side. The number of BDT's depends on how many each Council needs. There are tables to lay out inventory lists, market research data, whatever.

SBDT's cost the user ¢.50 per time and are typewriter entered but have a more complicated language than the Possession slaves (PD's) and will require some training to use. They record magnetically and can communicate directly with the Library Central. The SBDT slave is the one used by Bank Tenders to find out the odds on a business succeeding, for example.

BDT's are free and to use one of these slaves, you not only need your Card and thumbprint but bring your head along as you also need to put on the crown which checks your brain wave pattern against the one on your Card. All transactions are recorded on magnetic tape and on a cassette type which you can bring and carry away with you for your record. Since the T means Telephone, you'd have a record of any telephone deals you made. Besides transferring Credits from B accounts to other B accounts, BDT's are used to pay dividends. Let's say a Corporation is ready to pay a dividend. Its authorized representative sits at a BDT, uses the T (Telephone) feature to call the Business Central and says, "We're paying a dividend of so much per share' to stockholders of record as of the end of D Shift Saturday night," then matches thumbprints and the Credits transfer to the Business Central (BC) which transfers them to the Market Central (MC) which *knows* who all the stockholders are and pays the Credits into their Possession savings accounts.

In the process of separating Business from living, from People, it becomes necessary to discuss the relationship between Business and the P, Possession, configuration. It's simple.

THERE IS NO TIE-IN BETWEEN POSSESSIONS AND BUSINESS.

To transfer capital out of P savings to start or add to a Business, you have to see a Bank Tender and a Tax Tender who together can transfer Credits from your P portfolio(s) to your S account(s) using one of the 100 E to S circuits.

Businesses cannot own corporation stock, their own or anyone else's. They cannot own Leases or Annuities or Bank Shares. A representative, like the President of a corporation, as an individual, can own shares and Leases...even Homestead the Lease where the corporation is located with the Vice President as inheritor if they wish but the Member or the Council owns the Lease and Business leases from them. Generally, Business and industry will Lease land on which the Council owns the Lease.

On the other hand, in this process of give and take: ONLY THOSE STOCKHOLDERS WHO ARE EMPLOYED BY THE CORPORATION HAVE VOTING STOCK. This means that if a Council inherits a bunch of stock, a Corporation need have no fear that the Council could tell it how to run its operation as the Council wouldn't be employed by the Corporation (I hope). The Council would try to sell any shares it inherited to gain Credits for us, the People. So you as a Member can own all the shares you can afford and buy and sell them at will, but you can only vote the shares you own if you are employed by that Corporation.

OK, so that we can lead our multi-valued lives and learn to live without contention, we agree to separate People and Business. We need them and they need us but it's THEM and US. They can run their Businesses any way they want but the minute they sell us something spurious, screw up the Ecology, push us around in any way, we can Challenge and they must choose a representative to answer the Challenge. If the Challenge is proven, it can be played on TV for the People to decide their fate. What's our enforcer? Their Lease and their computer rentals; their bread. They cannot refuse a Challenge and stay in Business.

The Right of Challenge is guaranteed by the Councils but in the case of a corporation with Leases and accounts in many Councils, Central will get into the action. Once a Challenge has been settled, it would be a bug for a company to have to answer multiple Challenges about the same question. Take the weevily snuff Corporation. It might have received three or four hundred similar Challenges from all over the RNA but having answered one, it could apply to the Council Justice Office where the Challenge had taken place to send a copy of the video tape complete with public results to the Central Justice Section. The Central Head Justice Tender, if satisfied that the Challenges were really about the same thing, could give the Corporation permission not to answer any more of these same Challenges and to refer the other Challengers to the Central Justice Section. The Challengers can then request a copy of the tape and have it played on TV in their home Councils. This could also work for Senators, Councilors—just anyone who is Challenged en masse.

Central is located at the approximate geographical center of the RNA which puts it into the Central Time Zone. All its functions operate according to Central Standard Time, as do all its outlying functions in and out of the RNA so that all Central employees everywhere work their shifts based on Central Standard Time. For some employees this means that they are working yesterday instead of today. The stock market is open the four regular (A, B, C and D) shifts on Central Standard Time but everything else in Central is open 24 hours a day, every day, except Senators.

The Boundaries of the Central complex are around the outsides of three jet runways and are patrolled by the Boundary Patrol. No one can enter or leave except by air. Air transport is provided free by the Boundary Patrol and flights come in from the metropolitan areas two hours before the beginning of each regular Shift and leave two hours after the end of each regular Shift, like every three days. There are also Boundary Patrol feeder flights into the metropolae from outlying areas.

Central security is as absolute as it's possible to make it. Why? So we can take care of our People's Business without interference from any other kind...foreign or domestic. The only people with access to Central are the Senators, who are the representatives of the Councils, the Tenders, who are paid professionals and the Trainees who are assigned there. When you, as one of these, step off the plane, you get on a jitney and ride around the triangle until you reach your gate. Here you prove that you belong there and are the person your Card says you are. Once passed, you put everything you want to take in with you into a basket on the conveyor belt.

To orient yourself, here's a sketch:

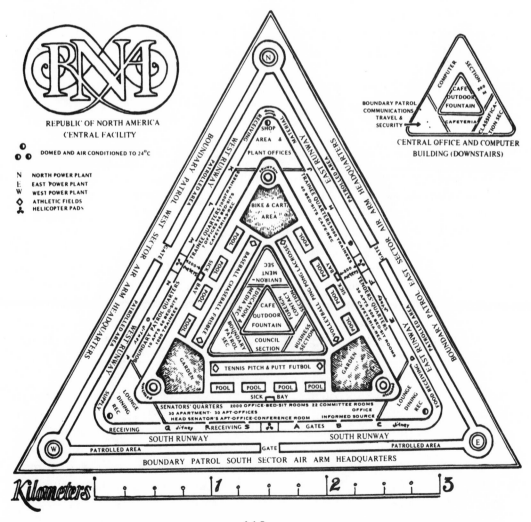

As your stuff disappears, you go to your locker, remove your clothes, walk past the scanners bare assed into the second locker room where you put on different clothes. (Coveralls are furnished and laundered for everyone but you do not have to wear them.) You pick up your thoroughly inspected basket, grab a bike (there are no cars in Central) and a bite to eat. (You wouldn't have eaten before, because everything in Central is free...there are no Exchange computer slaves there.) Now you have plenty of time to talk with the person you are relieving.

The Central facility is domed and air conditioned to 24 degrees Centigrade (about 75°F). Under the dome, the lighting is sufficient for sports and games 24 hours a day. The power for Central and the surrounding air arm headquarter units is supplied by three atomic plants, one in each angle of the outer complex. The top of the dome has the air traffic control center and the many, many antennae of the computer relay nets and Boundary Patrol communications.

To see how Central is organized, please consult the Chart where you'll find twenty-one committees which are made up of about 80 Senators each plus a Committee Head. Remember that each Council has chosen one of its Councilors as a Senator to represent it at Central. The Senators choose one of their number to be Head Senator whereupon the Council this person comes from must choose another Councilor and the Neighborhood must elect another Representative.

The Head Senator's Committee, consisting of the 21 Committee Heads, meets to settle disputes between Committees and has to do with Bills on subjects which affect all Central Sections—like it would make the final analysis on the annual Budget Bill and (hopefully never) Bills about war. In addition to acting as arbiter in Central, the Head Senator becomes the Social Head of the RNA dedicating Continental Treasures and environmental investigation sites, throwing parties (together with the Head Speaker) for visiting foreign VIP's and like that. If the Head can't make it, one of the eight Deputies will. These Deputies are Senators chosen by the Head Senator.

What do Senators do? They work. They find out what the People want, bring that information to Central and get it done. Since there is no Meeting Hall where all the Senators can gather, each Senator's office has closed circuit TV for either direct-watching or playback to hear what other Senators have to say. They will give their own speeches on video tape in their own offices and get them on the agenda. Each Senator is provided with an office-bed-sit with bath and kitchenette. The 21 Committee Heads have office-apartment-conference room setups plus one of the 21 Committee Rooms. The Head Senator has about the same setup as the Committee Heads but won't need a Committee Room. Each Committee can work it out so about 20 of its Senators are at Central during the four regular shifts. Thus they can work three days at Central and spend four days at home, one of which is vote day.

The Committees hire and fire the professional Head Tenders with whom they work. The professional becomes the coordinator of the Committee's efforts, giving it tasks like: logistics, public relations, personnel and the all important budget. In other words, Committees and professionals form a team which must cooperate toward getting the people what they want. The Committees and professionals cooperate in writing and presenting Bills on which the People vote, couched in the simplest and most direct language possible, framed as questions which can be answered *Yes* or *No* and state a definite time limit. Head Tenders are responsible to their Committees for the professional Tenders they hire, fire and supervise—especially for their eight Deputies who take their places when the Heads are not at Central. All Central personnel are paid by their home Councils which are then reimbursed by a Central Business Tender.

Notice on the Chart that most Central personnel come in multiples of eight. Why? Because there are eight Shifts and we need someone in charge on every shift. Also note that some columns of the Chart contain more than one Section. All 21 Sections and Committees are autonomous: no one has the say over any other and they each make up their own Bills to present to the People. Just because a Section is *lower* on the chart doesn't mean it's less important.

The Boundary Patrol furnishes air transport directly to their home Councils for all Senators to make sure they're home on vote day. The Head Senator, Head Tenders and Committee Heads can call upon the Boundary Patrol for transport to wherever they want to go at any time, for themselves alone or for a group— like a whole Committee might need to go somewhere to look at something. The rest of Central personnel use the regular flights. All flights to and from Central are arranged by the Travel Commander of the Boundary Patrol or one of the Deputies. Central security is supervised by the Security Commander while the Communications Commander supervises the Boundary Patrol Communications Center, which maintains constant contact among all units of the Boundary Patrol and from the units to Central. These are the three Patrol units assigned to the Central complex, a triangle of transportation, security and communication, located in the Central office building under the Boundary Patrol Section.

The Boundary Patrol Section itself is under the command of the Commander-in-Chief (hired and fired by the Committee) and is divided into three sectors, each responsible for the PCC's and Coventries in that sector and for patrolling the RNA boundary around that sector. These sectors are formed by drawing a straight line from the North Pole to Central and two other lines at 120 degrees to the first line, making three equal pie slices. Each sector's Commander commands and coordinates the various sea, land and air units necessary to do the Patrol's task 24 hours a day in that sector. The personnel making up a sector of

ORGANIZATION CHART
CENTRAL GOVERNMENT
REPUBLIC OF NORTH AMERICA

SECTIONS

BOUNDARY PATROL	FOREIGN CONTACT	COUNCIL	BUSINESS
COMMITTEE	SPEAKER'S		BUSINESS
COMMANDER IN CHIEF	COMMITTEE	HEAD SENATOR	COMMITTEE
8 DEPUTIES	HEAD SPEAKER	8 DEPUTIES	HEAD BUSINESS
WEST EAST	8 DEPUTIES	HEAD SENATOR'S	TENDER
SECTOR SECTOR	SPEAKER'S OFFICES	COMMITTEE	16 DEPUTIES
COMMANDER COMMANDER	AND 8 SPEAKERS IN	OF THE 21 COMMIT-	AT LEAST 8 BUSI-
8 DEPUTIES 8 DEPUTIES	EVERY CAPITAL AND	TEE HEADS	NESS TENDERS
BOUNDARY BOUNDARY	LARGE CITY OUT-	JUSTICE COMMITTEE	LOCATED IN
COVENTRY COVENTRY	SIDE OF THE RNA.	HEAD JUSTICE	SPEAKER'S OFFIC-
PCC PCC	TOURIST COMMITTEE	TENDER	ES OUT OF THE
SOUTH	HEAD TOURIST	8 DEPUTIES	RNA, 8 IN EVERY
SECTOR	TENDER	HEAD COUNCIL	PORT OF ENTRY
COMMANDER	8 DEPUTIES	COORDINATOR	INTO THE RNA
8 DEPUTIES	AT LEAST 8 TOURIST	WITH 8 DEPUTIES	AND 8 IN EXTEN-
BOUNDARY COVENTRY	TENDERS IN EVERY	FOR EACH OF THE	SION SCHOOL OF-
PCC	SPEAKER'S OFFICE	FOLLOWING COM-	FICES IN THE RNA.
IN CENTRAL PLANT	OUT OF THE RNA	MITTEES:	TRAINEES
SECURITY	AND DITTO AT	WATERFRONT	
COMMANDER	EVERY PORT OF EN-	COUNCIL	
8 DEPUTIES	TRY INTO THE RNA.	COMMITTEE	
CENTRAL TRAVEL	TRAINEES	CITY COUNCIL	
COMMANDER		COMMITTEE	
8 DEPUTIES		TRANSPORTATION	
COMMUNICATIONS		COUNCIL	
COMMANDER		COMMITTEE	
8 DEPUTIES		SUBURBAN COUNCIL	
TRAINEE OFFICERS		COMMITTEE	
TRAINEES		FARM COUNCIL	
		COMMITTEE	
		RANCH COUNCIL	
		COMMITTEE	
		TRAINEES	

EDUCATION	ENVIRONMENT	COMPUTER	CENTRAL PLANT
COMMITTEE	COMMITTEE	COMMITTEE	COMMITTEE
HEAD EDUCATION TENDER 8 DEPUTIES	HEAD ENVIRONMENT TENDER 8 DEPUTIES	HEAD COMPUTER TENDER 8 DEPUTIES	HEAD CENTRAL PLANT TENDER 8 DEPUTIES
AT LEAST 8 EDUCA-TION TENDERS AND AN EXTENSION SCHOOL IN THE 75 OR SO LARGEST CI-TIES OF THE WORLD. STAFF FOR PCC'S.	HEAD MEDICAL TENDER 8 DEPUTIES	8 LIBRARY TENDERS LC	8 MAINTENANCE TENDERS
	HEAD TREASURE TENDER 8 DEPUTIES	8 STOCK MARKET TENDERS MC	8 ELECTRICAL TENDERS
MEDIA COMMITTEE	HEAD MARKETING TENDER 8 DEPUTIES	8 NUMBERS TENDERS NC	8 DISPOSAL TENDERS
HEAD MEDIA TENDERS 8 DEPUTIES	HEAD STANDARDS TENDER 8 DEPUTIES	HEAD RELAY TENDER	8 PROCUREMENT TENDERS
8 MEDIA TENDERS LOCATED IN EXTEN-SION SCHOOL OF-FICES.	HEAD CONSERVA-TION TENDER 8 DEPUTIES	8 MICROWAVE TENDERS	8 STORES AND LAUNDRY TENDERS 8 CHEFS
TRAINEES	AIR-SPACE-WEATHER COMMITTEE	8 RADIO TENDERS 8 WIRE TENDERS	24 MEDICAL TENDERS
	HEAD AIR TENDER 8 DEPUTIES	CLASSIFICATION COMMITTEE	8 TRAINEE ASSIGN-MENT TENDERS
	WATER-OCEAN LAKE-RIVER COMMITTEE	HEAD CLASSIFICA-TION TENDER 8 DEPUTIES	FOR EACH SUN SIGN = 96 LIVE IN TRAIN-EE QUARTERS.
	HEAD WATER TENDER 8 DEPUTIES	8 CLASSIFICATION TENDERS FOR EACH OF NINE SORTER SECTIONS = 72	MATCH TRAINEES TO JOBS IN CENTRAL
	EARTH-RESOURCES COMMITTEE	TRAINEES	TRAINEES
	HEAD EARTH TENDER 8 DEPUTIES		
	FIRE-POWER-FUEL COMMITTEE		
	HEAD FIRE TENDER 8 DEPUTIES		
	TRAINEES		

the Boundary Patrol will organize themselves into Councils of 200,000 people with a Council Center and the whole schmutz. Thus they will have direct representation and their own Council computer configurations but the land they occupy is leased by Central from other Councils.

The duties of the Boundary Patrol are to be cognizant of everything that crosses our border, which is practically all ocean, and stop anything that means us physical harm no matter how high or how low. **The Boundary Patrol will not leave our boundaries.** The slogan of the Patrol is: WE, THE BOUNDARY PATROL OF THE RNA, PROMISE TO DEVOTE OUR ENERGY AND INTEREST TO ELIMINATING THE NEED FOR A BOUNDARY PATROL.

The Foreign Contact Section has two Heads: the Head Speaker and the Head Tourist Tender. There will be Speakers and their Offices in every important city and capital of the world outside of the RNA. The three Tenders making the triangle in Speakers' Offices are: a Speaker, a Tourist Tender and a Business Tender. Official contacts with foreign States are made by Speakers. They are, in reality, our complaint department. The Head Speaker and the Committee will appoint RNA representatives to World Organizations the People decide to join. Foreign policy of the RNA is decided by vote of the People; that is, the official position of the RNA involving foreign States is determined by vote on Speakers' Bills which can come along almost any vote day. Speakers handle immigration; quotas set by RNA Bills. Each immigrant, before being made a Citizen and allowed to enter the RNA, must agree to serve the three years required for Membership. These three years will be served in different locations to give the immigrant a better chance to choose where to settle.

The Tourist Tenders in Speakers' Offices handle problems RNA tourists and wanderers have overseas like getting into jail, losing their Cards (passports) or shooting off their mouths. There are also Tourist Tenders in every Port of Entry (air, sea and land) and here they handle problems connected with visitors to the RNA; you know, they issue Cards, orient tourists to the computer exchange system—like that. In Ports of Entry, the triangle of Tenders includes a Tourist Tender, a Business Tender and a Council Port Tender. The Tourist Tender deals with people, the Business Tender with money, being the interface between RNA electric Credits and all other money. After the Tourist Tender makes out the visitor's Card, the Card and the foreign currency to be changed into Credits go to the Business Tender who puts the Card into a **Type TED**, Tourist-Exchange-Direct, computer slave to put Credits onto the visitor's Card out of the Central Business Computer (BC). Visitors leaving can exchange their unused RNA Credits for their own money either with the Business Tender in the Port they leave from or with the one in a Speaker's Office. They can keep the Card as a souvenir. RNA tourists also exchange their money through the Business Tender at either

Port of Entry, Extension Schools or Speakers' Offices.

Businesses have to work through Business Tenders in order to have any foreign financial dealings. The procedure is simple. You, as a Business person, wish to pay a foreign concern for a diamond ring, a camera, a shipload of scrap iron, just anything that costs a lot or you don't want to pay taxes on. Just walk up to a Business Tender's desk at a Port Office, an Extension School or a Tourist Office and state your request.

"You said three million yen to the Yokahama Trading Company?"

"Right."

"Tokyo Bank, OK?"

"Right."

"Put your Card in the proper slot. Is this scrap iron for personal or business use? If it is business, you may use the S slot and thus pay no taxes."

"Right."

"Put on the headset so we can be sure you're who the Card says you are."

"Right."

"You certainly are! WOW, what a balance!"

"Right."

"Today's rate on yen is 300 to one, so that'll be 10,000 Credits. Just punch the seventh button once. That's right. Now your thumb. Very good. Let me make a copy of this check and tear off my stub. Here's your check; have a good day."

"Right."

A copy of the check is sent to Central by facsimile using the Tourist Tender's **Type TND**, Tourist-Numbers-Direct, computer slave. There one of the Trainees files the check after punching the amount into the Business Central (BC) computer which automatically deducts the amount from the Tokyo Bank balance and adds ₵10,000 to the total showing on the *IN* section. When Credits are received, they're ecology *IN* and when they're paid out, they're ecology *OUT*. On Sunday, the *IN* and *OUT* totals must balance. Business Tenders try to even the balance every day but sometimes the end of D Shift gets a little fraught. The idea is that each week the RNA imports *IN* exactly to the Credit value it exports *OUT*. This way we avoid an unfavorable or even favorable balance of trade with the rest of the world. If there is an unavoidable imbalance, the following week is started out on that note. If the stuff which is bought and sold is grown, mined or pumped, this system will keep us in balance with the ecology of our neighbors on the planet as well. By the way, this foreign exchange is one of the ways that our total number of Credits can get out of whack.

The Business Section in Central has a Head Business Tender plus the all important Business Committee to make sure that both internal and external financial dealings leave us with the same total number of RNA Credits each week in addition to determining the week by week, even day to day, value of the Credit as compared with foreign currencies. As well as making sure that imports balance exports, this Section makes foreign trade possible by having RNA bank accounts in every foreign city which has a Speaker's Office. The balances of these bank accounts are kept in the Business Central computer at Central and one of the tasks of Business Tenders is to keep these accounts from being overdrawn by transferring funds from one to another. Like in the scrap iron episode, the next morning the Business Tender in Tokyo might receive instructions to write a check on the Bank of Berlin to cover the check for three million yen that was written at the San Francisco Port Office the night before. I hope we don't operate this closely, but it has a rather familiar feeling.

The Head Business Tender has two sets of eight Deputies: one set has to do with matters external like the balance of trade and the other set with matters internal like the people's interface with RNA Business. The Business Committee (also known as the Budget Committee) and the Head Business Tender are the active driving forces behind the annual Budget Bill which determines how much each Council is going to have to pay each week to run Central and support those Councils whose economy doesn't allow them to make their weekly nut.

There are no Credits in Central except in the Business Central (BC) computer. Central has accounts in all Council Business Masters (BM's). Every Council pays into Central's account in its BM a weekly amount fixed by the annual Budget Bill. Central Business Tenders juggle these Credits to wherever they are needed. The Head Business Tender with support from the Budget Committee can make small interim adjustments in a Council's economy by depositing Central Credits into the deficit Council's B Master computer. Since every Council collects one tenth of 1% of the amount on deposit in its BM every week, the ailing Council's funds would be upped by this percentage.

The Head Business Tender and Committee can make up a Bill for the People's approval to increase or decrease the total number of Credits in circulation, giving very simple reasons.

The Council Section consists of the Head Senator's Section which keeps the peace among all the Committees, **the Justice Section and the six Council Coordinating Sections** whose Committees plus their professionals provide information, communications and liaison among all of the Councils of the RNA.

The Education Section is in charge of education for all people over 18 years old with the exception of trade, shop and lab learning which the Councils provide. One of its duties is to keep a file in the Library Central (LC) of all audio-visual educational material available in the RNA and elsewhere and to furnish copies upon request. It also runs extension schools in the 75 (or so) largest cities throughout the world and staffs Psychiatric Care Centers. PCC's are managed by a triangle of an Education Tender, a Medical Tender and a Boundary Patrol Officer.

The Media Section is part of the RNA's public relations team as well as an important part of the education function. Everywhere there's an extension school, there are Media Tenders and Trainees to collect news for the Council TV stations. They also gather and collate information by reading newspapers, magazines and watching TV to keep our LC file complete. The Head Media Tender, the Head Senator and the Head Speaker form the RNA public relations triangle. These three present a common front, have excellent TV presence and love the spotlight of publicity. I am not going to define public relations because they change with the wind but this triangle knows everything about RNA affairs, releases it to the media and serves to protect the other Tenders and Senators from the public eye wherever possible.

The Environment Section consists of six divisions that work with the Environment Committee. Each has a Head Tender and eight Deputies at Central plus Tenders in the field.

Environment: coordinates environmental investigations and studies for the RNA, the planet and space and publishes the results. It also gives the results to the Media Section for release and to the Computer Section for filing in the L.C.

Medical: investigates human and animal health.

Continental Treasures: obtains financing for and represents each Continental Treasure at Central.

Marketing: investigates internal and external markets.

Standards: keeps and makes available exact standards of weights and measures and standards of quality for foods, medicines and other consumer goods.

Conservation: takes the viewpoint of all living species on Earth, other than humans, so we can live together in harmony without any of us becoming extinct.

The Air Section investigates the envelope of air around our planet and the space beyond and provides weather and communication satellites and a chain of weather stations. A space probe, for instance, if voted *yes* by the people, would be handled by this Section. It would also be in a position to report on any areas of air pollution.

The Water Section investigates oceans, lakes, rivers—all bodies of water— for growing fish to eat, irrigation, transportation, human· consumption, pollution, flood control and like that. It would make studies in which several Councils were involved and report on the results.

The Earth Section investigates resources in the ground like oil, minerals, soil and plants, including trees. It would do many kinds of earth experiments—dams, model farms, erosion patterns, etc. In general, its job is to determine ways to make our earth support us indefinitely.

The Fire Section investigates ways to conserve Earth's supply of stored energy and ways to substitute the energy producing atomic reaction for other types of energy so our power needs can continue to be filled.

These five Sections cooperate with each other so their experiments and investigations take into account what the other Sections are doing. The available-amount-of-oil information from the Earth Section would be given to the Fire Section so it could figure out how to conserve what there is. Earth would work with Water on dams, irrigation and water erosion. Water would work with the Conservation division on fish population. And many more examples which could fill a book. Projects which cost a lot of bread will become subjects of Bills and approved by majority vote before they are begun but mostly these Sections figure out how much they'll need and have it put on the annual Budget Bill.

Located underneath the above offices in the middle triangle (the Central Office and Computer Building) is the **Computer Section** which has to do with programming, operating and repairing the computer systems and relay nets at Central.

The Classification Section is next door and here requests for Trainees and requests for assignments are matched. There's a sorter section for each Trainee category, except category 0 (acceptable non-service).

At the northern end of the Central facility is the **Central Plant Section** which runs and maintains Central including the three sick bays staffed by Medical Tenders plus cafeterias, stores, laundry, et al. Living with the Trainees are Assignment Tenders who tell Trainees already assigned to Central where to go to work.

One of the surprises in Central is the average age level. Look at it this way: you would pick the sharpest, young business or professional person in your Neighborhood to represent you in your Council, the People's Business—eager and on the go all the time. This is a well-paid, responsible, interesting job for someone just starting out. Guess whom these Councilors choose to represent them at Central? Some old fuddy-duddy like me—set in my ways and habits? Impossible. They'll elect the one with the most fire, someone who speaks their language. When the People vote on everything that goes down, the necessity for old weighty heads in our government is gone. Remember, WE tell them what we want and their success depends on how well they get it done. So with young Senators between 25 and 40 years old—my guess—and 12,000 Trainees and 1,000 Boundary Patrol Trainees mostly between 18 and 21, the Central dome will be throbbing with vitality...note swimming pools and other athletic facilities. I'm pretty sure that Business will recruit its young executives from Central personnel—look at the experience they've had. The professional Tenders will undoubtedly be older because they need to be the most knowledgeable people we can find in their chosen fields and will be balanced by the young Committees. Please note: no space or budget has been provided for anything like spy, enforcement or interference agencies. If the Media Section doesn't find it out in the Media, we won't know it. Conversely, we have nothing to hide. Scientists all over the world can again exchange theories and knowledge without being incarcerated.

The RNA presents to the world a many headed front of knowledgeable people so essential, contention-free communications can be made either by them or through the Media. A Treaty or any sort of agreement between the RNA and another nation would be signed by all the Section Heads whose area of expertise the agreement affects—after the People had agreed to the Treaty with a majority vote. If we agree to exchange educational ideas with someone, the Head Education Tender would sign. Fishing rights agreements would be signed by the Boundary Patrol Commander-in-Chief, the Head Environment Tender and the Water Tender. We, as a government, might make certain agreements with the representative of RNA Business to our mutual advantage and this agreement would be signed by the Head Business Tender and maybe the Head Marketing Tender. We can eliminate contention between the People who make up and are the North American Republic and Business and between the RNA and foreign States by providing first, a separation, then accurate communications and honorable agreements.

How does Central fit into the idea of modeling governmental institutions on the human organism (human symbiosis)? Business tends to think of its central organization as the brain of the whole with the branches obeying the brain. Central is the brain, OK, but it doesn't make the decisions. The Councils are not branches but are individual organs each doing their own tasks with Central, the brain, giving one a shot of oxygen here, helping another eliminate poisons there. Central is an information and data gathering, sorting and disseminating entity so the decisions made by each individual person include *all* the data.

After the decision has been made, Central becomes an action, balancing and coordinating agency. This interaction among molecules, cells, organs and brain allows our symbiosis to reflect changes instantly: changes in technology and changes that come with Understanding ourselves so

HUMANKIND CAN PROGRESS WITHOUT CONTENTION

HIS SEGMENT is about giving up the right to limit learning. In the RNA we will give kids all the opportunities there are, lay the world out in front of them, then step aside and watch, so they can go on from where we are to whatever they can be. To do this, we'll have to change our ideas about *teach* and *educate*. **TEACHING is the process of passing on Knowledge from an older person (on high) who knows *more* to a younger person (lowly, non-knowing) who knows *less*.** Having more Knowledge doesn't mean *better*. We don't even Know (much less, Understand well enough to Teach) great glomps of knowledge our children need to survive so our teaching them is a little silly. Furthermore, the ways in which we teach are by identification and rote; these methods are hampering, not educating. **EDUCATE, to lead out into learning.** We must change the idea of *teach* to *help to learn* in order to bring out the ability to create in everyone. It is much more important to make information available so people of all ages can learn *how* to do what they want to do instead of teaching them *what* to do.

The process of learning goes on through all of our alive lives. When we stop learning we may continue to live OK, but we stop being alive. The invention of the *boob tube* bears the same relationship to the science of education as Whitney's cotton gin did to the Industrial Revolution. Audio-visual (A-V) doesn't *teach*, it makes impressions on our senses that either stay with us or don't. In the Dark Ages of *teaching* education, we only ever had one chance. If we were reasonably intelligent and passed the course that was the end of it, whether we learned anything or not. Using A-V, the Council is going to repeat courses over and over again and if you didn't learn it the first time, you have another chance and another and another and when you're 40, you can retake Elementary Math if you've forgotten. No more need to feel foolish if you decide to take High School subjects at 50.

I had the task of developing an A-V method for training welders to weld micro-electronic components. The course was poorly prepared, the sound barely matched the picture and the welders had to continually look up from their microscopes to the screen, but they became welders in six days instead of in the six weeks it took without A-V and the quality of the welds was so much better that we ran the experienced welders through the course, too. I'm sold!

And look! To make A-V courses, we can use people who glow and bounce and know that their subject is the most important and interesting one of them all. These experts are excited about their subjects and love what they're doing. This love and excitement gets passed on through the video tapes they make.

Think of the way we *teach* geography now compared to how A-V can take you there. You can see real Brazilians, for example, instead of just a pink place on the map with *coffee* and *rubber* written on it and a picture of a man shooting a poisoned arrow out of a blow gun. Take a geology field trip; go to the moon! How about History with clips from movies; cartoon Mathematics? Animated Geometry and Trigonometry make working the problems easy as Pi.

The biggest objection to A-V that I hear mouthed is that children educated by it don't learn to read. Who the hell cares except you? Using the number of words a child can define and spell as a measure of educational level is bullshit. After seeing and hearing, they know much more about the subject than if they had read about it. Audio-Visual education leads to Understanding more quickly and the beauty of it is we can take our own path. The way to eliminate identification and rote (not to be confused with repetition) from Education is to take an A-V course several times until we really Understand. There'll even be different tapes on the same subject made by different people presenting different viewpoints. Thus we'll be able to see the Civil War, for example, from both the North and South sides.

Since audio-visual presentations of knowledge on TV have made our children able to pick up concepts more quickly than we can, we must continue to use this effective process from age 0 to 90 plus, wherever and for whomever it works.

There are two kinds of learning: the kind that can be learned audio-visually and the kind that needs actual contact with other people and with materials. By watching someone on TV do photography step by step, for example, you can see what it's all about but, of course, to do it, you need a camera, film and use of a darkroom plus someone around to answer questions if you're not sure. Educators, gurus, are needed for human contact and guidance in learning. Especially when you're young, you need someone around who smiles and encourages you.

Remember the Councils all have two television stations. They will broadcast on the regular channels, if they're not full, or use UHF channels since they would not broadcast beyond the Council limits. Councils in cities will probably use UHF channels, one for every Council, and a regular channel which covers the entire city. Council stations will continue in the *honorable tradition* of selling as many truth telling commercials as they can to pay for their programming and give everyone time to pee. At any rate, the stations become just another part of the Council complex. I visualize that there will be four one-hour news and commentary sessions with all of the material furnished from the various Central Media Offices throughout the world. Here's a *sample* of a TV schedule: Monday through Saturday—Sunday is vote day. All programs are on video tape.

0700-0800	Morning news
0800-1200	A-V courses for the under 12's (a course is one hour per day, three days a week for six weeks)
1200-1300	Noon news
1300-1800	A-V courses for the 12 to 18 year olds
1800-1900	Evening news
1900-2300	FFTests, Council voting news and Council affairs. Can be filled, if necessary, with travelogues or like BBC specials.
2300-2400	Night news
2400-0200	More FFTests or a movie
0200-0700	Extension courses and *adult* education.

There are about 200 six-week courses full of material in which children under twelve would ordinarily be interested. Take Math, for instance: divide the subject of Mathematics into about 20 courses which cover from basic digits through fractions to quadratic equations, exponents and complex numbers and make

each course six weeks long. Thus the basic language of Mathematics is fairly well explained to any child willing to watch and listen for 360 hours over a six year period—explained unboringly, too. A-V courses will follow one after the other and repeat. I realize all the courses won't be exactly six weeks long, but time and experience will help us learn the most efficient and best received lesson spacings and durations.

From birth to twelve, children are under the care and eye of their parents, the Neighbors and the Neighborhood Education Tender. As Neighborhoods are as individual as People are, there's no telling what Rules of Order or way of life they will encounter in the relatively short but extremely influential time they spend there.

As a parent or Neighbor, your total responsibility to the under 12's is to love them, keep them alive and healthy and allow them to watch TV. When they're very young it doesn't matter what kind of TV they watch as they can't help but learn something but when they reach four, five, six, like that, they'll start watching the A-V courses and leave the commercial television for you, for whom it is designed. When they show interest in a program, buy them a Work Book for that course from the Council so they can practice what they see, as long as interest dictates. The name of the new game is: let them learn at their own speed. If they drop out of the course and don't complete the Work Book, it might be up to you to pay attention to the course schedule, turn the tube on when the course starts again and remind them that they haven't finished it. Work Books should be kept if you want to keep a record of a child's education. Children who need help in a course or courses or whose parents don't want a TV or both work can go to the Neighborhood Center where the two television sets are on, one at each end of the Meeting Hall. There are Trainees and Learnees there to answer questions, smile and be comforting.

After lunch, the Education Tender, the educators (as many as your Neighborhood can afford), perhaps some Neighbors, the Trainees and the Learnees help the under 12's learn how to play together, use a library, "make and do," and take them on tours of industries, zoos...all the things which need contact to learn. In a Neighborhood where a lot of people work at jobs, they can afford to pay educators; in a Neighborhood where few people have jobs, they'll have time to spend with the kids and won't need as many professional educators. There is no activity in the afternoon session that contains anything that you and your Neighbors have not considered and decided in a Meeting.

By the way, Learnees are young people between 12 and 18 who assist Trainees to referee games, mix paint and clay, help keep Order on tours and, in general, bring our class sizes down to about ten kids per group. They will supply a floating population, sometimes too many, sometimes not nearly enough, but as they will be active and eager, they make valuable allies and cost us nothing.

When children reach twelve, the Council takes over their care and feeding and they get their own Cards, ₵15 a week and the right to live for free in the Council Houses which are miniature Neighborhoods, remember. All Council House doors open to Cards with blanks in the Service Number space. Here, they will learn to make their own rules, schedule their own lives, do their own thing— at least, start to find out what their own thing is. They don't have to leave home; however, our new goal as parents is to let them develop enough self-reliance, confidence and the ability to make their own decisions and to cope so they have a chance of making it in the world without us. We want to make sure it's a world of their peers and not one in which they are constantly being put down by adults just for being kids. Let them wear off the raw edges on each other, like pebbles in a rotating can. By having Council Houses in conjunction with every Speaker's Office, we're going to free them not only to move all over the RNA but the whole world as well, to help them find their educational direction. If they come home dressing and acting, talking and being different from us—that's the way it is where they are. We get to take care of where we are. AS CHILDREN GROW UP THEY ARE EITHER FRIENDS OR STRANGERS DEPENDING ON HOW WE ARE WITH THEM.

The 12 to 18 year olds get the more regular education, too—A-V, of course. From 1300 to 1800 hours both Council Television stations give courses that contain what we now call Jr. High School, High School and Jr. College material. These, too, have Work Books obtainable from the Council for the cost of printing plus 10% and will be kept, upon completion, as a record of the courses taken. Kids can travel OK, but they will stop in a Council House long enough to finish a course and build up enough bread in their accounts to be able to pay their fares to the next place they want to be. If they're going overseas, they might even have to take several courses, like the languages of the countries they plan to visit. I hope all RNA kids will be trilingual from an early age. I'm going to guess that there'll be about 500 six week long courses in this 12 to 18 category and I think I'm high.

Your Neighborhood Education Tender is directly concerned with how well the children learn; the Council Education Tender is concerned with making as much knowledge as possible available; and they both cooperate to see that the A-V courses in their Council and Neighborhood are the most comprehensive, most exciting, well presented ones they can find. The 200 Education Tenders from the Neighborhoods will meet with the Council Education Tender to decide which A-V courses will be given in the morning session. The Council Education Tender will schedule the afternoon A-V session largely according to student requests.

The Councils will present every opportunity to youths to use both their heads and their hands. The Council Shops, which actually do the work of maintaining the facilities and equipment in the Councils, are run by professionals and staffed with mechanics and Trainees. Kids between 12 and 18 can work in these shops as Learnees, probably recruited by the Trainees they help. Also, they can witness and actually perform experiments in the Council Labs that illustrate what we know about our environment.

OUR CHILDREN MUST BE ALLOWED TO LEARN EVERYTHING THEY CAN AS FREELY AND AS OPENLY AS WE CAN PRESENT KNOWLEDGE TO THEM.

At eighteen, youths become Citizens and get a vote. They also become eligible to Serve. They can serve earlier than 18 if they can convince two Council Tenders of their ability and need but mostly they will start at eighteen. Within certain bounds, the choice of Service is theirs. If you are interested in something and learn something about it, you will get to Serve in your chosen field. Like if you want to Serve in the Council Shops, you study mechanics and practice a little, even earn something when you're 15, 16 and 17 as a mechanic's Learnee so when you reach 18, you can truthfully say you have had three years of mechanical experience. You get to choose but you have to think ahead a little to get your choice.

The process is this: Phone the Council Justice Office to make an appointment for you with one of the four Fact Finder Operators in charge of Classification. At the appointed time, you sit in the Chair, put your Card in the slot, don the Crown and grasp the Brass Balls. The Operator will punch your E and A Numbers out of a computer card and ask you questions about the way you've decided to Serve. Be prepared to give three choices and to tell about your qualifications for these choices. You will also state the condition of your health, the various courses you've completed, the Learnee experience you've had and what you plan to do after Service if you know, like go on to University or whatever. As you talk, the Operator punches the card and when you're both finished talking and punching, the card will give an accurate reading of your dreams, hopes and desires. If you have paired and wish to Serve with your partner, make your appointments together so both cards are made by the same Operator at the same time and are fastened together. Your card is sent to Central Classification where it is put into the sorters and matched with a *request for Trainee* from a different Council than your own. A card in the mail will tell you where to go and what to do. If, after three months of Service, you find that what you're doing is not your thing, make another card with different dreams and choices.

After a year's Service, your supervising Tender will take you to the Tax Office in any POB and have a number put in the first blank and increase your People's share by ¢5.00 per week; the same after the second year and the third so after you complete the full three year tour, you have three Service Numbers, ¢30.00 a week and two votes for as long as you live. You become a Member of the RNA and with two votes are twice as effective.

If for some reason you decide not to serve at eighteen, no one will say anything (maybe Dad), but at nineteen your first Service blank is filled with a dash (-). This dash means your carefree ways in the Council Houses are over: no more free board and room or free hospital or medical care. Your status is that of an adult Citizen with one vote and ¢15.00 per week for the rest of your life or until you decide to Serve, which you can do at any time. After a year of Service, the dash will be replaced by some number. OK? If you never Serve, you'll never have to learn to use the Possession computer configuration. If you want to save money you can buy Bank Shares and to earn money you can have a job or run your own business just like Members.

Those who don't want to Serve but want to continue their education will probably join some sort of educational commune where they can live on their ¢15 a week and learn from someone who has something to say or show and needs someone else to lay it on. There's a place in the RNA for everyone.

However, the regular route to increasing knowledge and understanding through learning is through three years of Service with extension courses and on to a University. The Central Head Education Tender (in charge of all *book learning* type education over eighteen) has extension schools in conjunction with the Media offices in the 75 or so largest cities of the world. These schools are free. The primary goal of the Central Education Section is to provide opportunities so all Citizens and Members can continue the learning process for as long as they're interested. More specifically, this Section makes educational facilities available so at the end of three years of Service, all Trainees can have what we now call a Bachelor's Degree. (Note: no degree is awarded, however.) These can be A-V courses, actual lectures and seminars in the extension schools or correspondence courses. You get to choose which best fits your time and location. Trainees and other RNA students abroad can take special foreign courses taught by local experts who are hired and paid by the local Central Education Tenders. On the home front, anyone can study the A-V courses which are broadcast in as many Councils as the Central Education Tenders can persuade to show them. Tenders will also do groovy things like show 15 minute A-V courses on how to change an electrical plug, a faucet washer, like that.

The Council Shops and Labs are for adults, too. Shop, Art and Craft operations will be on video tape with a viewer for the students. Let's say you're interested in making pottery; you pull out the tape on *How to Wedge Clay*, watch how different professionals do it, choose a way to try and go at it. Next, you'd pull out *How to Center* which if you're like me, you'll have to watch several times. The same kinds of tapes will be available in all fields—to do an engine overhaul for whatever make, for example. If an A-V course tells you to do some lab work or you have an idea to try—go to the Council Lab.

Universities are Businesses. You have to be a Member to attend one and they deal totally in studies which we now call *graduate work*. They will do the research for Business and Government, provide them both with professionals and for this Universities will be recompensed by them. Physicists for advancing our knowledge, Engineers, Doctors, Justice Tenders, Ecology experts, Oceanographers and on and on will all be University graduates. Let's let Educators and all experts get their PhD's for coming up with new, wiggy A-V courses. Some genius might even come up with a course that actually lets children learn to read. Because reading cannot be taught, only learned. *Are you identifying the word* **course** *with the verb* **to teach**?

Universities are Businesses, all right, but they need not have to be geared to turning out technicians for industry. While I'm trying to make as few suggestions to Industry as possible, I would like to say: Why don't you set up schools to train technicians, factory workers, maintenance workers and all the various types of personnel you need in each Council that's heavy with industry? You can all cooperate in paying this bill and let everybody take all the courses and training programs they wish. You pay them nothing and it costs them nothing. When they finish a course, give them a certificate which says that they are qualified to run a punch press, be a quality control inspector, an assembly mechanic, an electrical maintenance person or whatever. This will give you a backlog of trained personnel to assure that all your shifts are staffed. It also makes it easy for a worker to find someone as a substitute in case of illness, vacation or just not wanting to work at a job for a while.

What I have been saying is that Education is a hell of a lot easier than we thought it was. Like, teaching is having it done to you and learning is doing it. Teaching is creating habits and learning is conditioning your own reflexes. It isn't only children who need Education, it's you and I. Perhaps we're just a little frightened to give our children their chance to learn more, to know more than we do. If we can find a way to force ourselves to stay out of their lives and go to the Council Shops and dig some of those early morning A-V programs ourselves, perhaps our kids won't say to us anymore, "You're dead, you old fart. You're dead and you don't know it."

WHEN YOU STOP LEARNING, YOU DIE.

HUMANKIND MUST LEARN TO PROGRESS WITHOUT CONTENTION

IN WHICH
TRANSPORTATION
GROWS UP

MY ACTIVE imagination would love to conjure up various forms of transportation to be developed in the future. Like, if someone does build a flying, floating VW bus, I'll be first in line to buy one but in this book I will stick to transportation concepts presently available to us.

In the new Establishment People, their shitsy witsies, written communications and merchandise will be transported through sun, mud, snow and etcetera, comfortably, safely and quietly, using minimum natural resources, maximum unemployment and without bunches of laws. We have to expand our thinking about travel and people moving about in the RNA. First, we work at jobs only three days a week; second, with the motto MAXIMUM UNEMPLOYMENT, there will be many more people loose than there are now. If we take an approx-

imate figure of 20 times more kilometers traveled per year, we might come somewhere near the actuality.

I will divide transportation into four categories: Council owned People and things transportation; privately owned transportation; Business owned People, their things and bulk transportation; and services provided by the Transportation Councils.

Council owned and operated People and things transportation: Since one of the things we need is thorough, safe and frequent public transportation, the Councils will provide 24 hour, seven day Peripheral and Direct bus service. The Peripheral buses go round and round the edges of the Council (remember every Council's boundaries are roads or parkways) always clockwise, hugging the kerb, stopping at all stops to pick up people and their things. Once each round, the buses will cut into their circles to go past the Council Center. Peripheral bus routes will probably be different for each type of Council. In City Councils, divided from each other by a double parkway, smart Councils would provide parking on the grassy, park side of the street because the lane closest to the Council would be reserved for Peripheral buses which could come by as often as once every ten minutes. Suburban Councils might provide two circles, one smaller and further in and the circles could meet at Council Center. In Farm or Ranch Councils, it might take three or four such circles so people could get around easily. In these Councils, the buses could be combination petroleum-electric: petroleum on country roads and electric in the towns. They might come by every half hour or so. Some Councils would have Peripheral boat service. In the Northern wilderness, where the mind gasps at the immensity of the Council areas, hovercraft could be used. These don't need roads but make a helluva noise. The northernmost Councils would only provide transportation as far North as there are people. Whatever the solution, the minimum is clear around every Council. People will be depending on it.

Direct buses cover three routes: between Council Center and the Council Shop area, between Council Center and a neighboring Council Center and between Council Center and the Council Way Station on the closest Transcontinental Hiway. Buses on the last two routes will haul mail, parcel post and express besides People and their things.

The buses will be powered electrically and free to passengers. When the bus operator, a Trainee, stops the bus and opens the People doors, the same circuit opens the thing doors on the kerb side so people can remove their skis, bicycles, packages, bags from the baggage compartments under the seats The stops will necessarily take time but will make public transportation more feasible. All Council owned transportation will allow pets, as I hope Business owned transport will. WE, PET LOVING PEOPLE, PROMISE TO MIND OUR PETS' MANNERS AND CLEAN UP AFTER THEM IN ALL PUBLIC SITUATIONS. Non-pet lovers, please mind your own business—not try to pet the pretty little tiger, like that, and we promise it won't bite you. We'll even let you Challenge us for our pets' actions. OK? It would be groovy not to have to own a car just because of all those silly rules about pets and public transportation.

Privately owned transportation: One of the lovliest privately owned means of transport is feet. We've gotta stop thinking People are weird because they walk. People who walk are similar to and probably slimmer than other People who don't. To take a simple walk nowadays is like taking a chance of being molested. By whom? The fuzz.

Personal transport, as interpreted by the modern motor car, has been allowed to become a necessity; that is, to get around, we need a car whether we want one or not. With public transportation that is complete, tasteful, cheap and safe, we can cut down on the numbers of privately owned petroleum users. While we are building the public transportation of the future, we can lower exhaust emissions by refusing to buy cars with huge, wasteful engines: engines over two cubic liters. Since we already have a status symbol in the new society, we need not waste our limited resources on monster cars. The status symbol? Our tax rate, right? Every time you buy something, it tells the people around that you're a wheel or a happy flat tire. If cars no longer need to be ego boosters, they can be made to get us there with the minimum of fuss. If you don't have to shift going up a steep hill, you just plain have too much engine for our resources.

Small fuel injected, air cooled engines use less fuel and make less smog than other engines now being produced. In the future, maybe we can use the new *rotaries* which reburn the petroleum product until it is smog-free. The rotary types need more development as they wear fast and are inefficient. While we're developing, think about making interchangeable engines so drivers could have a new one installed in any gas station when the red light goes on saying, "Your engine has reached its wear factor limits." The engines thus traded can either be rebuilt to *new* standards or recycled. Eventually, we will want to develop petro-electrics which will allow a vehicle to use either petroleum to generate the power to turn the wheels or to pick up the atomically generated electric power in the insulated roadbeds by induction transfer.

THE ONLY WAY TO DEAL WITH POLLUTION IS ABSOLUTELY

Boats, planes, motorcycles, cars: we love them all, but with engines that will not emit anything harmful to the rest of us.

What about those books and books of laws about speeding and rights of way and all that crap? If we keep building cars to have wrecks in, we're going to make highways into one huge *dodge 'em* game. First off, let's settle one thing about traffic:

THE LEAST MANEUVERABLE VEHICLE OR, IF EQUAL, THE ONE ON THE RIGHT, HAS THE RIGHT OF WAY.

Thus, the Porsche is supposed to avoid the Cadillac.

Next, let's change driving from a competitive sport to a cooperative effort where everyone on the road is committed to the idea that all drivers and pedestrians arrive safely with the minimum time expended. There are tracks built especially for competitive driving but in regular transit let's be polite.

THE INDIVIDUAL WHO OBJECTIVELY SEES THE CAUSE OF A TRAFFIC SNARL WILL PAUSE AND GET SOME KICKS DIRECTING TRAFFIC UNTIL THE JAM IS ON ITS WAY.

The only uniform needed is a smile! If a sticky traffic situation happens often in the same place, the Council can rent a cop for those hours.

WE ALL HELP EACH OTHER GET TO WHERE WE'RE GOING. To illustrate, here's a story: While walking along the traffic laden, many laned beach highway in Rio, I saw a car stall. By the second light change, the drivers of the cars in the other lanes stopped, left their cars, pushed the stalled one in front of the traffic (now stopped by their vehicles) over to the shoulder. The five gentlemen then returned to their cars and traffic flowed once more...minutes only and just a few beeps. Or, in London on a crowded road, a man actually stopped his car and the traffic in back of him to let me back out of a driveway and start to where I was going. So let's add cooperation to driving and stir in a little Consideration for Everyone.

The rate of speed that we, as individuals, can drive safely is determined by a machine at the Council Shops which tests our driving knowledge and reaction time. This test is free and you can take it as often as you want to...just sit in the driver's seat of the simulator and do what the Trainee says. The machine tests your reactions to determine the distance it takes you to stop, make a steering correction, handle emergencies, like that. After taking the Driving Reaction Test, you are given a colored card and the following table shows at what speeds you can safely drive under what conditions...for yourself? Of course, but for the rest of us as well. If your reactions test out so badly that the machine operator can not, in conscience, give you any color of card at all, you'd better not drive. If you are Challenged, you could be Consequenced heavily by the People who would, for sure, see you in living color. The only way you can be forced to take a Driving Reaction Test is if you've never taken one, get Challenged and the FFOperator tells you to take one as information for the People. Also, if you never take one, what do you think the first question will be if you are Challenged for some driving peccadillo? Right! Now for the table:

Cards for Personal Speed Limit Determination

Road Condition Traffic	Roadside Letter and Color Code	Red Card Speed Limit K/Hr.	Yellow Card Speed Limit K/Hr.	Blue Card Speed Limit K/Hr.	Green Card Speed Limit K/Hr.	White Card Speed Limit K/Hr.	Order-Fire Card Speed Limit K/Hr.
Children Danger	D Dayglow Orange	10	10	15	20	25	None
Residents Heavy Traffic	R T Yellow	15	20	25	30	40	None
Roads and Light Traffic	L Blue	30	40	50	60	80	None
Highways	H Green	70	80	90	100	110	None
Freeway Transcon	Signal Lights	100	110	120	130	150	None

Drive sensibly for both of us.

All highway signs will be according to the International Convention in pictures—speed limits per table. So...if you are given a yellow card it means that in a zone marked with a green H or otherwise color coded green, YOUR top limit, determined by your reactions, is 80 Kilometers per hour (50 mph).

When you get your Driving Reaction card, you can put it in your car where it's visible, throw it away or light a fire with it. No one cares, but you know what color it was and within what limits YOU are able to handle your vehicle— right? If a Neighborhood really wants to slow traffic down, it can put metal bumps in the road, called *topes* in Mexico. If a *NO PARKING* or special traffic control sign is needed, let's put the reason on it. Like, *SLOW—BRIDGE OUT* tells me a lot more than just *SLOW*.

Councils where enough people have boats and/or airplanes to set up a reaction and knowledge tester (like a flight simulator) can help people classify their own talent by suggesting limits to them: *no passengers, around the airport only, OK for cross country* and like that, but the actual actions taken are left up to the individual—and Challenging peers, of course. If you own a plane and your Council doesn't have testing facilities, you can fly to another Council that does.

And how do we make vehicle safety as absolute as pollution? We can't really but we can make sure that every vehicle of every type is inspected and brought up to some 80 to 90% of its *as new* specifications every year and that all operators know how to operate their vehicles. To explain this I have to tell you how vehicles will be registered. Registered vehicles will include anything that is motor driven but exclude like bicycles, gliders and boats with sail power only.

EVERY VEHICLE MADE WILL HAVE A NUMBER STAMPED OR OTHERWISE PERMANENTLY MARKED IN EASY TO SEE SYMBOLS IN TWO PLACES.

This number is filed in the Library Central (LC) under the manufacturer's B Number. When the vehicle goes to a dealer it's registered under its number in that Council's Numbers Master, showing the dealer's B Number as owner. There it remains until it is paid for by some individual or Business when the new owner's E or B Number is put after the vehicle number in both the Council N Master and the LC at Central. The new owner goes to a Council ID Room to do this. All vehicle numbers follow the same pattern. A little hard to stamp on motorcycles but we'll do it somehow. The first letter indicates the type of vehicle. Even though it's obvious from looking at it, we still have to file it under something so C is a car, A an airplane, J a jet, M a motorcycle, L a motor scooter or motorbike, T a truck, B a bus, U outboard motor, N inboard motor, Y auxiliary powered sail boat, S a ship, F farm machinery and like that. The second symbol is not a letter but the Astrological sun sign for the month in which the vehicle was made; third, a letter designating the manufacturer; fourth, a letter for the model number and finally, a five digit number to indicate the number of that particular vehicle. Therefore: CC6FA00123, a ten digit ID, tells the whole story of a car made in Capricorn, 1976, Ford, Model A, the 123rd of that model made in that month. Car makers will have to change models ten years later but if they don't improve quality, it won't make any difference. This number would probably be stamped CC6FA123 on the actual car but the computer would need to have the zeros as well. AG5CL54 or AG5CL00054 describes an airplane, Cessna, the 54th made of Model L in Gemini 1975 and so forth.

What these numbers have to do with safety is simple for the Custom reads:
EVERY REGISTERED VEHICLE IN THE RNA MUST BE INSPECTED BY THE APPROPRIATE SHOP IN SOME COUNCIL DURING IT'S BIRTH

MONTH OR THE OWNERSHIP OF THE VEHICLE PASSES TO THE COUN-
CIL WHEREIN IT IS FOUND.

This Custom will lead to some interesting happenings because if a vehicle is not inspected and the inspection coupon is not taken to the ID Room to inform the LC of the inspection, the data bank never gets the word that the vehicle is safe for the year. The first of the next month (giving like eight days grace past the end of the sun sign period), the LC puts out a list of uninspected vehicles via ID Rooms all over the RNA. An entrepeneur can set up with a tow truck, a tug and/or an airplane tractor, pick up the list of uninspected vehicles and start cruising. The Council will pay the towing charges and put the vehicle through the standard inspection and repair course. When it's ready and safe, the owner will be notified and can come and claim it before a month has passed. If not claimed, the Council can keep it for its own use or sell it on the Council owned used vehicle lot. If a vehicle is beyond saving (maybe why the owner didn't both-er to have it inspected in the first place) the Council can sell it for junk. Vehicle inspection will become a habit.

Let individual drivers be responsible for safety belts, neck cracker preventers, extra heavy truck type rubber baby bumpers. How in the hell did we get into the business of protecting the fools in this world? We must, however, make sure that every vehicle is safe to operate, with treaded tires, brakes and lights that work, an engine that isn't fouling up our air, meets boat and aircraft safe-ty standards...like that.

As for driver instruction, remember I said that your Card is also your driver's and pilot's license? It is proof of who you are in case of accident but tells noth-ing of your driving ability. By Custom: the original vendor of a vehicle is respon-sible to the rest of us for the new owner's ability to handle the vehicle with safety. A seller must wait for the proceeds of any sale until the buyer can oper-ate the whatever including all its equipment: navigation, safety and all that. The Councils give the first courses in driver education and when you're twelve, live in a Council House and start fooling around the shops, you will be encouraged to learn how to operate all the vehicles used in the type of Council you're in. There will be car, truck, bus and farm machinery driving and maintenance courses, flying and airplane maintenance courses, boat dittos, depending upon the type of Council but when you buy a motorbike, car, airplane, boat, etc., the original seller must be sure that you know how to operate the damn thing. Don't forget, if you're making payments, they'll own the vehicle until you pay for it. If you feel you weren't properly instructed, you can Challenge.

IN THE RNA, YOU WILL BE CAREFULLY AND LOVINGLY EDUCATED AND INSTRUCTED IN THE OPERATION AND MINOR MAINTENANCE OF EVERYTHING YOU BUY BY THE PEOPLE YOU BUY IT FROM.

When a vehicle changes hands between two individuals, the buyer takes the dealer's course in that type of vehicle. Things take more time this way but allow us to relax a little about whether the damn fool behind us knows where the brake pedal is. Dealers can use some of the money they save by not needing bookkeepers or tax consultants on operating and maintenance courses.

Privately owned planes, no matter what size, if they are not in the Business of transportation, will have well equipped air fields for their use. They will not use the large commercial airports or the airbus strips provided by the Transportation Councils except in emergencies. There's a custom that says that these private planes cannot be flown in the landing and take-off patterns of a commercial airport without being Challenged. Councils will provide the facilities for private aircraft according to use and ability to make a profit. I see a lot more private flying in the future because kids will have instruction more available to them, and there are already excellent build-your-own-plane kits on the market. These would need a Council inspection to fly.

Business owned and operated People, their things and bulk transportation: Commercial airline and bus services will still be provided by Business. The difference will be that reservations won't be needed as they are now. In the RNA, no flight leaves without being full of passengers or freight or a combination of both. This means that if you're on the way to somewhere, just go to the nearest bus station or airport and WAIT until a bus comes by or a flight headed to where you're going is full, then climb aboard. You can call the dispatcher at the airport to find out if there's a plane going where you want to go, like Peking, and how close to full it is. But you have to be there, ready to go in order to be put on the passenger list. When you arrive at the airport, tell the dispatcher "Peking" and WAIT until the plane is full. When it is, they'll call you so you go to the gate they told you to and take a short form FFTest, gratis. The short FFTest is to assure the rest of us that you're planning no harm to the flight. **NO MORE HI-JACKING!** Weigh yourself and your baggage and pay your bill. You will be charged per kilo/kilometer traveled. You or your porter wheel your stuff out to the plane or are elevated to it, put your luggage into the cannister marked *Peking* and board the plane. If there is no flight to Peking being made up, wander around and find one going to San Francisco or Hawaii or Tokyo to get you started in the right direction and continue from there. Remember there'll be lots more people traveling and more transportation than there is now.

The services in commercial planes can only improve and the rates will be a lot lower. Look at the fancy downtown offices, computerized reservation services and travel agents we won't have to pay for. Today, a plane flies on schedule whether it has a pay load or not but it isn't the operation of expensive, near empty flights that bothers me as much as the thousands of people who spend their job lives making sure we have seats and will arrive somewhere at some particular minute.

Airports will be entertainment centers provided by the Transportation Councils and people will go there even if they're not traveling. They'll have movies, bars, restaurants, dance halls, sleeping cubicles with TV and call service, writing and office rooms for working, complete with phones and secretaries and anything else you can think of to keep the passengers and non-passengers entertained, happy and busy 24 hours a day.

Commercial buses may or may not use the routes and passenger fun stations run by the Transportation Councils. Bus services provided by commercial companies, freight shipments and Business to Business shipments will use the system provided by Business about which I, as a People, know nothing. If Businesses use ours, they'll have to pay us. Freight includes anything that doesn't fit into the parcel post or express categories. Businesses will set up their own freight stations on the Transcontinental Hiways where their things will be picked up by freight planes for the fast stuff, Transcontinental buses for small shipments and their own combination petroleum-electric trucks for the long hauls. These trucks will probably consist of one cab pulling three or four trailers.

I see Business using large containers that will be lifted by cranes or fork lifts onto trucks, trains or ships. These can be sealed to stop all the pilfering. With no customs checks, the containers won't need to be opened until they reach their destinations. There is no such thing as contraband in the RNA.

What about trains...the railroads? They will belong entirely to Businesses to do with as they will. If they want to provide passenger service, especially for commuters, we'll ride them and if Businesses decide to use railroads for bulk shipments only, we won't ride them. If they decide not to use them at all? Goodbye, railroads. The roadbeds might provide safe places to run hovercraft.

I'd like to make a suggestion to Business. Industrial complexes and other places where a lot of people go to work on shifts can happily provide bus service to and from their gates along all the main roads to save wasteful parking space and to eliminate a whole pile of gas burners. Of course, if you live up some weird canyon, you would have to make it down to the main road but, in general, you'll not have to drive to work if Business takes my suggestion. It will be a transportation advantage to work in the Council you live in but never a requirement. People who work at offices and stores downtown can use the Council free bus service. Or FEET or bicycles?

Services Provided by Transportation Councils: The Transportation Councils stretch out along both sides of the Transcontinental Hiways (Transcons) until a

Council includes about 200,000 people with their Council Centers approximately at their half-way points. They include towns, villages and even small cities along their routes whose economy depends for the most part on the Hiway. So, unless a town or a city has enough population to be a Council of its own and it's on a Transcontinental route, it becomes part of the Transportation Council with perhaps huge Ranch Councils adjoining it that use the town as their buying, selling, shipping and receiving center. Tax-wise, remember, your home Council gets the tax, no matter where you spend the bread.

Transportation Councils are in the business of building, operating and maintaining Transcons and will keep their services in peak condition. Transcons are the East-West, North-South fibers that hold the RNA together. Two or three of their lanes in each direction will be electrified for buses and trucks to pick up their free power and two or three lanes will be for vehicles that run on petroleum. Eventually all lanes will be electrified. To ride them will cost the same whether you use the electricity provided or buy petroleum products in addition to the toll. You pick up a ticket at an automatic station as you enter the Transcon and pay with your Card at a scale station as you leave it: so much per kilogram/kilometer. Business vehicles will be provided with separate weigh and pay exit lanes where drivers can use their B Numbers to pay the toll.

Where a Transcon runs along a coast, it becomes part of the services of a combination Waterfront-Transportation Council. These combo Councils will be shorter and fatter in more ways than one. They provide ferry service where necessary to keep the transportation threads of the RNA continuous.

Where a Transcon meets a city or metropolitan area, it either goes around the area, perhaps forming part of the circle that divides City Councils from other types or, if it has to go through, it becomes double decker with the petroleum users on the top deck and electrified traffic underneath. These Circles go around the edges of the heaviest population concentration like between city and suburb. No off and on ramps through cities; you have to go on the city street and highway system to meet the Transcon. The Way Stations of the Councils making up the metropolitan area are located outside of the City, either on the circle or where the Transcon has room to spread out. We can make the land transportation circles around our cities serve as walls used to around Medieval towns. That is, we can provide large parking and storage areas, places for gas stations, car sales, service and accessory stores—like that—on the outside of the dividing circle. People arriving at the city gates in cars could park them and use the Council Peripheral and Direct buses plus the spokelike subway or surface transportation to get around. We can provide thousands of free bicycles for People to use and leave where they will. These can be repaired in the Council shops by the 12 to 18 year olds. We can insist on electric cabs, electric rent-a-cars or rent-a-pickups and provide service vehicles that run around carrying fully charged battery units so quick power supply changes will be available all over the city. NOW, our cities can be clean and quiet as they should be for easy living. Besides, bicycle riding and walking are healthy and cause no noise pollution.

While talking about noise pollution, I would like to suggest that we adopt the European two-tone emergency vehicle warning horn to replace the sirens and wolf calls we now use that tend to produce heart attacks along with warnings.

The building of Transcontinental Hiways will be a four phase operation. We are naturally going to start with what there is now, like the present U.S. system of Interstates and put facilities on them. During the second phase we will extend these to cover the entire RNA from Tin City to the Columbian border while at the same time, starting the third phase which is to electrify two or three lanes. The third phase will probably start from the large population centers and fan out. The fourth phase brings total electrification and more automation. During all design for construction we must keep the finished product in mind.

Transcons have two service roads, one on each side, that serve as the Transportation Council's Peripheral and Direct bus routes and possibly the Peripheral route for the adjoining Council. These service roads have motels, hotels, rest stops, restaurants, stores, business centers, warehouses, Council Way Stations, the Transportation Council's Center and Shop area—also the land and airbus passenger stations and airports. Each Council, separately or in conjunction with another Council, provides a road from Council Center to the nearest Transcon. These routes will have a tendency to gather where Transcons cross each other so more than one direction can be served. Where this route meets the Transcon, the Council has a Way Station: a drop-off and pick-up point for passengers, mail, parcel post and express hauled by the Direct bus system.

Transportation Councils provide airbus service along the Transcons together with land bus service. The buses themselves can be owned either by the Council or concessionaires but the Councils provide the passenger facilities and airbus landing strips near population centers, at every Transcon junction and sometimes in between. The landing strips run along the Transcon and are long enough so an airbus can land, taxi up to the passenger center, load and unload, then take off in the same direction. Airbuses land only where there are freight or passengers to pick up or leave and must be flagged down by radio like trains at whistle stops used to be. They will fly low. If one is full, it won't stop and you'll have to wait for the next one. Their schedules? Whatever they can make money providing. Their rates are the same for freight and People—so much per kilogram/kilometer—pay the conductor on board. Airbuses have the right of way (less maneuverable) and there's a Custom which says that private planes need permission from airbus traffic control to cross an Intercon. The long distance Transcon land buses never leave the Transcon, cover the same routes as airbuses but are slower and cheaper. If you pay between each stop, you can alternate between land and air depending on your whim, pocketbook, passenger load or terrain.

Airbuses, land buses and hovercraft buses are all cut out of the same pattern: luggage and stuff below with hydraulic doors that open to let passengers put things in and take them out and places for people and their pets above. The land type that ply the Transcons will probably be hooked up three or four trailers together pulled by a tractor so one operator can steer it all. Eventually, airbuses may not need more than one pilot for emergencies; the routine operations being handled by automatic controls.

Transportation Councils are also in the commercial airport business. They provide the passenger dispatching and recreation centers, services for commercial airlines and feeder routes with Transcon buses to airports not directly on a Transcon. In cooperation with commercial airlines, they will help provide air safety and navigation equipment. On a coast, the airport may be part of the Waterfront Council's facilities and act as a terminus to the Transportation Council's responsibilities. There are airbus landing strips at airports for transferring people and things in and out of the commercial air transport system and to provide fueling and maintenance services for the airbuses.

Transportation Councils will learn to provide for a new type of phenomenon: the traveling Neighborhood. These Neighborhoods come into a Council to build a Transcon, an airport or are just traveling through and are assigned an area by the Council. They act like regular settled Neighborhoods: make their own rules, care for their under 12's, etc., but the people will probably live in trailers, buses or even tents and get their Shares from some *home* Council. Traveling Neighborhoods will also be found in Farm Councils at harvest time.

Let's take a look at how mail, parcel post and express travel. You can mail your letter at any Neighborhood Center. If a Neighborhood has voted to provide parcel post and express service to and from its Council POB, these can be mailed there as well. Neighborhoods collect for postage using their B (Business) Cards, Credits to their S (Small Business) accounts. This Card goes with the mail to the POB so the carrier can pay the Council. Neighborhoods could decide to charge more than the actual postage in order to pay the carrier.

OK, let's say that one way or another your mail, parcel post or express is at the Council POB and paid for. There it is sorted into receiving Councils and is either sent directly to adjacent Councils or bussed onto the Transcon Way Station for further distances.

At the Transcon, the Council pays the Transportation Council and it's put on a long distance bus or airbus, if air rates have been paid. Off continent mail is dropped off at an airport or Port of Entry and goes from there by plane or ship.

Along or above the Transcon it goes and when it reaches the receiving Council's Way Station, it is dropped off where the Council Direct Bus picks it up to take to its POB.

Remember the original and one copy label on parcel post and express? At the receiving Council POB, the original is torn off and sorted with the mail into Neighborhood bags. The Neighborhood carrier picks up the bag and takes it to the Order Office where mail and labels are sorted into bins. When you receive a label you know there's a package waiting for you at the POB and what the charges are, if any. The receiving Council might charge the receiver pick-up distance from Way Station to POB if this is a long trip. Your package can be picked up at the POB, the Neighborhood Center or brought to your home, depending on what sort of arrangements you've made. My guess is four days for mail from Vancouver to Mexico City and five days for parcel post and express at land rates. Air mail rates could drop this time to two and three days.

To have our mail forwarded is easy, but not free. We'll buy *Forwarding Strips* from our Neighborhood Order Offices, write our E Number on each one and leave them there. This can be done over the phone if necessary, and a Trainee will write the E Number on each strip. They cost the same as to mail an ordinary letter and don't expire. When mail or a parcel post or express label arrives to be forwarded, a Trainee will put the new A Number on the Forwarding Strip, paste the strip over the old receiving address and off goes the letter or label back through the system. A forwarding A Number can be phoned in at any time.

If *Home* is defined as the place they *have* to take you in, then any Council in the RNA is home. They might frown a bit if you're the 275,001st but they can not refuse you. There's a Custom about it. When you move from one Council to another and want to change your *home* Council, go to your new ID Room and ask for a **change in registration**. The Trainee will take your fingerprints and other ID and check them against the ones in your old Council, request the Trainee there to remove them and make you a new card with your new A Number on it, "¢ 5, please." At the same time the Trainee will change your vehicle registration(s) and add the new A Number to your crossfile(s). This procedure is different from just getting a Card in another Council which you must do in every Council in which you buy Land Leases or have a Possession, Small Business or Business account. A change in registration means you are actually changing the Council in which you receive your Share and pay taxes. Remember we can only be registered and receive Shares in one Council.

Take your new Card to the Tax Office and request that your Exchange account be transferred. Once this is done, your old Card will just make the light on any Exchange computer slave glow red. To change your P account(s), you have to see a Bank Tender at the POB. If you are a Citizen with Bank Shares, a Bank Tender will either help you convert them to Shares in your new Council's banking ability or will have the A Number on Shares held in another Council changed. If you are a Member, the Bank Tender will help you transfer your financial possessions into portfolios in your new Council if you so request, Leases excepted. Generally, we will keep our old Cards for access to Possession portfolios in our former Councils of registry. To change the location of a Business from one Council to another, go first to a Bank Tender to lease a computer slave, then to the ID Room for a Card with that B Number on it and back to the Bank Tender to open your new account.

With the idea of transportation comes the idea of Travel and its buddy, Tourism. If you come from overseas, you will need a Tourist Card which you can pick up in any Port of Entry. The requirement is a return ticket to your place of origin and a short form FFTest to show you mean us no harm. These Cards are good until your birth date, renewable upon an FFTest to show how you've spent your time with us. You get no People's Share, pay no taxes and can earn any money you wish—work at any job you can get. Tourist Cards have the visitor's Number which is made up of sun sign and two digit year of birth number, just like ours. Instead of the Council of birth number, they next have a T plus a three digit Port of Entry number, then a four digit order of entry number; that is; order of entry into that Port born under that sun sign in that year. There are two types of Tourist Cards: the regular Card for Tourists aged 0 to 12 and 19 and on and the Youth Card for the 12 to 19's. The regular Card has a dash (-) in the first Service number space while the Youth Card has a blank in this space so youths can live in the Council Houses and have free medical care. The money the Tourist deposits into our system is kept in the **Types TEM**, Tourist-Exchange Masters, at Central. There will be twelve of them, one for each sun sign, in order to have room for two million or so accounts. These accounts are supervised by a Business Tender at Central.

The Tourist's Number and ID are relayed to Central to a bank of twelve **Types TNM**, Tourist Numbers Master computers, one for each sun sign; thus they can be counted. The A Number for mail on a Tourist's Card is whatever the Tourist gives the Tender and can be changed at any Council ID Room or Port of Entry.

Tourists' Cards work exactly the same as ours. *Holds* can be put on Tourist E accounts by Business Tenders in charge of the TEM's at Central at the request of a Tourist Tender or any Justice Tender. The Tourist would call a Central Business Tender free of charge to find out the reason for the *hold* and have it removed. Visitors are Challengeable. Tourist Tenders will have this phone number on the tips of their tongues.

Business people from overseas would see a Central Business Tender in a Port of Entry or an Extension School Office to make large transactions. Overseas, they'd go to a Speaker's Office. Tourists with errors to correct would go to the same places plus any Council Tax Office.

Travel in the RNA can be accomplished in many different ways—even free. The natural starting point is our Council Center where we can transfer a little bread out of savings, have another Card made, you know—tidy up our affairs a bit. We can travel the whole RNA riding the free Peripheral buses, boats or hovercraft from one Council to the next. This makes for a slow trip but it is a way to get to see everything, especially for kids who have all those Council Houses to stay in.

Transcons are only the bones, the structure of the transportation system with none of the interesting places on them. They are meant for transportation, not for travel, and are a cheap, fast way to get close to the things we want to see and do. To really see and feel the Continent, we have to get into the open spaces between Transcons and use Peripheral and Direct buses, commercial buses, hovercraft, ferries—we could even drive.

GOOD ROAD

This Segment completes the VISION. The picture of the New Establishment has been painted and from here on out the work starts. If you dig the Vision or part of it enough to try to Seek Agreement with others to make an Establishment that fits our present and future needs, one that gives the People the right to make the decisions, let's you and I start to take some steps.

HUMANKIND MUST LEARN TO PROGRESS WITHOUT CONTENTION

REMEMBER that in order to change, you have to dig it where you are long enough to build up some Juice of Change, then when you have the strength and juice to change and have decided the direction of change, do it. Changing the heads of the majority out of about 340 million People won't be easy but there is a way and the way to start is what I want to lay on you in this Segment. Baby Steps: steps to take while we are waiting for this information to reach enough People so we can actually start to move. You say I said to mind our own business and how can we do both? That's right, but minding our own business and the business of our kids' kids is what I'm talking about. Remembering: Timebinding, Hooray!...Missionaryism, Boo! The most important Baby Step is silence—that's right—SILENCE!

NEVER GATHER IN GROUPS.

Never admit to anyone that this book is any more than a normal part of your library.

No speeches, no rousing cheers, no bullshit.

Then what is our task? First we gotta dig things the way they are; join movements that seem to be heading in the direction we want to go, like groups dealing with pollution, with Audio-Visual education and like that. OK? The admonition of silence is all important, especially when dealing with groups. Dig it where you are, dig it like it is, make the best life style you can. Live with love; love the life you live and the People around you; smile and enjoy. That's what we do first.

The next Baby Step is to sell and circulate this book. Get the information out—without qualification, without indicating preference, with love, but without prejudice. Think of sneaky ways to get books into the hands of People who would never buy one, like, "I'll loan you this book and if you decide to keep it, you can pay me later." You don't have to explain the book nor say whether you agree with it or not.

We are going to use the sales of the book as indicator points to tell us what to do next: to tell us where we stand. Of course, this is going to make me as rich as the inside of a dog but, you see, my conscience is clear, my life style set. A VW bus, a house, travel and the time and leisure to continue to write, that's my thing, so the money will go to provide for the People who help get ready to make the change: the information funnel. This I promise you.

The first indicator point will be at sales of 250,000 when we can start to feel that there is enough interest being stirred up by the book so we can, as a beginning, start the rest of the Baby Steps, the first of which is:

REGISTER AND VOTE.

Write in candidates if you don't like the ones on the ballot. Vote on Bond issues, propositions, Vote on everything so as to get totally immersed in the system to know enough about it to change it. Go through the absentee bullshit, if necessary, to get your ballot in time to vote. Get used to whatever rat race They make you go through to vote. This is what I call practice voting. OK?

The next Baby Step: Buy Land! That's right, BUY LAND.

Get your hands on all the land you can afford. If will be important later to have a lot of the land in our hands. You can start, with a little help from your friends, the growing and producing of healthy food and herbs. The more plants we can grow in our cities, the cleaner the air will be. I don't know what is right in this way but you can find out, then do it. This will make the next Baby Step more possible:

EAT WELL.

The way to a healthy mind is a healthy diet and I don't even have any opinions—except for roughage—as I have already made up my mind about what's healthy for me and I try to eat that way—still, a little too much, but that is between me and my appetite. Eat well, please. Make the place where you buy stock brown rice, fresh fruits and vegetables, unbleached, unchemicalized, foods with vitamins and minerals that will help you and your kids grow healthy bodies and minds.

When we have sold 500,000 copies of the English version, the Spanish and French editions will be ready and you can take a few of whatever language and make a trip, passing out and selling in strange places. Make it fun and never commit yourself lest ye yourself be committed. Right?

The last Baby Step is a little involved but consists of passing along the art of Non-Communication to all who are ready to learn it. Non-Communication will eventually become a science, but now it is strictly an art. It is the way of communicating thoughts that contain feelings by just BEING for everyone to see and feel. It is communication using images with or without words and without preconceptualized ideas (like references to authority). We can spread Non-Com by spreading ourselves around. Lay on everybody the communication of love between People. This sounds pretty messy and probably is but what I mean is to relax the feeling of embarrassment that makes our communications unclear. It is OK to be understood; we just have to feel a little surer. We do it among ourselves but it needs taking out into the world. When we can BE it in all situations, we gotta move out and let others see and learn that it is possible and, therefore, possible for everyone. And what is IT? The art of feeling good together.

GO OUT INTO THE WORLD AND TEACH THE ART OF HANGING OUT BY DOING.

People who practice the art of Non-Com have a tendency to become a closed group and they truly must not, even unto feeling *alone* and *unquietened.* Non-Com is merely a term for being what you are wherever and must be spread like apple butter into all the nooks and cranies. I even know what I am asking, but also doing. Pay your dues, brothers and sisters. Some Baby Step?

LEARN THAT BEING WHAT YOU ARE IS INFINITELY MORE IMPORTANT THAN BEING WHAT ANYONE ELSE THINKS YOU SHOULD BE, THEN UNDERSTAND IT—BE IT.

One word about gathering in groups or rioting and demonstrating: *DON'T!*

OK, so the Baby Steps we are going to make between zero and one million copies sold are:

Be quiet, don't speak about VMW at all. Just push books.

Register in local, state and national elections, then VOTE.

Buy Land; grow nutritious food.

Eat, live and love in our own styles.

Mind our own business and keep our heads intact, our eyes unburnt, our lungs ungassed.

Learn the art of Non-Communication, really Non-Conceptual Communication.

OK, learn to hang out and let others see us hanging out. Thus we take a few tiny(?) steps toward mankind learning to progress without contention and being part of something else by BEING something else.

Barbara's Carrot Cake

2 cups dark brown sugar
1½ cups oil
*2 cups flour (add more for higher altitudes)
1 cup chopped pecans (optional)
4 cups grated raw carrots
4 eggs (separate and beat whites)
*2 teaspoons soda
*2 teaspoons baking powder (subtract some for higher altitudes)
*2 teaspoons salt
*2 teaspoons cinnamon
*1 teaspoon ginger
*1 teaspoon nutmeg

Cream sugar and oil, add egg yolks, beat well. Sift * together, add to sugar mixture and beat. Fold in carrots and nuts, then the stiff egg whites. Bake in three 8" or 9" pans oiled and dusted with cocoa or flour at 300°F or 150°C for 50 to 60 minutes—the higher the altitude, the higher the temperature.

Icing

12 ounces cream cheese
3/4 stick of butter
3 teaspoons of vanilla
1 pound (½ kilo) powdered sugar—you can substitute part powdered milk

Sift sugar, cream with cheese and butter, add vanilla. Spread on cooled cake. Voila!

SOON AS sales reach a million, my task will be to set up a corporation; a real growling, money making, stock-share corporation called VMW, Inc.

This corporation will get income from: 1) the sales of the VMW; 2) sales of the VMW comics, our information and action periodical; and 3) the publication and sales of other books, pamphlets, design brochures: anything allied to our direction. The Corporation will act as liaison for all those who are engaged in the design projects about to be described. It will not tell people *what* to do, but will keep people who are working on the same projects in communication with each other and put out progress reports. You get up the word and the corporation will put it out, at a profit, OK?

I cannot say at this time just how the information network will be fashioned but I sug-

159

gest to the corporation that it make all statements of progress and intent available to everybody, like in a small newsletter to be sold at newsstands all over. The language could be impressionistic imagery—a comic book would be perfect, but you decide and I will help. For the purposes of this book, I am going to assume a comic book will be used.

Once VMW, Inc., is in business, it'll be time to take the first Giant Step which is: **ELIMINATE HAND GUNS.** Use our new found position of collective opinion, our Gestalt, to originate, formulate and get passed national laws which outlaw weapons that are less than 76 centimeters (30 inches) long. Take time to think of the reasons. Death is portable enough without it being hidden as well. Hand guns are useful only for killing and maiming People. They are OFFENSIVE WEAPONS. People can protect their homes and families better with shotguns, which will still be legal. If guns can be seen and identified from a distance, they can be run from or defended against. Even militaries won't have to make real changes—maybe increase the muzzle length of whatever horrible automatic weapons they are now handing out to 18 year olds.

Rifles and the right to bear arms and all that jazz we gotta keep on account of maybe needing rifles some day. If people want to be armed, make them be obvious about it; show their intentions in front. We'll not have personal peace until we do. The Law, for now, might read:

THERE WILL BE NO WEAPON MADE, MANUFACTURED, POSSESSED, CARRIED OR EVEN COPIED LESS THAN 76 (SEVENTY-SIX) CENTIMETERS IN LENGTH THAT IS CAPABLE OF DISCHARGING PELLETS, BULLETS, GAS, HARMFUL RAYS, BALLS, ARROWS OR PROJECTILES OF ANY SORT.

The penalty for possession or manufacture will be imprisonment, changing to Coventry in the new system. There are no exceptions. I recognize that some people and museums might have great-grandfather's pearl inlaid dueling pistols, like that, but these must be totally disarmed, made unuseable for discharging anything and, if carried, the person would be treated as if the gun were real. Use the present system to pass this law. The statement will become a Right in the new order of things, one which will be guaranteed along with the Right of Challenge.

If national laws could be made right away, the task would simplify itself but alas and alack, we have to move step by step. First, pass an ordinance in your town, village, city—no hand guns, not even toy ones. Make your cops carry rifles and shotguns and give them permission to arrest anybody they catch with a pistol. *A shotgun hanging over every door but not one pistol in town* can be your motto. I would sure love it if the lawmen in my town carried rifles and shotguns and shot those carrying hand guns. I am strictly a defensive person and tend to run like hell when I see somebody with *any* gun, which I can see better if it is more than 76 centimeters long.

Next, make States or Provinces or whatever the next larger political division is, pass similar legislation. When enough of these are free of the hand gun, VMW, Inc., will spend money and whatever influence it has getting the same legislation passed at the national levels. You know, lobbies or whatever it takes. The communications system (the comic book?) will let everyone know how the battle is going.

Just for fun, let's say we will start the second Giant Step when sales of the Book have reached two million. Of course, it's silly, but fun is what we are trying to have with all this because:

ANYTHING THAT'S NOT FUN IS NOT WORTH DOING.

But that's just a comment on life, not the Second Giant Step. The step is running for office. The First Step might only be started because when 1,000,000 copies have sold, all that has to happen is for each book holder to go out and sell one, thus 2,000,000 could happen in about one day, that is, if we have been doing our jobs and have books available. There may be a hiatus period or two while some printer waits for paper, but we hope to keep them coming. OK, the method is simply:

RUN, RUN, RUN FOR OFFICE, ANY OFFICE.

Find out what it takes to have your name put on the ballot, whatever party you choose. A day or two before the actual election, meet with the other candidates for that job face to face. This is the time you'll have to make your stand known, underplayed, if possible. If it turns out that more than one of you are VMW, you'll have to draw straws or somehow decide who is to be the ONE VMW candidate for that post. Before the election, the VMW candidate will have to let the People know. This can be done on TV giving the Sign, a picture in the newspapers, maybe even hanging around the polls wearing a VMW sweatshirt. Work it out, but the voters will have to know you are the ONE VMW candidate for that office. Please do not campaign, do not spend your money, do not gather People in groups where they can be gassed or maced or even machine gunned. Use your head. We are trying to cool the whole scene, not make another. We want to get out of politics altogether, not just start a new brand. You know about how many people are interested in VMW by the book sales figures in the comic book, right? You also know you will get every available VMW vote in your district. All you have to do is subtly let the People know you are running for VMW.

Everyone can buy the comic book at the same newsstand where you buy yours. There will be no secrets but the big one, where each of us personally stands.

When you are elected (IF), you must not rock the boat, but keep your ears and eyes open. Take NO action that might indicate you are anything but another person who wants a job in government. Don't start any great bullshit of making speeches, just do your job as the job description indicates and try to hang on to it and use it as a springboard to a post where you can hear and see more.

If you fall into the trap of declaring your sentiments, you might be persuaded to settle for small changes to take care of some of the immediate beefs we all have. Remember, we are trying to fashion a society modeled on the human organism, something no *small* changes will do.

However, this doesn't mean you cannot lean. For example, if you have been elected Sheriff, you swear to uphold and enforce the law and this you must do, even if it means putting your friends in jail but you can give all the breaks there are. As a County Clerk, you might take steps to register property more simply, by numbering each piece. Like that.

WE HAVE TO BE PART OF THE ESTABLISHMENT IN ORDER TO CHANGE IT.

We will need people in responsible positions throughout the Government, the Armed Forces, Business (big and little), the various Chambers of Commerce... everywhere. For example, if you are a Captain in the Air Force and if you read this book and are in agreement with its ideas, please DO NOTHING, except get promoted so you are like a General at Change Time. Improve your position on the Chess Board so you can be helpful, but do not talk about what you feel. You can get as rich and as high as you can, have the fullest life you can stand...then wait. If enough people, like a majority, agree to these ideas, the sooner we can get it on, the less you will have to wait.

We do not seek publicity in the press, on TV, nowhere. Some media people will probably become interested and they can keep our exposure to a truthful minimum.

When sales reach four million (or even the day after you read the book), we can have enough confidence to take the next Giant Step, the Education of our Children. Not reeducation; just a few things for them to know in addition to what they are learning in the outside world.

1. For racial survival, Mankind must learn to progress without contention.
2. For racial survival, Humans must learn to speak truth about what they did or agreed to do.
3. For racial survival, Mankind must allow a natural process of selection to determine the direction of evolvement.
4. For natural evolvement, no one may profit by another's death.
5. For individual evolvement, People must learn to mind their own business.

6. Freedom and Responsibility are the same thing.

7. To serve and be served with humility is expanding.

8. To work is a privilege and an honor. To have something meaningful to do is everybody's Right.

9. Everything that is happening or that has happened is exactly where it's at, so learn from everything.

10. Cooperation is the very breath of life. Contention is the very breath of death. Playing the game is the important thing, not winning. When the game is over, explain what you did to win so next time the scales can be balanced.

11. A definition of Love is: do and feel everything so that the one or ones you love can become what they can become.

12. Earth, Air, Fire and Water cannot be classified as possessions, but only as things to be used while we're here, then passed on, augmented, or at least undiminished.

13. Money is to buy things with so people who make cars can buy lightbulbs, not to have power over other people with. Money is also to buy shares with so people collectively can do larger things than individuals can do.

14. Make your own decisions, now and forever. Other People's decisions can not be used by you except to learn from. In other words, pick out the toy you like, not what the other kid buys.

15. Seeking Agreement is a groove but has a limit. If two people totally agree on everything, one of them is not thinking.

16. Voting is a privilege, not a chore. Government is an extension of your will so keep it clean and shiny. Your vote is like polish. Polish itself is cheap; polishing takes time.

17. Computers and machines are slaves to our will but people never.

18. You are a Human who lives on the planet Earth, which is being wasted so people can live beyond the planet's means. Learn to live within your means—personal and ecological. Learn also to recycle to increase the means.

19. It's perfectly OK that you are the way you are and that others are the way they are. You can learn new ways of being by watching the way others are and if you are being what you are, they can learn from you.

Children are very important in the process of getting a world free of wars, strife and confusion. If it weren't for my kids, I wouldn't be sitting at this smoking typewriter in the first place.

When book sales reach 8,000,000 including the Spanish and French editions, we have another Giant Step to make, which is: be counted. When you find out from the Comic Book that it's time, mail a postcard to the corporation if you are voting for these ideas. Don't pack it; simply send one postcard saying like "yes" and you might send a little LOVE. No names, no addresses, please. The idea here is so we can tell how many voters there are per copy sold. The results will be printed in the comic book and the cards themselves will be either recycled or used to heat the office.

By 10,000,000 copies sold, we'll know how many there are of us (from the postcards) and by this time, the small arm should be starting to disappear in a lot of areas and we can start to eliminate pistols, hand guns on national levels. Also, a lot of you will have started to work in the Establishment.

If we figure 150,000,000 voters in North America, 80,000,000 would make a majority. Depending on the results of the postcard survey—let me guess two voters per copy sold– at 20,000,000 copies, we will be half way toward a majority and can start the next Giant Step which is **super running for office**; have a candidate up for election for every post in government. If someone cannot get on the ballot by ordinary means, we set up for write-in candidates. The way to do this is send your name for the position you want to run for and the location. If there is more than one person for a position, VMW, Inc., will put the names in a hat and pick one. The comic book will tell the voters what name to write in. It will work. I figure by 40,000,000 books sold, we will have enough people in the Establishment to make the Change. By this time, everyone will know.

Meanwhile...back at the Corporation office, another Giant Step has been taking place. One thing that can be started as soon as VMW, Inc., exists, or even before, is design. We have to interest some of those people, the experts that is, who know about things others don't. For instance, there is the division of the continent into population groups of 200,000. This must be ready to go and will take time and knowledge to map out. There are also computers and computer slaves to design and build working models of. The thing to do is when you have an idea, write the corporation which will put you into direct communication with the others who have chosen work on the same project. You should be able to get the thing designed among you so that at Change Time, the necessaries will not only be designed, but even tested and proven (using corporation funds) and ready for production. Just do your own thing. If, for example, there are twenty of you computer imperts doing a design together by mail on the Exchange Master computer, your correspondence must concern nothing but the business at hand, OK?

The corporation will set up these design sections sensibly secure so there is never material in the office that might cause it to be overcrowded. So if you write, don't send your ideas, just mark your letters with the number of the design section you wish to communicate with. Like VMW, Section 1, Box 1295, Santa Fe, New Mexico 87504, will get your letter to the Geographical design section.

Here is a numbered list of the design sections. If you find an area of interest on the list, read about it. If not, you can go on to the next Segment but you might miss something.

DESIGN SECTIONS

1. Geographical: division of North America into Councils, locating Central and Central Leases.
2. Human Engineering: ways and means.
3. Education: Audio-visual courses, Extension Schools and other design requirements.
4. Media: News, TV stations, public relations.
5. Justice: FF machines.
6. Boundary Patrol: organization, equipment, defense methods.
7. Finance: some guesses; also plans for conversion to computers.
8. Central: plant.
9. Computer, Data storage: LC and N configuration. Classification sorter.
10. Computer, Exchange: E and S configurations
11. Computer, Business: B configuration, foreign bank accounts, BC.
12. Computer, Stock Market: and P configuration.
13. Computer, Relay Net: cross-ties.
14. Computer, Vendor: special machines for loans, insurance, mail, etc.
15. Power: reactor and safety design.
16. Transportation, Land.
17. Transportation, Air.
18. Transportation, Water.
19. Council Centers: POB, Meeting halls, offices, security room, etc.
20. Council Shops: hospital-mortuary, labs, library, etc.
21. Council Houses
22. Council Trainee and Public Housing
23. Neighborhood Centers: general ideas.
24. Protection Organizations: Rent-a-Cops, fire companies.
25. Disposal and recycling
26. Other

The organization of the design sections is entirely up to you. There need be no leader, for example, unless you designate one. The design section's final, totally agreed upon results will be published for further criticism and perhaps change so the whole ball of wax will be ready when needed.

The specifications I am about to lay on you must be considered customer specifications, which means they are made up by the idiot who wants to use the thing to be designed and his wishes, while valid, are not necessarily the final word. Idiocy must always be tempered by Newton, at least on this planet. Please remember that if I have managed to think of everything, that's bullshit in front.

1. Geographical Design Section

This section must work with Section 2 to delineate the boundaries of the RNA, then divide the continent into about 1700 Councils of approximately 200,000 people each. This division is a critical part of the plan. It must be done right and must be ready when we are. I feel the actual work should be done by people who live in an area, as no one can know it all intimately enough. Each Council must provide for the people who live there; that is, make its weekly nut and a profit. Also, Councils should be populated by people who are interested in the kind of work there is available in that Council so factory workers don't have to get into forestry, for example.

If you're interested, you'll need really complete maps that show contours, land resources, population density, sea depth and like that. Then I suggest using those blank maps kids use in Geography class for rough work and the small scale Geodetic Survey maps to draw the finished product. Once you have an area drawn up, let the P.O. Box know and we'll tell you where to send it.

The first digit of A Numbers indicates the continent. If the second digit is a zero, it means Central, so A Numbers from 10000 to 10099 are for use by Central for Boundary Patrols, PCC's, Continental Treasures and other Central Leases. Part of this section's work is to figure out where Central is and delineate areas for Coventries and PCC's. Each of the three sectors will have a Coventry.

If the second digit is not a zero, it indicates the closest megapolis. It's a general location digit. This design group will draw the borders exactly, but for now they are roughly drawn so:

1. New York, Montreal, North to the Pole and East. It will include Greenland and Iceland (if it comes in).
2. Washington, Savannah, Pittsburgh, Ottawa, Philadelphia.
3. Detroit, Tallahassee, Mobile, South Bend and North to the Pole.
4. Havana, Jacksonville, Mérida, Tapachula, South to the Columbian border and including the Caribbean Islands.
5. Chicago, St. Louis, Kansas City, Winnipeg, and North to the Pole.
6. Dallas, New Orleans, Houston, Juarez, Albuquerque, Denver, Wichita, Oklahoma City.
7. Mexico City, Veracruz, Tehuantepec, Culiacán, Monterrey, Matamoros.
8. Los Angeles, La Paz, San Blas, Nogales, Phoenix, Las Vegas, Morro Bay
9. San Francisco, Salt Lake City, Edmonton and North. Also includes Hawaii and other Pacific Islands.

A sample Council number would be: 11000 - North America, megapolis area 1. The third digit indicates the Type of Council, like:

    0. means Central. 10111, Central group No. 11.

    1. City

    2. Suburban

    3. Farm

    4. Ranch

    5. Waterfront

    6. Transportation

    7, 8 and 9. Combination Councils. Each area cannot have more than three mixed types.

The fourth and fifth digits are for individual Council numbers. So 11503 means North America, New York area, Waterfront Council No. 3. The general specifications for Councils are:

- There must be a boulevard, double street, highway, road, hovercraft swath: some place where the Peripheral buses can operate all around every Council. Even wilderness areas will be totally surrounded by some sort of route for transportation, except for the Councils whose boundaries run up to the North Pole.

- City Councils will be totally contained within the heavily populated urban area, within the circle made by a highway around the city. Since City Councils should not be concerned with sea bottom to care for, the ports and people who live off and around the sea should become part of Waterfront Councils.

- Large manufacturing zones will naturally become part of whatever Council they are in but would contain no Neighborhoods as no one lives in these zones.

- Waterfront Councils are each responsible for an area of the continental shelf. Their land areas include the port towns, villages and port areas in cities until they have a population of about 200,000. The shore between ports can be parts of other Councils. When an airport is in a Waterfront Council, it becomes part of that Council's facilities.

- Transportation Councils are described in Segment XI. Where Transcons meet, the two Councils will cooperate to run the communal area and the people decide, by Neighborhood vote, in which Council they want to be counted.

- Suburban Councils take in the areas around cities outside of the highway circle and reach out until they mix with Country, Small Town and Farm Councils.

- Farm, Country and Small Town Councils start where Suburban Councils end and include areas where the predominant industry is producing food. They include the towns and small cities in their areas, except when they are part of a Transportation Council. One of the towns near the geographical center will become the Council Center.

- Ranch and Wilderness Councils contain most of the rest of the RNA. Try to keep Forest land together, as it's advantageous to have this land cared for by a few Councils that hire experts and thus become expert in tree management.

- The sea area managed by the RNA must be delineated so we have a fair share of *The Sea Around Us* to support us and for us to care for. Remember, we have to patrol and defend it.

- Councils will be better served if they tend to be long and thin in shape rather than squarish so Council Centers are near the Peripheral transportation.

- In this beginning division, City Councils should be started out near maximum (275,000 people) and Ranch and Wilderness Councils near minimum population (125,000) if we want to look ahead at the probability that many people will split from the cities as soon as they don't have to have jobs to eat.

2. Human Engineering Section

Those who work in this section must devise ways and means for people to happily, even laughingly, make the adjustment to different ways of earning. How to persuade people who have jobs in, for example, life insurance, politics or Labor that their talents are useful and needed in other jobs?

There are millions of people who have accepted the *fact* that other people are always going to tell them what to do. This will no longer be true. Many of these people have not yet learned to read, but most of them can be communicated with using comics, radio and television so they (especially their children) can learn to make decisions. The interest and the ability to control their own actions will come at the same time. You provide the interest and they'll provide the action.

This section must figure out how to assure the same basic standards of living throughout the RNA. Remember it costs more to live in the cold North than in the warm South.

There are some small political divisions contained in the North American continent that have been totally controlled by a man or a group of men for years. These men will not easily give up their power. Opening our borders will allow the brighter, more adventurous out to look around at the way things are in other parts, but how do we get rid of the borders entirely so everyone can move freely through the RNA?

We need answers to these questions and others like them. You figure it out and the corporation will print the answers so all can know. OK?

3. Education Section

One of this section's tasks is to make groovy Audio-Visual courses that cover the educational requirements of all ages, divided into 0 to 12, 12 to 18 and adult—not only make them up but record them on video tapes and try them out on local University and Educational TV stations plus any commercial stations that can be persuaded to show them. Another task is the design of Extension Schools for adults.

The requirements for the designs of Council Labs, Libraries, Shops and Council Houses fall to this section as well, so sections 20 and 21 can do the actual design. Keep simplicity and maximum learning in mind if you decide to work in this area. Also: find out what cannot be taught by A-V so as to be ready to handle that efficiently when the time comes.

Some of those who feel to work with this group must decide where, how many and what types of Psychiatric Care Centers (PCC's) we'll need and feed the data to the Boundary Patrol design section so they can design satisfactory complexes. There will be different kinds of PCC's for different types of disturbances. There is little use in using the numbers of People presently behind bars in institutions for the *mentally ill*, because many of them will be able to make it in some Neighborhood on their Shares. My friend, the psychologist, says that more than 60 percent of the People now in mental institutions are there unjustly, put away by a heartless society simply because they are a little different from or older than the rest of us and no one wants to take care of them, financially or otherwise. So maybe knock 60 percent off in front. I would like to see PCC's provide at least one hectare of bare survival land for every disturbed person in a PCC. My theory is that when a person lives under bare survival conditions, fantasy has a tendency to disappear but I'll leave design requirements to the experts in the education and medical fields.

4. Media Section

What do we want from our Media in the new Establishment? First, with a Media Office in every major city of the world, we want total coverage of all the important things that are going down throughout the world but never mind the blood, OK? Our Council TV Stations have four hours of news from all over every day. We want programs that everyone will watch because Our news is complete, honest, unbiased and clear. This design section has the job of laying out a net of news collecting agencies and deciding how many Trainees will be needed to absorb all the local news, then finding out the best way to get it into an interesting form to present to the People on video tapes.

The second item is the program for nonprotagonistic promulgation of the ideas contained in this book. Ways to get the ideas out. Ways of widening views. For example, some Churches advocate that their members shouldn't read books containing the word *evolution* because they feel it will change members' heads about Adam and Eve and all that. They have millions of members and what kind of a message can we give them that might convince them there is nothing in the VMW that will try to change their views? In fact, they might find herein a society where they can live by their principles a lot more easily than before. There are

many such public relations challenges that the Media design section can provide the rhetoric for people to rap about.

The third item is the design of Council TV programming and what personnel will be needed. By taping everything, station personnel could be kept at a minimum. Don't forget commercials.

5. Justice Section

Read the description of the FF in Segment VII but don't forget a toilet in each trailer. The units will need not only the comfortable chairs mentioned for the Challenger, Challengee and Operator, but also three loose, straight-backed chairs for two advisors and a Trainee. You may want to make the back of the Operator's chair tall so brilliant hair doesn't screw up the video tape with unwanted reflections. The lighting must be sufficient for making video tapes. How about putting lights in the ceiling behind ground or faceted glass, then cooling the area?

The sensor-senders of the system are: the crowns with temple plates to measure pulse, brain wave pattern variations, etc.; the two brass balls which, I think, are largely for psychological effect but can determine perspiration rate changes in the palms of the hands plus changes in grip intensity; and the pick-up microphones over the heads of the principals. These mikes are a major source of lie determination and must be totally effective. They measure differences in voice pressure as well as the variation in tonal wave length.

Each FF unit has two video tape recorders so the spare can be switched on if the first malfunctions. The cameras are fixed, angled so they show the two principals, the two indicator panels (one in front of each principal) and the Operator's control console.

The indicator panels show all of the physical measurements taken translated to something everyone can understand. The receiver-transducer section of FF's is in the Operator's control console. The transducer's product will be changed to voltage to be read on a volt meter or to a visual representation of the signal to be read like on an oscilloscope. These representations need no recording facilities but need to be big enough so viewers can easily read them. During the whole time the principals' Cards are in the slots in the FF, their Numbers and brain wave patterns recorded on their Cards show on the TV screen. The brain wave patterns they make from minute to minute are then projected over the one on the Card to show the variations.

This section will need not only engineers but also physiologists. It must be determined, for example, how people's brain wave patterns vary when they are telling 100% lies. The same with the other indicators: sweat, rate of heart beat, voice pressure, etc. Within what limits are changes *normal for each person* and outside of what limits do they show agitation? When these lie indicators and limits are known for sure, the machines measuring them must be designed so the Operator can change the limit indicatorsfor each person, as we're all different.

When the *normal* limits have been surpassed, a transducer makes the lie alarm go off: the super loud bell sounds and the lights flash. This transducer must be able to be set by the Operator so the lie alarms are activated when one, two or three of the sensors show over-reaction. As some people are naturally jumpier, perspire more or whatever than others, one sensor might be setting the alarms off a lot and these people might need two or even three out-of-limit indications to tell when they're actually lying and not just nervous.

The Operator must be able to push a button that sets off the lie alarms for demonstration purposes, but this button must be clearly marked and visible so the TV viewers can plainly see that it is not touched during the actual FFTest.

FF's need three types of Exchange computer slaves: an ED and ESD to be used when the trailer is at Council Center and an ESR for the times it's out in the field.

At least two FF trailers in every Council need computer card punching facilities so prospective Trainees' desires and dreams can be expressed to the cold-hearted Classification Sorters in Central.

When the sales of VMW reach 10 million and this design section can show that it has an easily operable FF which is *unbeatable* either physiologically or psychologically, the corporation will furnish the bread to build one—if only to have it outside the office for demonstration purposes. Two things we need to know are how much an FF costs to build and how much one costs to run.

The other machine this section needs to design is a portable FF which can be operated by a Trainee for short form FFTests. It will probably be about the size of a large portable radio, battery powered with places for the operator's and one subject's Cards. The sensor is a rig like pilots use with the two temple plates and the sensitive microphone in one assembly that slips easily over the head. The Tests are recorded on cassettes and can be erased immediately if there's no complaint from the Testee. The short form FFTest first produces positive identification by comparing actual brain wave pattern with the one on the Card, then, by measuring differences in voice pressure, brain wave pattern, pulse rate and pressure, can determine if the subject is telling a 100% lie when asked one question like, "Have you agreed with yourself or anyone else to do harm to this flight (or person or whatever)?" This machine need not be as sensitive nor as adjustable as the regular FF because there is a tremendous difference in the states of Being in people about to commit hijacking, bombing or murder and in those who have committed an act in the past. The short form FFTest will be used in security situations and may cause a certain amount of inconvenience for the readily agitable but we have to remember that its basic purpose is to keep us from harm.

6. Boundary Patrol Section

I am totally the last person to know anything about defense patrols but what I figure we need is a well organized, well trained DEFENSE organization, with not too much power that keeps anything harmful from first, passing our boundaries and second, from doing any damage, if it does squeak through. Are Polaris submarines an answer?

The Patrol engineering and construction function, using outside contractors, designs and builds Coventry and PCC facilities and builds Central. The design specs for PCC's come from the Education design section and the designs for Central from the Central design section.

We need the Patrol in the same breath as regretting that need so have it ready. Remember they are divided into Councils. You also have to decide about uniforms: what kind or if just an arm band on a T-shirt will suffice.

7. Finance Section

What are needed from this section are some wild guesses. What will be the total of Credits made available in North America? What will be the overall effect of closing down a lot of factories until they emit zero pollution? It does seem silly that Business doesn't try to clean up its scene pollutionwise without being forced to do so but so has experience shown us. What will be the effects of corporations losing their legal status as individuals and of their not being able to own their own stock? How much will the cost of things be cut because Business pays no taxes, tax accountants, personnel or supervisory people plus the reduction in their advertising costs because of the same overhead reductions? How many computer slaves will each Council need—by type of Council? Work on your educated guesses, agree on them and VMW, Inc., will publish them and let others second guess you: the old executive game.

In addition to the above guesses, this section can do concrete planning to tell us *how* to do the *what to do's* in Segment XVIII. We will need:

- A step by step procedure for Councils to set up two different kinds of banks while we're still using paper money so individuals can make the division between their personal money (for the Exchange configuration) and their business money (for the Small Business configuration) in time for computerization.

- A more detailed plan for collecting taxes in the Personal Banks (later to be E configuration) and ways and means of persuading people to keep their cash in banks instead of shoe boxes.

- An approximation of the credit-debit balance we will experience when settling debts with every country on the planet outside of the RNA. How much do we really owe?

- A plan to redeem all RNA currencies with gold and silver from reserves and mines. What kind of agency are we going to create in foreign countries to make the exchange—like that.

- A plan to convert old system Bank shares into those in the new system.

- Advice to loan, insurance, holding, mutual fund and other superseded financial institutions as to how to get their holdings into the hands of individual subscribers, policy and share holders in an equitable fashion.

- Preparation of Central Bills regarding the amount limits, interest rates, time limits of conversion and types of certificates that will be accepted in exchanging public debts for low paying Council Annuities.

- Preparation of Central Bills regarding conversion of Social Security, Veteran and government retirement funds into high paying Council Annuities.

- The amount in dollars of a Citizen's Share based on the economy at that time. This amount must yield an integer when divided by three and will be used until superseded by Central Bill.

If you, as a cog in this design section, feel there are other plans or guesses we might need to smooth the transition, please submit them and they'll be published.

8. Central Section

Central has been laid out by me but I expect to be second guessed—everything can be revised.

There is a lot of work to do on the plant: drawings, specifications, estimates and all that jazz so it can be published and ready to go. It's one of the first things we'll need.

9. Computer, Data Storage and Transmission Section

The Bear is the LC. The Library Central will be tough to design, perhaps largely because it will need so many in and outputs to make it useful to the greatest numbers of people. It'll probably need to be huge to contain every bit of available data on every subject and make that data available instantly. You'll have to come up with a simple language so ordinary people can ask like, "Where can I buy navel oranges?" and have your beauty be able to look it up and print the answer two thousand miles away in under a minute. How's that for a customer specification? You need miracle engineering. You have to figure out how data should come to the beast, like from a Bank Tender or from whom? In what form? Don't forget the vehicle register.

Members of the Computer, Data Storage section have, in addition to the Type LC, the N configuration (but not including the Card making machine), the facsimile transmission setup and the Classification Sorter in Central to design. For the Classification Sorter, we can probably use the old FBI ID sorter to start with, with the exception of those people who want to Serve together. I don't think the FBI sorter will have provisions for these people so you have to come up with some way of sorting the computer cards that come in stapled (horrible thought) together.

BLOCK DIAGRAM

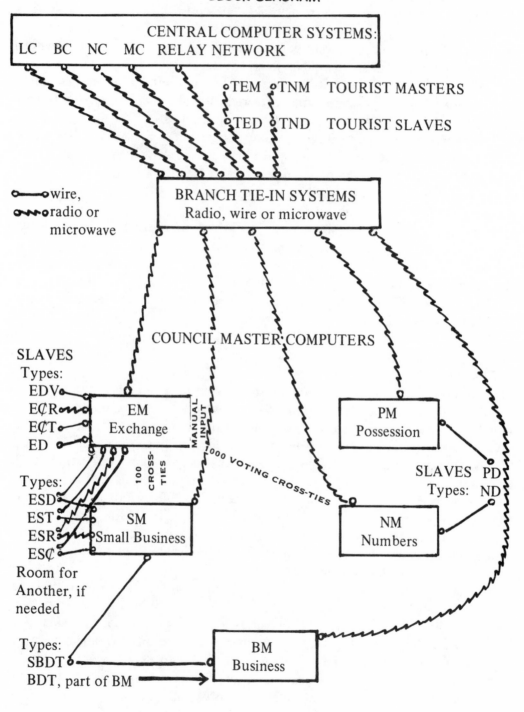

CENTRAL COMPUTER SYSTEMS:
LC BC NC MC RELAY NETWORK

TEM TNM TOURIST MASTERS

TED TND TOURIST SLAVES

wire,
radio or
microwave

BRANCH TIE-IN SYSTEMS
Radio, wire or microwave

COUNCIL MASTER COMPUTERS

SLAVES
Types:
EDV
E¢R
E¢T
ED

EM
Exchange

MANUAL INPUT

1000 VOTING CROSS-TIES

100 CROSS-TIES

PM
Possession

Types:
ESD
EST
ESR
ES¢

SM
Small Business

SLAVES PD
Types: ND

NM
Numbers

Room for
Another, if
needed

Types:
SBDT
BDT, part of BM

BM
Business

COUNCIL COMPUTER CONFIGURATIONS

Council computer masters—located in the Computer Security Room in the POB with access to Tax Tenders only, triple powered, bomb sheltered, if you wish.

E, Exchange Type EM	S, Small Business Type SM	N, Census, ID, Voting Type NM	P, Possessions and Savings Type PM

Capacities:

EM: 200,000 accounts per side in parallel. ₡9 999.00 per account. Records magnetically, in twelve divisions (one for each Zodiac sign), each division has own multi-track recorder.

SM: 100,000 per side in parallel. ₡99,999,999.99 per account. Records magnetically, 10 divisions—first digit of B Number. Each division has multi-track magnetic recorder.

NM: 500,000 ID and Numbers storage units, not in parallel. 1,000 voting circuits cross-tied to EM. As many units as a Council needs to record and cross-file vehicles and Land Leases.

PM: 100,000 portfolios not in parallel. ₡999,999.99 in savings plus nine other items per account. Completed transactions recorded magnetically.

Tapes to last a week. 100 automatic transfer circuits from EM to SM. When ₡9,900 are built up in the Council's, telephone company's or local transportation's accounts, they are automatically transferred to the SM.

Capabilities:

EM: Stores personal Credits. Calculates: tax rates and taxes on every transaction, pays People's Share, gives weekly Credit total. Transfers votes to NM for counting. Manual input to correct computer errors, add new accounts,

SM: Stores Business, Council Credits. No taxes. Gives weekly Credit total. Takes one tenth of 1% per week or weekly slave lease fee (whichever is greater) out of every account and adds it to Council S account. Manual input

NM: Stores and cross-files basic data: Number, fingerprints, brain wave and eye retinal for every person in Council from birth to death. Transmits by facsimile to other NM's, and NC to LC. Stores vehicles under ten digit

PM: Keeps savings without interest and registered possessions and gives weekly savings Credit total. Manual input through PD.

E

subtract dead ones, put holds. *Weekly chores* might have to be started manually but once started, the machines will take over and do them automatically.

Tourist Exchange Masters (**TEM**) located at Central. Supervised by Business Tender. Does not collect taxes or pay Shares. No voting capabilities.

S

through SBDT.

N

numbers, cross-filed under owner E or B Number. Stores Leases under seven digit numbers, cross-filed under owner E Number or Council number. Can give current population figures broken down into under 12's, 12 to 19's, in Service, with children, Citizens, Members, Business people and by Neighborhoods. Counts votes by Neighborhoods. Reports totals to ND slave.

Tourist Numbers Master (**TNM**) counts tourists but not votes otherwise same as above.

P

Type PD

Members only. Located in Possessions Room and in Speakers' Offices. Records all transactions on paper roll for user. Costs ₡.25 per user. Thumbprint. Tax per time. Thumbprint. Tax

Slaves and Purpose:

Type ND

Located in ID Rooms. Operated by Trainees under the supervision of a Tax Tender. Issues Cards, Order of Registration Nos, checks and replaces ID's.

Type ESD

Transactions from EM to SM, from EM to EM, from SM to one or two EM accounts, from SM to SM without tax. Records all transactions on magnetic tape. Thumbprint and capable of checking brain wave pattern.

E

Type EST

Belongs to telephone company. Records magnetically in telephone office. Transactions from EM to SM, from EM to EM, from SM to EM, from SM to SM over the phone. Thumbprint.

Type ESR

Radio connected EM to SM transactions only, tax to Council EM account. Does not record. Thumbprint.

Type ES¢

Transactions of ¢.99 or less, from EM to SM, tax 10 percent and SM to SM, no tax. Thumbprint.

Type E¢R

Portable radio transmitted EM to EM transactions of ¢.99 or less, tax 10%. No thumbprint.

Type E¢T

On every telephone. Thumbprint telephone calls ¢.99 plus 10% tax or series of them.

Type EDV

Each Neighborhood furnished three by Council; more by request. EM to EM transactions with tax. Has voting feature: call

P

free tie to E configuration. Typewriter entered. Buys and sells shares and annuities from savings. Deposits dividends and annuity payments into savings when told to by Bank Tender. Homesteads Leases. Used by Tax Tenders to enter PM to add and subtract accounts, give weekly Credit total.

N

Finds people through ID and through cross-file of A and E numbers. Finds vehicles and Lease owners through cross-file. Facsimile transmission. Types out answers to current census questions, types out vote count by Neighborhood for broadcast by Council TV station. On Central Bills, counts votes by Neighborhoods and transmits totals to Numbers Central. Registers and files all protectable creative efforts, transmits this information to the LC.

Type TND

Located in Speakers' Offices and Ports of Entry. Operated by Tourist Tenders or Trainees. Registers and cross-files tourist ID's and Numbers.

E

ID Room to be switched.
Vote indicator in thumb-
print hole: to the right,
YES; left, NO.

Type ED

In Council Centers only.
₵ to Council without
tax. Thumbprint.

Type TED

In Ports of Entry, Speak-
ers' Offices and Exten-
sion School offices tied
to tourist EM's at Cen-
tral—enters new accounts,
deletes old ones.

BUSINESS COMPUTER CONFIGURATION

Type BM

Located in Business Room of POB. 10,000 accounts per side in parallel. ₵999,999,999.99 per account.
Holds Central Credits for giving one tenth of one percent to Council, Clearinghouse Credits, Corporation
accounts, Council Credit storage. Takes one tenth of one percent out of each account weekly and puts it
in Council BM account. Gives weekly Credit total.

Slaves:

Type BDT

Senses E, A and B Numbers. This slave is integral part
of Master. Records magnetically, also on tape brought
by user. Has brain wave ID attachment in addition to
thumbprint feature. Makes BM to BM transactions,
without taxes. Used by Tax Tenders to enter BC only

Type SBDT

Located in Business Room at POB. Costs ₵0.50 per
transaction. Typewriter entered. Records on paper
roll with copy to user. Makes SM to BM and BM to
SM transactions. Taxless. T is a telephone connection. Ties into LC. Can be used to order things, pay

business bills, like that. Used by Tax Tenders to enter SM to add and subtract accounts, fix errors and get weekly Credit total. Thumbprint plus capable to check brain wave pattern. when Cardholder is there.

CENTRAL COMPUTER CONFIGURATIONS

Located at Central. Owned, operated and maintained by Central for the Councils and for Business. Triple powered, bomb proofed(?). At any rate, well secured.

Type LC
Data storage Library and Communication facility for exchanging every kind of information in and out of RNA. Stores and re-ports everything patented or copyrighted. Holds all vehicle registrations and inspection data. Finds vehicles.

Type BC
Stores Credits not in circulation. Receives Credits from Business to pay dividends. Makes weekly Credit census.

Type NC
Tied to ND's. Transmits by facsimile. Gives instant current census. Totals votes on Central Bills by Councils, posts results by Councils in Central and returns totals to Councils' NM's, so ND slave can make a tape to send to TV stations. Finds people through Council cross-file.

Type MC
The Stock Market wherein all corporation shares are bid, bought and sold and stockholders Numbers are listed. Pays dividends to stockholders of record. Tied to PM's and BC only.

CENTRAL AND BRANCH RELAY AND TIE-IN NETWORK

These are located at Central and where needed to accept, amplify, switch and retransmit signals from Types EM, SM, NM, PM and BM into the Central computers, or directly to the Council Master involved. They are operated and maintained by Central. May be connected by wire in a Metropolis but probably transmit and receive from Central by microwave or radio.

10. Computer, Exchange Section

This section has the E and S configurations to design as they work together. Part of the design information is in Segment VIII, the rest is on the Block Diagram, the specifications tables and in your heads. One thing not explained earlier is what happens when you put your Card into a slave so here's a story: As you put your Card into the slot, it pushes the switch built into the back of the slot. The switch turns on the scanning light which shines through the Card to the sensitive photoelectric elements on the other side and lights them up everywhere, except where the Numbers are blocking the light out. The blocked out areas make a signal which is amplified and transmitted at the speed of light and radio waves to a Master computer. The Master checks the Council Number part of the A Number and if the Number is out of its storage banks, the signal is immediately switched to the closest relay net and transmitted at the speed of light to the *home* Council. If the A Number is in the Master's storage banks, the Master seeks out the E or B Number in its data banks and waits for the next signal. Every slave, except for the less than a Credit ones, has a pickup head located immediately over the brain wave and eye retinal space on the Card. This pickup leads to two external jacks on the side of the slave. A store can lease an attachment with a headset that plugs into the jacks and compares the person's actual brain waves with the one on the Card and, if they match, a contact closes and sends the signal to light up the Balance window. If this attachment is not plugged in (the usual case), the pickup head merely senses that there is a brain wave pattern on the Card, closes the contact and sends the signal. If there is no brain wave recording there, it will not send the signal. (Why a Child's Card will not operate over one Credit slaves.)

The Tax Rate window shows the rate at the same time the Balance window lights up. The Card receiving the Credits is put in and the Master/slave go through the same process. When the paying person punches the amount on the buttons, the Master waits one full second, then multiplies the Amount by the Tax Rate and sends the signal to the Tax window.

The thumb hole on the slave has an image comparator and when the actual thumb matches the one on the Card, the comparator clicks a microswitch in the slave which sends the signal to the Master or Masters to transfer the Credits from buyer to seller and the tax (if any) to the Council. As the Credits are exchanged, the numbers in all the windows except the Balance window go to zero and a recording is made. Tax Tenders need a decoder to read out the tape to find errors.

The vote section of the Exchange Master must be set to 0 for children and youths under 18, to 1 for Citizens and to 2 for Members with a memory bank that allows each Citizen and Member to vote only their alloted times per Bill.

Remember to make the Masters self-repairing, but I am already in over my head. As we'll need 1700 of both types of Masters plus a mountain of slaves, twelve Tourist Exchange Masters and TED's, it would be nice if you could get some bids.

11. Computer, Business Section

This section must design the BC which is just a fancy adding machine with a memory. It holds only one account, ours. It sits there in Central full of Credits and hums occasionally when someone adds to it to pay a dividend or a Business Tender writes a check on a foreign account or transfers Credits to a Council's Business Master. It also adds up the total Credits in the RNA when told to.

Another computer for this section to think about is the one that handles the foreign bank accounts. It's a kind of computer that banks now use and allows the Head Business Tender or Deputy to keep our balances in these foreign accounts above the line. It has to allow for the time lag of a check going by mail or by carrier. Like when it's in the mail, it's out of one account but not yet in another. It also helps the Central Business Section balance import Credits with outport Credits and figures out what the foreign currency exchange rates are. The Head Business Tender or Deputy must figure the rates of exchange every day and report the information to this computer which then lets all Business Tenders know by phone or facsimile.

The other configuration this Section has to design is B, 1700 (or so) Masters plus their slaves. BDT slaves live in the same hardware as their Masters and need not only a thumbprint but brain wave ID as well. SBDT's tie in B and S Masters, are typewriter entered (three languages) and if we have to take a special course to learn how to run one, it's OK. See Spec table and Segment IX.

12. Computer, Stock Market Section

There's already one of these around. At least, I saw a picture of a stock market computer in the paper. Maybe a few adaptions to make it into the MC is all you need to do. This section has the PM's and PD's to design as well and find out how much they'll cost. Don't forget the big TV closed circuit screen in every Possession Room and the three languages on PD's.

13. Computer, Relay Net Section

There's not enough information in my head about relay nets to even make me dangerous. We need some sort of relay equipment so Credit transactions, information, facsimile transmissions and other can go from Council to Council, from Council to Central and every whichaway with a maximum of accuracy and minimum of time. Probably the ten main branch relays, the ones for Council area numbers listed under section 1, would be enough relays to start with, then expanded as needed. Ideas, please.

14. Computer, Vendor Section

I'll just list them:

- *Loan Vendor:* loans Credits on People's Share and Council Annuities. Automatically collects from either the PM or EM so will need circuits and tie-ins. Talk to the related design section.

- *Vehicle Insurance Vendor:* needs the facility of describing in risk terms every vehicle we are willing to insure. This can be a punch button selector. Next, it must have an actuarial computer that can determine the odds on what the Vehicle can have happen to it over the possibility of it happening. The rate then can be calculated by this factor times the length of the policy to determine cost. This vendor needs storage capabilities to hold all the policies until they expire, plus print-out facility to give policy holders their policy numbers and conditions. I have no idea of capacity, so Councils with heavy vehicle concentrations may need several machines.

- *Lease Insurance Vendor:* much like the one above, but having to do with what can happen to houses, property and also to People who wander around on them.

- *Risk Insurance Vendor:* a real dilly but about the same kind of thing with maybe different models for the types of Councils. Crop insurance for Farm Councils, cargo insurance for Waterfront Councils—not exclusively, just a kind of division of effort sort of thing. We expect to make a lot of bread out of these so the more types of insurance each machine can handle, the more Credits it will take in.

- *Card Insurance Vendor:* insures against loss of Credits due to someone else using your Card to spend your Credits. It is a simpler form of the others.

- *The parcel post machine* in the POB is described in Segment VIII.

- *The mail sorter:* designed to handle black edged RNA envelopes. The first sorter senses the first digit of the A Number. If this digit is 1, the letter passes to the next section. If it is other than 1, it gets kicked into the foreign mail bin where it's hand sorted or machine sorted by continents. Depends on how much foreign mail each Council has. These letters are bagged and sent to their respective continents for further sorting there.

   2 - South America
   3 - Europe and the Near East
   4 - Africa
   5 - Indian Asia
   6 - U.S.S.R.
   7 - China and Japan
   8 - Pacific Islandia, Indonesia and Australia
   9 - Antarctica(?)

0 - Earth Central, if time gives us enough sense to have one. It would be a groove to have Earth Central in Venice.

The second sorter senses the second digit of the A Number (area) and puts the letter into one of 10 sorting sections attached to it. There is a human, the first needed, to judge whether or not there's enough mail in any of the ten areas to warrant using the third sorter. Anyway, after it's sorted into area and type of Council, off it goes and the first Council of that type in that area it reaches will sort it into Council number, maybe using a sorter at its Way Station that senses the last two digits of the A Number so mail gets to the exact right Council it was addressed to.

These sorters are all the same and can be set to sense a certain digit so they can be used interchangeably. Some Councils may need only one and others, like a bunch.

This design section could also figure out mail, parcel post and express rates; the ones to start with, anyway. Remember when setting the rates, both the sending Council and the Transportation Council have to make a profit.

- If anyone can think of any other handy dandy items for use around the Council, design them and get some bids on them, OK?

15. Power Section

Our task is to design a simple 220 volt, about 10,000 KVA generator that will furnish enough juice to light, wash clothes, heat and cook for about 30,000 to 50,000 families. Councils can use one, two or three of these strategically placed so as to give maximum service to the inhabitants. We could use a design for a smaller model, too, that will put out about 1,000 KVA for from 3,000 to 5,000 families to be used in spread out areas. These generators can either be powered by a small (old-fashioned) uranium reactor or by a breeder type reactor.

The power plant and generator will be double-ended which means that a reactor can be placed at either end of the generating equipment. I have suggested for safety that we dig deep wells, like maybe 300 meters deep, install explosive bolts, quick disconnects and a power pack retro-rocket on the reactor so if it ever reaches out for its critical mass, it will automatically drive itself to the bowels of the earth where either the water and pressure will cool it off and it can be hauled back up again and reused or it will go off causing some minor disturbances (which you can tell us about), but the reserve reactor is calmly hooked up and service is resumed. Check into tiny fusion reactors and into solar or nuclear energy to create hydrogen to replace natural gas.

When you design what we need and agree upon it, depending on which way the wind is blowing, maybe we can get a grant to build and test one. We'll try like hell anyway.

16. Transportation, Land Section

There are two allied design requirements: the roadbed and the things that ride on it. I have talked about the buses a little with their luggage compartments under the sitting places and when you get off the doors open so you can get your stuff out—would you believe a bicycle? The long distance buses could hook together to lower the number of drivers.

I have a picture of the Peripheral and Direct buses using regular roads around the Councils with an overhead wire pickup but it may not need to be true. The Transcons can have power embedded in the roadway if an induction transfer pickup can be designed—you know, like two parts of a transformer, one part of which is moving. With a workable design for power transfer, power cables could be laid near the surface and, with a totally even roadbed, the pickup (maybe riding on its own little wheel) can be close to the power supply which would make juice transfer to the vehicles easy and efficient. The combination petro-electric vehicles (which use petroleum to generate electricity) would have to have pickups that can be raised on ordinary roads and lowered when moving on the Transcons.

I would like to see the whole roadbed made of vitrified material. It lasts, has fairly good expansion characteristics and surely, we can make it non-skid by now. Can you imagine the monster paving machine which melts the rock, pours the roadbed and roughs it up after? Can you? I hope so, because we're going to need some. The slag can be skimmed out, put on the side of the road, then ground and spread to make the shoulders.

The facilities along Transcons for people (land/airbus stations) and for mail, parcel post and express (Way Stations) have to be designed keeping in mind minimum employment and maximum machine use of the order of difficulty that allows Trainees to handle the job. Those bus passenger entertainment centers will be a gas to design. Have fun.

The standard cross section of the Transcon at an airbus strip location is: airbus strip, two lane service road, two or three electrified lanes, three petro lanes, all going one way. The same going the other way. The petro lanes are entered from tunnels under the electrified lanes with plenty of acceleration strip. Truck and bus lanes are entered directly from the service road with just a pause to pick up a ticket from the machine. There are no airbus service facilities on the airbus strips only at airports. Land vehicles will need electrified turnouts for emergency servicing like flat tires but, in general, land buses will be serviced and cleaned at the ends of their runs.

The design of Ports of Entry falls to this section as well. These are located at RNA Intercontinental airports, water ports and one at the Columbian border. They are occupied by Central Business and Tourist Tenders, Council Port Tenders and Trainees. An office for the Port Tender and one big room will do the job. The Tourist Tender will need ID equipment, Card making machines, TND slaves (Tourist-Numbers-Direct) to register visitors in the Tourist Numbers Master at Central and short form FF's. The Business Tender will need Types TED, Tourist-Exchange-Direct, computer slaves to open and close Tourist accounts and put Credits into them out of funds in the BC in exchange for the Tourist's currency, cash or check. The Port Tender will need Council Exchange computer slaves (ESD's) plus places to stash ailing or undesirable animals and plants for inspection by a Council Medical Tender. Ports of Entry must be numbered using three digits.

17. Transportation, Air Section

The airbus is the roughy and I see literally a bus with wings, fixed landing gear, faired to minimize resistance but down and ready to land all the time. They fly directly over their side of the Transcon all the way, probably never exceeding 300 meters in height. They must be very stable landers and take-offers because they don't pay attention to the wind direction at all. If the wind velocity is very high, the next Transcon junction will provide them with another pair of landing strips going in the opposite direction. The power plant, maybe three, super-quiet jets in the tail, would probably be left running except when they refuel. OK, a bus with wings with room for people and pets above and baggage and freight below and engines or engine out back so the business of loading and unloading can take place without shutting them off, that's what we need and a lot of them. They can be as automatic as you care to make them. They have their own special service strips at airports and don't get into the regular landing-take-off pattern at all. They will use ESR Exchange computer slaves to collect the fares and some kind of automatic weighing equipment that puts out a weight slip as you leave the service area so the conductor knows how many kilos to charge for. I don't know how much speed you can build into such a fat beast but I assume about 500 kilometers per hour. With about 20 stops at 15 minutes each and two refuelings at 30 minutes, an airbus would take about 15 hours from San Francisco to New York along Transcon 80 and that's reasonable, don't you think?

With airbuses taking over all the local air traffic, the commercial airlines can concentrate on the longer flights, like the same trip with a stop at Chicago would take about five hours and you might be able to get some sleep.

Hovercraft are noisy beasts and I know nothing about their economic considerations. I rode one from France to England on a rough day. A forty-five minute roller coaster ride I got. However, we can use them to make rapid transportation possible where there are no roads, like all over the Caribbean and in the far North but passengers sure have to be insulated from the noise. It seems to me they could be adapted to carry bulk cargos, too, like bauxite from the Bahamas right up the Mississippi to Chalmet and like that. Don't forget container hovercraft.

Airports with complete facilities to sleep or play—do something besides wait—and up-to-the-minute safety and navigation equipment are part of this design section's task as well. Get it together for printing, OK?

18. Transportation, Water Section

All over the RNA there are applications for rapid water transportation and we had better get going on hydrofoil buses that ply the coastal and inland waterways and rivers as Peripheral and Direct transportation for many Waterfront Councils.

The main thing the Water Transportation design section has to do is make all our port facilities ready for containers and practically automatic loading facilities. Outside of wheat, scrap iron and other bulk stuff like that, there is absolutely no excuse for not containerizing everything shipped, really by either land or water, but especially for the port facilities furnished by Waterfront Councils, efficient designs are needed.

Another thing this section must do is design smog-free, nonpolluting commercial fishing equipment that can selectively fish the right size fish out of the sea without, for instance, harming our fellow intelligent race, the porpoises. In the RNA, they are going to be protected by Custom and anyone can Challenge you if you harm one.

19. Council Center Section

The one thing that characterizes the RNA is movement. Look at it! From the end of Panama to the North Pole there's not a single border. We are seeking *maximum unemployment* and each person has enough to keep body and soul glued without recourse to a job. What the hell do you think is going to happen? We are going to move into the opener spaces, move south, move north, move east; Greeley couldn't even imagine!

OK, the Council Center consists of a meeting hall for the Councilors and the POB, described in Segment VI plus places for several FF's to park and hook in. When we start all this, we will gain a lot of experience in a hurry as there will be 1700 to put together and get working but before we finish setting up these, the great Movement will start. When a Council loses People to the 125,000 point, it has to join its neighbors and when it gets to 275,000, it has to split into two. That's what we are agreeing to do. The Council Center's location is at the whim of the majority so we have to be prepared to move the machines and computers as the population eddies about. Hell, one of the problems with the present Establishment is its tendency to make government institutions so ponderous they can not be moved where they can properly serve the People.

This means that the equipment a Council uses must be designed so it is portable. When you know the sizes and weights of the Master computers and other machinery, you can design wheels under it all. Containerized! that's the word. Design their containers so they can be loaded on trailers, moved like fifty kilometers and set onto their already perpared foundations. Say 12 hours from disconnect to connected and working. The containers can have breakaway sides and removable wheels to be stored or used somewhere else. You can use forklifts, cranes, whatever needed to move and install a Council Center. Step by step procedures must be written so an idiot could follow them, including the estimated cost in Credits and labor—then published.

This section must also design the ID equipment needed by the Councils and Tourist Tenders: the fingerprint machine, the eye retinal pattern machine which reduces the pattern to a magnetic record, the brain wave machine which does the same, the Card making machine—everything to do with ID and Cards.

There is an item of equipment not mentioned in the text, the Banker's Memory, that must be designed. This machine sits in the middle of the Bank with four entrance typewriters on which Bankers and Tax Tenders record their special transactions. It operates only for their Cards. Each typewriter has two magnetic recorders connected to it so each entrance has two sides and is easily switched from one to the other. They go like this:

Entrance One is for Leases: one side for E Number Leases bought and sold, liens, lien payments, land use changes, lease fees and like that; the other side is for Council owned Leases used by Business. The transaction is typed out in duplicate, one for the customer and one for the Bank Tender and taped for the record.

Entrance Two has one side for Council Annuities and one for Bank Shares. The recordings are the only permanent record of who the owners are. When the Council Bank pays a dividend, the Bank Share tapes are put on a different machine to be read out and the Bank Tender credits the shareholder's savings in that portfolio. If the holder has no Possession account, the amount of Bank Shares held are increased by the amount of the dividend. You wondered how all this fancy stuff got done, didn't you? The Annuities tapes are read out once a week and the payments credited to the holder's P savings. The Bank Tender may have to sit down at a PD once a week and punch these payments out, portfolio by portfolio, until one of you comes up with an automatic machine. When Bank Shares and/or Annuities are bought, the permanent record is changed with the transaction.

Entrance Three contains loans: one side for B Number loans and the other for E Number loans. Every time the situation changes, the whole transaction is recorded. Like, if you make a payment, the recording is changed to show your new balance—no record of payments made or not made, just what is owed and what the interest rate is. Who the hell cares how fast or well we make our loan payments? We have to pay the extra interest, don't we?

The loan vendor machine needs to be read out weekly and E account deductions given to the Tax Office. Can this be done automatically? Let's work on it.

Entrance Four is for special transactions. The Tax Tender gets one side for recording *One Time Transactions, holds,* including the *hold* requester's Number, corrections made to an account due to computer error and like that. The Bank Tender's side is for recording special P to S transfers, repossessions, bad debts written off, insurance claim pay-off's and so on.

The Banker's Memory is actually just a recorder and playback machine, not a computer. Remember, it has to be able to be moved.

20. Council Shops Section

Council shops with their hospital, mortuary and perhaps high-rise, cross or star shaped crypts, athletic field, library, shops, studios and laboratories are not mobile, except for Bookmobiles and ambulances, of course. A spread out Council might need two or more shop areas, each designed to take care of some proportion of the Council's People. In general, you have to figure on facilities to handle the ailing and beyond, out of 200,000 People. I don't even know where to look for the statistics, but you will.

Try to make the auto shop big enough so everybody and his brother or sister can work on their cars and remember that Farm Councils will have a lot of farm machinery to repair—like that. Provide the most complete training ground you can so People can learn to use their hands. Don't be afraid to slant shops toward a Council's interest, like Waterfront Councils toward learning about boats and diving equipment, Ranch Councils toward learning about airplanes and veterinary medicine, OK?

21. Council Houses Section

The task here is to design standard Council Houses that are reasonably inexpensive and indestructable (barrack type?) and can be knocked down and set up on prepoured foundations, as they'll be moved about a lot, at least in the beginning. Designs must include: houses warm enough for ski time, with floors that sand won't hurt at beach time, houses in high-rise buildings, overseas, on the Yukon River, near Mayan ruins (mosquito proof). I figure about 300 of these Houses per Council but check this figure—75 to 150 kids per House, remember.

The kitchens, pantries and baths must be specially designed for their purposes. The kids are going to need fresh vegetables and fruit which need special storage plus things they can cook themselves for a well-balanced diet. The equipment must be easy to care for and use—juice squeezers built into a sink top that can be lowered out of the way and sprayed with water for easy cleaning—things like that. Food stocks must be made easily available—also easy for a Trainee to see what's needed. Room for lots of wiggy ideas and you'll get input from the Education design section.

22. Council Trainee and Public Housing Section

Each Council will provide housing for about 2,000 Trainees in Neighborhood sized units. Trainees are Citizens. Rooms will be made for double occupancy with baths down the hall. In addition to the usual Meeting Hall and Order and Education Offices, study and recreation rooms need to be provided. Food will be served in cafeterias, labor by guess whom—more Trainees.

Council Public Housing is designed for Citizens and Members to rent cheaply from Bank Tenders. Where, how many and made out of what are the questions. There'll be three types needed, each in its own building in Neighborhood sized units. If there's not enough demand for a Neighborhood of one type, combination units can be built. The first type are for two people consisting of an all-purpose room including kitchen and half-bath, the second type for three people with one bedroom and the third type with two bedrooms for four people. All have tubs and showers down the hall (bath houses?). There will be enough people waiting for this almost free housing to Challenge us out of there if we try to overextend the facility design.

There will be some in cities, a lot in the country, some near Universities, up in the mountains and down at the beaches.

23. Neighborhood Centers Section

Suggestions are needed here so a portfolio of Neighborhood Center Designs can be made up for every type of Neighborhood you can think of. The standard things needed are a Meeting Hall with room for about 400 voters, an Order Office with 22 pigeon holes for mail and 24-hour facilities, an Education Office with plenty of storage space for paint, clay, paper and all that, a Representative's Office plus two super size TV screens for kids taking courses. Maybe a dorm and kitchen for Trainees, a coffee shop, music for dancing on the Meeting Hall floor after the chairs have been folded and put into the chair closets. Craft booths? Basketball? Suggestions on what old buildings could be converted: old warehouses, school buildings, whatever, and how and out of what to build new ones and what's the bite? Also, we'll need a booklet on *How to Get Together to Make a Neighborhood.*

24. Protection Organizations Section

These are going to be Businesses in the new society, right? OK, but the existing fire and police departments might as well get in on the ground floor. How to make a local tax supported fire department into a volunteer one or into a Business? How to change a police department into a rent-a-cop setup? How to operate a private detective service?

25. Disposal and Recycling Section

As I write this, the state of the arts of recycling and disposal seems to be barely above Neanderthal standards. This design section needs to produce some literature to explain just what recycling is all about and how to make individuals conscious that part of the task is theirs—the first part. You've probably heard that we waste billions of calories in our daily garbage and some ways of converting them into useable material for farms or heating or something must be presented. Sewage recycling and/or disposal plants, too, need to be designed so they can make money either for the Councils or private Business, however it works out. Recycling services come right after the logistics of food provision and we need ideas NOW—no need to wait.

26. Other Design Sections

If you see something we will need for the new Establishment, please go to it. If it becomes a big deal, it'll be assigned a number of its own; there are plenty left.

OK on design sections? You create the ideas, design them so they'll work, even get bids on them and VMW, Inc., will keep you in touch with each other and publish what you've come up with. What are needed are the most efficient whatevers you can agree on and the publication is with the deliberate intention of getting even more efficient ideas. A new society needs all the help it can get.

HUMANKIND MUST LEARN TO PROGRESS WITHOUT CONTENTION

WE, AS INDIVIDUAL RESIDENTS ON THE CONTINENT CALLED NORTH AMERICA, take upon ourselves the **Right** to form the Republic of North America (RNA) and to divide our Republic into Councils of about 200,000 People which are divided into Neighborhoods of about 1,000 People.

We who live in the RNA have the **Right** to govern ourselves according to a definition of government which says: GOVERNMENT IS THE SCIENCE AND ART OF FINDING OUT WHAT THE PEOPLE WANT, THEN HELPING THEM DO IT.

We take upon ourselves the **RIGHT OF CHALLENGE** which gives every individual the Right to Challenge any other individual in the RNA to a Fact Finding Test to determine the truth.

The Consequence for refusing a Challenge is expulsion from the RNA.

We give ourselves the **Right** to state that no weapon or replica thereof capable of any type of projection or emission (gun) can be made, owned or used that is less than 76 centimeters long. The Consequence for Action contrary to this statement is expulsion from the RNA.

Strangers who live closely packed together can generate and maintain an aura of friendliness if they can assume that the People around them have agreed to similar concepts of action. If Fulano knows that Joe Doe is going to smile back and that he won't be considered weird for smiling, Fulano will probably smile. If Jeanne knows that if she smiles, Joe won't take it as an invitation to screw, she'll probably smile. If we all agree to smile at each other, the pleasure of being able to smile and of being smiled back at will cause psychiatrists to find something else to do. The Customs in this book can offer us the confidence that the strangers we see on the street will not violate the secret places where we live. Each of us who decides to agree on these Customs has to confidently assume that the strangers we encounter have agreed to act according to this pact of non-violation; that they have read the same book we have.

Given the Right of Challenge, Customs would ultimately be developed by People but it would be a lot of hassle. Customs are things we can agree on, in front, making for fewer Challenges. Each Custom is designed to eliminate certain bodies of law, delineate certain areas of responsibility and add the idea of Seeking Agreement to human relationships and organizations.

Let's take a couple of Customs and work them over a bit to show a little about how they come into being and how they work.

WOMEN CHOOSE WITH WHOM THEY LIVE.

This is a simple statement involving very complicated bodies of legal thought and many men I have exposed to this idea have to be *sold* on it with a lot of hemming and hawing before they agree that our new Establishment will work only if we have some solid agreement on this point. The statement could as easily be written so men would choose but that doesn't make it, as women have really been the choosers since the beginning. Why not just agree to that and eliminate volumes and volumes of law books and a lot of CONTENTION?

"Why does anyone have to choose?"

"A relationship is an agreement, like a fight."

"What if a man doesn't want to be chosen?"

"Does that mean she can kick me out of my house? Off my land?"

"How about if she is my business partner?"

And on and on and on. The answers to these and other questions and arguments are contained in the original statement of the Custom. Perhaps, for clarity, the entire Custom should read: "If there is any argument, women choose with whom they live but this doesn't give them any rights about property, possessions, business dealings or anything else not directly connected with the idea of living together." But dammit, the simpler statement is simpler. Neighborhoods can make rules about marriage and divorce and keep records and all that, but the RNA Custom is that she gets to choose. If her choice violates Neighborhood Rules, she can leave the Neighborhood.

Customs, then, are definitions, pre-made and agreed upon decisions and bits of communal understandings. They are lubricating salve to let us rub together without friction. Then there's:

CHILDREN ARE REGISTERED ONLY ON WOMEN'S CARDS.

Nowhere does this say that a Child must be registered on the mother's Card so there will probably be a lot of putting the third child under twelve on granny's or older sister's Card and like that but without making a bunch of laws, we have to expect this. Basically this Custom is a statistical device. The Census statement is not how many men and how many women the society has to gear to care for but how many People with children and how many without. The position of the genitals, internal or external, has no bearing at all until they are in use to produce little additions to the population when they become remarkable and countable as such. If you, as a father, are having to raise the kid and need the bread to do so, a simple Challenge will make mother hand the Credits over to you, if she hasn't done so voluntarily.

For those of us who are going to start all this, the Customs may be a stone drag but, remember, that if we do it lovingly the next bunch will have it a lot easier, so surviving and agreeing to survive can become practically synonymous.

So that we can intermingle and get our communal job of living together done without rubbing each other the wrong way, bad tripping each other or putting each other down we, each individually, make these AGREEMENTS:

That I accept a majority vote as unanimous until changed by another vote.

* * *

To make my own decisions and allow other individuals (over 12 years old) to make theirs.

* * *

To classify myself into occupational, social, financial, sexual, racial and/or any other category I wish and to refrain from classifying others.

* * *

To accept and use the following RNA classifications and a Citizen's Weekly Share of the economy (amount to be determined by Central Bill).

Census classification and amount:

Child - birth to twelve years old;

Youth - twelve through eighteen years old, receives one Citizen's Share;

Citizen - at eighteen years old, gets one Citizen's Share and one vote until death;

Trainee - a Citizen serving the People, receives one Citizen's Share plus one third of a Citizen's Share for each completed year served up to three;

three months in one location is required in order to be counted toward a full year;

Member - a Citizen who has served the People for three years, receives two Citizen's Shares, two votes on Council and Central Bills and the right to use the Possession computer configuration;

Woman with one or two children - can be a Youth, Citizen or Member, receives an additional two thirds of a Citizen's Share per Child.

Business Person - can be a Youth, Citizen or Member who rents any computer slave with a B Number on it.

Identification classification:

Child - retinal eye pattern, fingerprints;

Youth, Citizen, Member - eye retinal pattern, fingerprints and brain wave pattern

Numerical classification:

C Number - astrological sun sign plus last two digits of year of birth;

E Number - C Number, Council of birth number, order of registration number and three service digits; **each individual will have only one E Number and be registered in only one *home* Council at a time.**

A Number - Address number consisting of: Continent, Council, Neighborhood (or industrial complex) and last three digits of phone number which is the final locating number; if these last three digits are 000, it means the individual has no phone but can be reached by message through the Neighborhood Order Office;

B Number - the number stamped on certain computer slaves leased by the individual in Business.

Child - has one C Number plus 'Woman with one or two Children's' E and A

Numbers;

Youth - has one E Number without Service digits plus A Number:

Citizen - has one E Number without Service digits plus A Number; when a Citizen becomes 19 years old without having completed a year of Service, a dash (-) is put in the first Service digit place;

Trainee - has one E Number with one Service digit for each year of Service completed, plus A Number;

Member - has one complete E Number plus A Number(s);

Woman with one or two Children - has one E Number which may or may not have Service digits, A Number and one or two C Numbers;

Business Person - has one E Number with or without Service digits, A Number(s) of Business location and B Number(s).

* * *

To use an everything Card containing my identification and numerical classification and to allow the Councils and Central to use computer configurations keyed to these Cards to exchange, care for and store the electronic medium of exchange (my Credits) and my financial possessions; to take the Census; count votes; register and crossfile my land leases and vehicles and to keep count of the number of Credits in circulation.

* * *

To use the Fact Finder (FF) operated by an FFOperator to make me tell the truth about what I did or agreed to do.

* * *

That the Challenge and subsequent FFTest deal with Principals only. Principals may have help from an Advisor to form questions but not to answer them.

* * *

That a video tape is made of every FFTest.

* * *

That there are two types of Challenges:

The Challenge which needs an appointment and an FFOperator and must be shown to the People for judgement unless settled and erased.

The Minor Challenge which needs no appointment, can be run by a Trainee and must be erased or changed to a Challenge.

* * *

That FFOperators ask questions only about what Principals did or agreed to do and, of course, are Challengeable.

* * *

That FFOperators are empowered to order a medical examination for any Principal they suspect has taken drugs or been mentally prepared (like by hypnotism) to beat the FF.

* * *

That with the help of an FF, FFOperators determine the truth about the Challenge and decide which Principal pays the Principal Fee (one Citizen's weekly Share) and the FF Fee (one Citizen's weekly Share per quarter hour).

* * *

To furnish my E and A Numbers to any individual who wants to Challenge me or I pay the cost of my own detection.

* * *

That if *FFOperators*, using their abilities and training as *mediators*, succeed in settling the Challenge to the agreement of both Principals, the video tape is erased in front of the Principals as soon as the Fees are paid.

* * *

That if the Operator fails to settle the Challenge (a Principal may refuse to settle) or feels that one of the Principals is likely to cause future harm to individuals or groups, the video tape of the FFTest must be played on television for the *People's Judgement.*

* * *

To accept the Judgement of the People, at least twelve who agree, and the Consequence they assign which can be:
1. Reparation, replacement or reimbursement for physical damage done.
2. Loss of Membership or Trainee time served from 3 months to 3 years.
3. Assignment of a dash (-) to individuals under 19 years old.
4. Assignment to a Psychiatric Care Center (PCC) from three months to a year with no change in Membership status.
5. Assignment to Coventry for three years with loss of Membership or any Trainee time served. A second assignment to Coventry can be from three years to life.

That the same FFOperator handles an FFTest from the time the Principals appear for their appointment to the termination of the Consequence, if any.

* * *

That a fight is a Contract between individuals or groups which is terminated upon surrender; further hostile action is considered harmful and Challengeable.

* * *

That a Job is a Contract between employer and employee.

* * *

To allow the Council wherein my E Number is registered to inherit my financial possessions at my death with the exception of land leases which revert to the Council they're in and the single Homesteaded lease which I can will to a Member and further to allow my copyrights and/or patents to become public domain at the same time.

* * *

To give the Councils the guardianship of the four elements: Fire (power), Earth, Air and Water.

* * *

To keep the boundaries of my lease clean and free of trash. What's inside the boundaries is my own business.

* * *

To place no limits on human learning.

* * *

That, before operating any self-powered vehicle without an instructor, to take the course of instruction and operator reaction and knowledge test for that *type* of vehicle given by the Councils and the instructions for that *particular* vehicle given by the vending agency.

* * *

That the least maneuverable vehicle and/or the one on the right has the right of way.

* * *

To take a short, one question FFTest, if asked to, before boarding a public carrier or for other security reasons.

* * *

To use envelopes and package labels especially made so they can be put through the mail mill by machines.

* * *

To be responsible for the care and protection of computer slaves I lease from the Council.

* * *

To care for or replace Council owned tools and equipment.

* * *

That Business has nothing to do with me unless I have something to do with Business.

* * *

To pay interest only to the Councils on the medium of exchange.

* * *

Not to kill porpoises and to think about eating everything I kill.

* * *

To show any living thing brought from overseas to the Port Tender at Port of Entry.

* * *

To consult with a Council Medical Tender before I bring into the Council any plant or animal not indigenous to it.

* * *

To live my own life style as long as it doesn't interfere with others and allow them to live theirs.

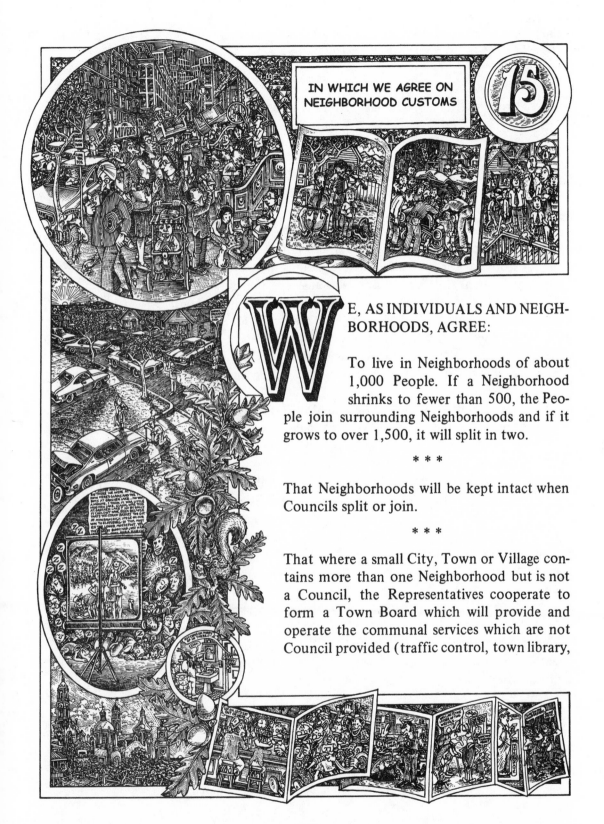

WE, AS INDIVIDUALS AND NEIGH-BORHOODS, AGREE:

To live in Neighborhoods of about 1,000 People. If a Neighborhood shrinks to fewer than 500, the People join surrounding Neighborhoods and if it grows to over 1,500, it will split in two.

* * *

That Neighborhoods will be kept intact when Councils split or join.

* * *

That where a small City, Town or Village contains more than one Neighborhood but is not a Council, the Representatives cooperate to form a Town Board which will provide and operate the communal services which are not Council provided (traffic control, town library,

199

park, fire department). The labor to keep these up can be volunteer.

* * *

That Neighborhoods have Meetings called by their Representative, a Neighborhood Tender or a group of Citizens.

* * *

That in a Neighborhood Meeting, Citizens:
1. Decide on their Rules of Order and enforcement procedures;
2. Choose a Representative who becomes the Councilor, gives Citizens copies of Council and Central Bills and answers questions concerning them;
3. Choose an Order Tender who is in charge of:
   a) enforcing the Rules of Order made in the Meeting(s);
   b) trying to settle disputes before making an appointment with the Council Justice Office for a Challenge;
   c) taking care of mail, including the selling and processing of Forwarding Strips;
   d) helping the Council with Neighborhood refuse;
   e) receiving telephone messages for People in the Neighborhood;
   f) leasing under ¢ 1.00 transaction, radio connected exchange computer slaves.
4. Choose an Education Tender who is in charge of education for the Neighborhood's Children and helps with problems concerning them.

* * *

That the Representative and two Tenders are each paid a minimum salary by every Person in the Neighborhood of two-thirds of a Citizen's Weekly Share per year.

* * *

That a Neighborhood must have definite geographical boundaries—a street, road, path, corridor, waterway, whatever—and post its unusual or far out Rules of Order for strangers.

* * *

That Neighborhoods provide a Neighborhood Center with:
1. a Meeting Hall with foldable seating for the Neighborhood's Citizens;
2. an Order Office with telephone facility, a mail sorting setup, a Bill duplicator and whatever is necessary to keep this office open 24 hours a day, every day;

3. an Education Office;
4. a Representative's Office;
5. facilities to board and room approximately 22 Trainees; this can be done in the Neighbors' homes.

* * *

That Neighborhoods also provide:
1. pick up and delivery of mail between the Neighborhood Center and Council Center; parcel post and express service to be decided by Neighborhood vote;
2. educational and recreational facilities for Children including two television sets; the Meeting Hall can be used for this purpose;
3. at least one computer slave to be used for Neighborhood business; the Small Business account so obtained is for use by the Representative and Tenders on Neighborhood business;
4. a stand outside of the Order Office for at least three Council furnished exchange and voting computer slaves and protection for them from the weather and vandalism;
5. a protected public telephone with a computer slave furnished by the Telephone Company so people can send money by phone.

* * *

That Neighborhoods are responsible for and care for their Children.

* * *

That a Neighborhood can eject any Person or animal not complying with its Rules of Order.

* * *

That a Neighborhood can hire Rent-a-Cops or whomever they choose to assist the Order Tender in maintaining order within its boundaries and collect the costs from the Neighborhood(s) or Council(s) whose residents are causing the breach of order.

* * *

That disputes between Neighborhoods are settled by Council Bill or by a Challenge between individual Tenders or Representatives.

* * *

That People can live their chosen life styles when they allow others to live theirs—without contention. With many different Neighborhoods, there's a place where everybody can BE.

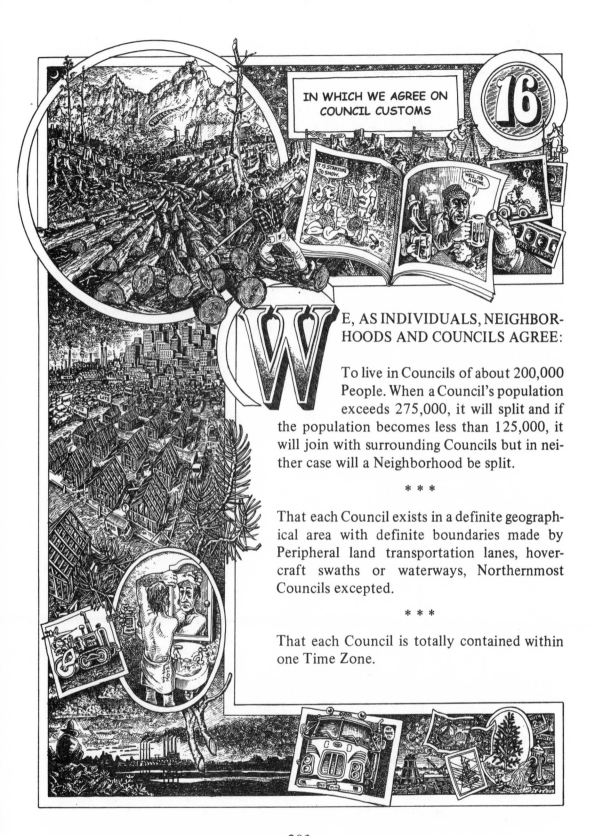

WE, AS INDIVIDUALS, NEIGHBOR-
HOODS AND COUNCILS AGREE:

To live in Councils of about 200,000
People. When a Council's population
exceeds 275,000, it will split and if
the population becomes less than 125,000, it
will join with surrounding Councils but in neither case will a Neighborhood be split.

* * *

That each Council exists in a definite geographical area with definite boundaries made by
Peripheral land transportation lanes, hovercraft swaths or waterways, Northernmost
Councils excepted.

* * *

That each Council is totally contained within
one Time Zone.

That no Council can refuse a request for registration or change in registration.

* * *

That Neighborhood Representatives from within the geographical boundaries of the Council become Councilors and represent their Neighborhoods in the Council.

* * *

That Councilors find out what the People want, then help them do it.

* * *

That Councilors choose one from among themselves to become Senator and represent the Council at Central. The Neighborhood represented by the Senator will choose another person as Representative/Councilor.

* * *

That there are ten types of Councils:
1. City
2. Suburban
3. Farm, Country and Town
4. Ranch, Forest and Wilderness
5. Waterfront and Shore
6. Transportation
7, 8 and 9. Combination types
0. Central Lease (Boundary Patrol, Coventry, Psychiatric Care Center, Continental Treasure)

* * *

That Council type is determined by location, area, types of natural resources and economic efforts.

* * *

That the Councilors form themselves into ten Committees. Each Committee (except the Senator's Committee) hires and fires the professional Head Tenders the Council needs to supervise its facilities. The Committees are:
1. Senator's Committee
2. Bank and Lease Committee
3. Tax Committee
4. Justice Committee
5. Education Committee

6. Medical Committee
7. Maintenance Committee
and three Field Committees:
8. Electrical Committee
9 and 10. Different for different Councils.

* * *

That the function of the Senator's Committee is to deal with the relationship between the Council and Central. It prepares the information of what the People want from Central and give it to the Senator who uses the information in helping to prepare Central Bills, especially the Budget Bill.

* * *

That all committees prepare Council Bills in simple language worded so they can be answered Yes or No and with a definite time limit.

* * *

That the functions of Bank Tenders (people who handle a Council's money) are:
A.   To provide a Council Center consisting of:
   1.   The Council Section:
      a)   a Meeting Room large enough for all the Councilors with a machine for duplicating Bills;
      b)   at least ten Committee Room-Office setups for the Council Committees plus at least one setup for special public projects and one for visiting Central Tenders;
      c)   a centrally located Trainee pool room where liaison and secretarial Trainees can be found when needed and where they can do their work;
      d)   Justice Office open 24 hours a day, seven days a week and a private office for the Head Justice Tender.
   2.   Post Office Bank (POB) Section - all services open 24 hours a day, seven days a week:
      a)   Post Office with machines and personnel to sort and handle mail, parcel post and express;
      b)   Bank containing an exhibit and leasing facility for every computer slave the Council leases, the computer slaves needed for use by the banking Facility and the "Banker's Memory;"
      c)   Business Room– door opens only to Cards with B Numbers on them—contains the Business Master computer with its attached slave computers which is the interface between People's Credits

and Business and other slave computer(s) which exchange Credits between Business and Small Business and tie in to Library Central;

d) Banking Office and a private office for the Head Bank Tender;

e) One or more Card operated loan machines which charge interest and make loans on Members' Shares of the economy and on Council Annuities;

f) At least one each of four types of insurance vending machines— vehicle, land lease, risk and Card loss or theft—but no fear insurance;

g) Exchange and voting slave computers.

3. Computer Section - all services open 24 hours a day, every day:

a) Computer Security Room contains the Council's Master computers, except the Business Master—door opens to Tax Tenders' Cards only and a Tax Tender must be present whenever anyone else is.

b) Tax Office with a private office for the Head Tax Tender;

c) ID Room contains the machines necessary to make Cards, take People's identification and transmit by facsimile. Also contains the computer slave necessary to register and crossfile:

People's identification
E, A, B and C Numbers
Land Leases
Vehicles

and has the facility to switch voting computer slaves to *vote*, send results to Council television stations and to Central and ties into Library Central;

d) Storage Closet to securely store video tapes of copyrights, patents and FFTests;

e) Possession Room—door opens to Members' Cards only—contains Possession computer slaves to transact all stock market business, store Members' financial possessions and land leases; these slaves have a tax free tie-in to the Exchange configuration, but no tie-in to any Business configuration.

B. To guard and hold the element, Earth, in trust for the People by assigning each cohesive piece of land within the Council's boundaries a lease number (L123xxxx, 123 is the Neighborhood number), then selling the lease to the People or leasing it to Business and Central and cancelling the lease upon proof of *misuse of land*, upon the lease holder's death (except for one Homesteaded Lease) and upon nonpayment of lease fees. Upon application by a Member, the Bank and Lease Committee decides whether or not to combine parcels under one lease number and whether or not to split a parcel into several numbers. (*Misuse of Land* will be defined by Council Bill.)

C.   To determine land lease fees.

D.   To cancel a land lease if land use has been changed without application to the Bank and Lease Committee.

E.   To make and keep the element, Air, absolutely pollution free by cancelling leases whereon air is being polluted.

F.   To make and keep the element, Water, absolutely pollution free by cancelling leases whereon water is being polluted.

G.   To provide land leases without land lease fees to every Neighborhood within the Council's boundaries to make a Neighborhood Center.

H.   In Transportation Councils only: to provide fee free land leases on both sides of the Transcontinental Hiway to all Councils which apply to build a Way Station. The Station facility can be built by the Council or by the Transportation Council and leased for a fee.

I.   To supervise the Council Banking facility which;
   1.   leases computer slaves;
   2.   provides Neighborhoods with materials to build or improve a Neighborhood Center;
   3.   makes interest bearing land lease liens available to Members;
   4.   makes interest bearing business and agricultural loans available to Youths, Citizens and Members;
   5.   makes convertible Bank Shares available to the People and pays dividends on them at the rate of some percent of the Bank's banking, insurance and computer lease business—the percentage to be determined by Council Bill; these Bank Shares are stored by Members in the Possession configuration, by non-Members at the Bank and revert to the Council upon the death of the holder.
   6.   makes nonconvertible high paying life annuities available to Members and pays them weekly, the rate determined by a Bank Tender dependent on the Member's age and physical condition; these annuities are stored in the Possession configuration and payments stop upon the holder's death;
   7.   uses high paying life annuities to finance new public projects like Council Centers, Council Houses, public housing, Trainee housing, museums, water works, sewers, etc.
   8.   exchanges with Members low paying life annuities for presently held public debts—the limit which any Member can receive from this type of annuity is ₵1,000 per week and the interest rate on them will be

determined by Central Bill; they, too, are stored in the Possession computer and payments stop upon the holder's death;

9. allows Members to store savings without interest in the Possession computer; these go to the Council upon death;

10. builds:
    a) one Council House for every pride of 100 Youths registered in the Council with extra Council Houses in recreational areas—doors open to Youth Cards only—and supplies beds, but not bedding, kitchens with food and cooking equipment, two study rooms with TV set(s) and bath and toilet room(s);
    b) Council public housing with units for two, three and four People and collects the rentals;
    c) Trainee housing for about 2,000 Trainees in groups of 1,000;
    d) Council shops and laboratories—kinds to be determined by Council Bill;
    e) Council Library;
    f) Hospital and Mortuary complex;
    g) athletic field(s);
    h) two Council television stations.

11. decides upon a set of building codes for its area for electrical, plumbing and construction work. If an installation is found which doesn't conform to this code, it can be made the subject of a Challenge;

12. provides an investment advisory service;

13. pays the Senator, the Tenders and the expenses of Councilors when on Council business;

14. pays the Central Tenders whose E Numbers are registered in that Council;

15. transfers Credits from Council accounts to the Central account in the Council's Business Master computer weekly; number of Credits to be determined by the annual Central Budget Bill.

J. To supervise the Council Postal facility which:
    1. moves mail, parcel post and express between Council Center and the Council Way Station;
    2. sorts incoming mail and parcel post and express labels into Neighborhood bags and sorts outgoing mail, parcel post and express into Councils and foreign countries;
    3. builds a Way Station with its Council number on it to handle mail, parcel post and express on both sides of the nearest Transcontinental Hiway or leases the facility from the Transportation Council; this Way Station also accommodates passengers if it is located far from a Trans-

portation Council passenger station;

4. Transportation Councils only:
    transship mail, parcel post and express from Council Way Station to receiving Council Way Station for the same kilogram/kilometer rate throughout the RNA; rate to be determined by Central Bill; sending Councils pay at time of shipment from Way Station.

* * *

That the functions of Tax Tenders are:

A. To collect taxes from People at the time of purchase of articles or services for personal use, rates proportionate to the average of the individual consumer's income for the past 50 weeks—the more the amount added to an account in the Exchange Master computer, the higher the weekly tax rate, *One Time Exchanges* excepted. Rates to be determined by Council Bill.

B. To collect a weekly computer use fee from Business which is a percentage figured weekly of the amount in an account in any Business Master computer or a weekly slave computer lease fee, whichever is greater.

C. To operate, maintain, guard and repair the Council's computer configurations 24 hours a day, seven days a week. These configurations allow us to:
    1. exchange Credits among us under all circumstances including overseas and over the telephone;
    2. store Members' financial possessions;
    3. split our earnings with another person;
    4. pay our taxes without figuring anything;
    5. vote quickly and easily and have the votes tallied immediately;
    6. be counted;
    7. receive our weekly Shares automatically every Sunday starting at 0615 hours Central Standard Time;
    8. store our land leases and Homestead one;
    9. make *One Time Exchanges*;
    10. correct computer errors, if any;
    11. provide automatic cross-ties for the Council, the telephone company, local transportation, etc.;
    12. total the number of Credits in circulation weekly;
    13. store our vehicle numbers and make sure our vehicles are inspected and brought up to practically *as new* safety and pollution standards once a year or become the property of the Council in which they are found;
    14. as Members, perform transactions in the Possession Room assisted by a Tax Tender or Trainee, if necessary;

15. as Business People, perform transactions in the Business Room with assistance, if necessary;
16. have access to the information in the Library Central;
17. enforce the Right of Challenge and perform emergency notifications by limiting spending.

D. To run the ID Room.
E. To staff the Storage Closet.
F. To check the crossfile in Library Central to make certain the Member requesting to Homestead a lease has no Homesteaded land leases anywhere in the RNA before putting an H in front of the lease number.

* * *

That the functions of Justice Tenders are:
A. To operate the Fact Finders (FF's) so we can be assured that Principals tell the truth about what they did or agreed to do.
B. To show unerased FFTests to the People on television for their judgement.
C. To give the Media any information they want on FFTests that will be shown to the People after the Test has been made but never before.
D. To make special Fact Finders available with computer card punching facility to those wanting to provide classification information for the Central classification sorters.
E. To make Fact Finders available to those wanting a pay-off on an insurance policy.
F. To supervise Fact Finder Operators and make appointments for them.

* * *

That the functions of Education Tenders are:
A. To provide education for all Youths.
B. To staff Council Houses, laboratories, athletic fields, shops, libraries and Trainee housing.
C. To provide nourishing food to be cooked (or not) in Council Houses and Trainee housing.
D. To program two television stations (one of which can be operated in cooperation with other Councils) to use for:
    1. audio-visual courses for all ages;
    2. Fact Finder Tests for the People's Judgements;
    3. four hours a day of news broadcasts consisting mostly of news gathered by the Central Media Section;
    4. information on Council and Central Bills.
E. To sell work books to students requesting them for audio-visual courses

for the cost of printing plus ten percent.

F. To provide instruction courses on operating self-powered land vehicles and performing minor maintenance on them. If a Council so votes, to provide instruction and minor maintenance courses for aircraft, farm machinery, boats or any other vehicle.

G. To set up knowledge and reaction testing facilities for drivers (pilots, boat handlers and others if a Council so votes) so individuals in the Council can know how fast they can handle a vehicle under what conditions. When testing pilot knowledge, to be sure the pilot knows that airbuses have the right of way and clearance must be requested to cross an Intercontinental Hiway and that private planes must stay out of the landing and take-off patterns of commercial airports.

H. To provide the facilities for inter-Council meets in sports, games, flowers, beef, handcrafts and whatever else the Council's People are interested in and provide the Media with notices.

I. Provide special educational facilities for the types of jobs available in the Council. This can be done in cooperation with Business.

J. To accept requests for Learnees (Youths to assist Trainees) from Neighborhoods and Council facilities and post the requests in the Council Houses.

* * *

That the functions of Medical Tenders are:

A. To run the Council's Hospital-Mortuary complex including medical, dental and counselling services and charge according to a person's tax rate. These services can be prepaid by labor. Youths and Trainees—no charge.

B. To supervise health in the Council Houses, Trainee housing and public housing.

C. To provide medical advice and assistance to an FFOperator who feels a Principal has been drugged or otherwise conditioned to beat the FF.

D. To control epidemics: human, animal and plant.

E. To give information upon request about animal health and importation into the Council of plants and animals.

* * *

That the functions of Maintenance Tenders are:

A. To maintain all Council buildings.

B. To provide balanced distribution of water to the People in the Council and maintain the waterworks.

C. To provide pollution-free refuse and sewage disposal by operating a plant(s) or paying another Council to have it done, if the Council has no disposal facilities.

D. To provide testing facilities for self-powered land vehicles and staff the shops where they can be repaired by the owner or by the shop or sold. This function helps guard the element, Air, from pollution.

E. To provide vehicle and vehicle parts sales in the repair shops.

F. To maintain Council owned equipment including Fact Finders, all vehicles, computer slaves and shop and athletic equipment.

G. To provide free Peripheral and Direct bus service.

H. If the People in a Council so vote, to provide an airport with flight safety equipment for private aircraft with aircraft safety testing facilities and aircraft repair and sales shops.

I. If People in a Council so vote, to provide boat storage, repair, sales, testing and water safety facilities.

J. If the People in a Council so vote, to have farm machinery for rent and farm machinery repair shops.

K. To help Neighborhoods build their Neighborhood Centers.

* * *

That the function of Electrical Tenders is to provide and maintain pollution-free electrical power (fire) to the People generated, preferably, by small atomic generators. In low population areas, individual users may have to pay for distribution from Neighborhood Center to point of use. If an electricity user uses Council provided electrical power for the production of a product for sale, this user can be asked to pay the Council for the electricity. In a Transportation Council this function also provides and maintains the power for the electric roadway.

* * *

That each Council provides Field Committees and Tenders according to the Council's needs.

* * *

That the functions of the Port Committee in a Waterfront and Shore Council are:

A. To operate the Port of Entry which has an office open 24 hours every day with a:

1. Business Tender from Central to exchange Credits for other currency and vice versa;

2. Tourist Tender from Central to make Cards for incoming Tourists;

3. Council Port Tender to supervise Port Business and check foreign plants and animals.

B. In a Council which has water safety responsibility, to decide on water safety equipment and personnel needed to take care of things like boats in distress and life guards.
C. To make sure the Continental shelf within the Council boundaries is farmed, not mined.

* * *

That Councils which are part of a city containing two or more Councils choose one of the Councilors as City Administrator to cooperate with the other City Administrator(s) in hiring and firing the professional Tenders needed to run the communally provided services. The Neighborhood whose Representative was chosen will elect another Representative. The Council pays the City Administrator and its portion of the cost to run the city (including Tenders).

* * *

That Councils which produce a major portion of their economy from the earth have an Agricultural (Petroleum-Mining-Lumbering) and Marketing Committee which offers advisory services to producers and in cooperation with the Council Banking facility trades in commodity *Futures*. This dealing in *Futures* is not limited to their local Council.

* * *

That Councils which need extensive road and/or irrigation facilities have an Engineering Committee which is responsible for roads, irrigation, bridges, dams, etc.

* * *

That Transportation Councils have a Transcontinental Hiway Committee with Transcon Tenders who build and maintain Transcons including airports and airbus strips.

* * *

That Transportation Councils have a Transcon Facility Committee with Transport Tenders to:
A. provide passenger bus and airbus stations and passenger facilities at airports which make waiting for transportation a pleasure. If the Transportation Council includes an Intercontinental airport in its facilities, to provide the Port of Entry.
B. advise their Bank and Lease Committees on what sort of services are needed along their strip of Transcon.

C.   if the People in the Council so vote, to provide the buses and/or airbuses to travel the Transcon.

* * *

That Waterfront and Shore Councils which handle the ultimate disposal of waste products from *several* Councils higher in elevation than they are have a Water and Disposal Committee in charge of providing sewage treatment plants, waste recycling facilities and a desalination plant and pumping facility powered by atomic power to sell and deliver potable water.

* * *

That disputes between Councils can be handled by a Challenge between Senators or by Central Bill.

* * *

That Councils are the People's Business and intend to make a profit each year.

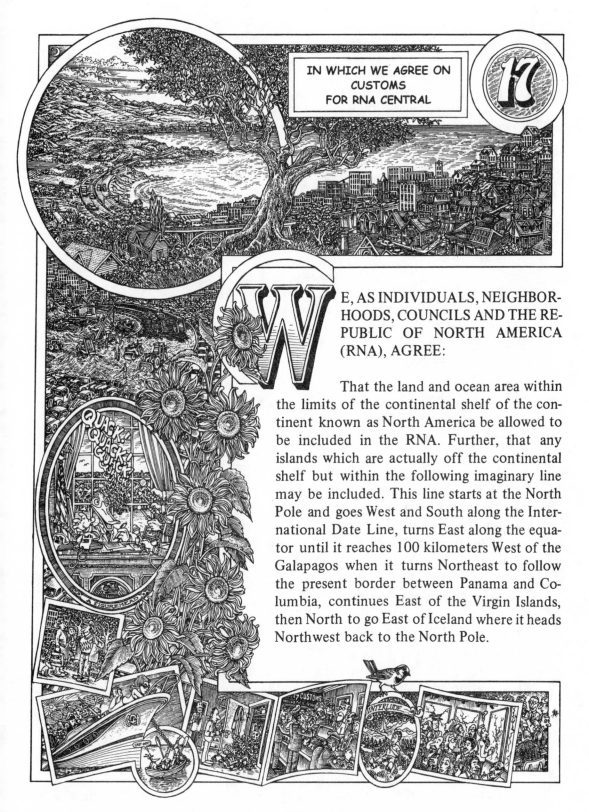

E, AS INDIVIDUALS, NEIGHBOR-HOODS, COUNCILS AND THE RE-PUBLIC OF NORTH AMERICA (RNA), AGREE:

That the land and ocean area within the limits of the continental shelf of the continent known as North America be allowed to be included in the RNA. Further, that any islands which are actually off the continental shelf but within the following imaginary line may be included. This line starts at the North Pole and goes West and South along the International Date Line, turns East along the equator until it reaches 100 kilometers West of the Galapagos when it turns Northeast to follow the present border between Panama and Columbia, continues East of the Virgin Islands, then North to go East of Iceland where it heads Northwest back to the North Pole.

To build a Central complex in the geographical center of the North American continent, this complex to: be accessible by air only; to operate its services on Central Standard Time, 24 hours a day, seven days a week, except for Senators and the stock market.

* * *

To divide the continent of North America into three sectors by drawing a line from the North Pole to Central and two more lines at 120 degrees from the first line.

* * *

To use the Central complex structure to give the People of the RNA the services Councils cannot provide. Many of these services will be determined by Central Bills and include the following:

1. Make agreements with foreign governments which must be ratified by the People before they are made and assist immigrants—number to be decided by Central Bills.
    (Foreign Contact Section, Speakers)
2. Aid Tourists, incoming and outgoing.
    (Foreign Contact Section, Tourist)
3. Patrol the boundaries of the RNA to insure continuing life in our ocean area and to intercept anything that might be shot at us in an unfriendly way. We assure the rest of Earth's People that those who do the patrolling will not cross RNA boundaries.
    (Boundary Patrol)
4. Provide an area called Coventry in each of the three sectors and build, operate, maintain and staff the services provided at the main gate of each Coventry and patrol its borders.
    (Boundary Patrol)
5. Lease from Councils areas to be designated as Psychiatric Care Centers (PCC's), build the facilities and patrol their borders.
    (Boundary Patrol)
6. Operate, maintain and staff the services needed in PCC's.
    (Education and Environment Section, Medical)
7. Lease from Councils areas designated as Continental Treasures and operate and maintain the facilities provided.
    (Environment Section - Treasure)
8. Furnish air transport for People and goods to and from Central.
    (Boundary Patrol)
9. Act as liaison between Councils with an eye toward the ecology of the

North American continent, including the continental shelf and the islands within RNA boundaries.
(Council Section)

10. Settle disputes between Councils.
(Council Section, Central Bill or Boundary Patrol)

11. Help Councils enforce the Right of Challenge.
(Justice Section)

12. Prepare Central Bills in simple language, worded so they can be answered Yes or No and with a definite time limit.
(All Sections)
Also, disseminate information concerning them.
(Media Section)

13. Balance Council economies so the same basic standard of living can be experienced throughout the RNA and reimburse the Council the Credits it pays to Central Tenders.
(Council and Business Sections)

14. Count the total number of Credits weekly so we can maintain the same number of them in circulation.
(Business Section)

15. Balance imports with exports every week.
(Business Section)

16. Collect complete, unbiased news from all over the world and make this news available to Councils and pass on complete, unbiased RNA news to foreign countries upon request.
(Media Section)

17. Provide extension schools in the 75 or so largest of Earth's cities for Citizens to continue their education.
(Education Section)

18. Provide and operate a classification sorter to match requests for Trainees with requests for assignments.
(Classification Section)

19. Help keep the primary agreement made between RNA Business and RNA People: that Business is self-governing and the People are self-governing and neither will govern the other except:
    a) that Business makes and enforces the Rules of Order in its plants, complexes and locations;

b)   that Business and People agree on the following job shifts throughout the RNA (or others as worked out by Business and employee in special cases):
- from 0600 to 1600 hours on three consecutive days, two per week,
- from 1600 to 0200 hours on three consecutive days, two per week,
- from 0200 to 0600 hours on six consecutive days for maintenance,
- from 0600 to 1600 hours, on Sunday,
- from 1600 to 0200 hours, on Sunday,
- from 0200 to 0600 hours, on Sunday.

c)   that a Job is a contract between employer and employee;

d)   to pay employees by the acceptable unit completed method wherever possible;

e)   that People in Business use their personal Exchange accounts to pay for articles and services not directly connected with their Businesses, thus paying the Council's tax—vendors responsible;

f)   that Businesses provide thorough operating and minor maintenance instructions on articles sold to People;

g)   that corporations are not required to give voting privileges to non-employee held stock shares;

h)   that Business charge the People no interest; installment buying is made possible by assigning differing prices to the article being sold dependent on how long the buyer takes to pay for it;

i)   that Business owns the article until it is paid for;

j)   that Business use the Business computer configurations provided by the Councils and Central as an interface between People's Credits and Business;

k)   that Business has no connection with the Possession computer configuration and pays dividends to Members through the Central Business computer and that all corporation shares offered to Members are bought and sold through the Councils' Possession configurations which are directly tied to the computerized stock market at Central;

l)   that Business allows the Central Business Office to regulate imports and exports so the two balance weekly;

m)   that Business allows no pollution;

n)   that Business makes no guns shorter than 76 centimeters;

o)   that whenever Business uses a patent or copyright it pays the holder ten percent of the gross profit or ten percent of the retail price.

p)   that Business agrees to limit its profit structure to approximately twenty percent net.

20. That the telephone company is a Special Business, a combination of government (giving the People what they want) and Business (with shares on the stock market). This Special Business makes certain agreements with the People:
    a) that the telephone company provides all wire and microwave services as requested by Central and bills Central at cost plus ten percent;
    b) that the telephone company provides an office near each Council Center and works with the Tax Committee and Tax Tenders to provide the Council, the Neighborhood and the People with total communication and computer service, some with recording facilities at cost plus ten percent;
    c) that the telephone company may receive Trainees, if available, to assist it in providing the People's services;
    d) that the telephone company also works with Business; however they agree between them.
21. Write Central Bill(s) so the definition of *pollution* can be decided by vote. (Environment Section)

22. Build and maintain a Library computer with all the information requested by Central Bill and to include:
    a) a file of all audio-visual tapes,
    b) patents and copyrights,
    c) census information.
    d) registration of all vehicles and annual inspection data,
    e) information and data for Business and agriculture,
    f) environmental information and data.
    (Computer Section)
23. Set up and maintain a relay network which ties in a Council's Master computers to the same kind of Master computers in all other Councils, the Possession Masters to the stock market computer at Central, certain computer slaves to Library Central and to Numbers Central, special Tourist slaves to their Masters at Central and computer slaves overseas to Council Master computers.
    (Computer Section)
24. Provide 12 Tourist Exchange Masters and 12 Tourist Numbers Masters with computer slaves.
    (Business and Computer Sections)

the Velvet MonkeyWrench

25. Make environmental investigations the People approve by Central Bill and propose investigations of our environment to the People.
(Environment Section)
26. Operate the Central Complex.
(Central Plant Section)

* * *

That the definition of government in the RNA is: the science and the art of finding out what the People want, then helping them do it.

YOU SEE how all this was done? I constructed it in my mind, wrote it down, then checked it out with the sharpest people in as many fields as I could find: people who feel as well as think, who dig it where they are and are ready for change. This makes this book not completely mine but then, I never thought it could be. For example, the sharpest con artist I know read it to see if she could beat the computer system. She could, so together we plugged the holes. The same with a psychologist, a businessman, a couple of lawyers (who didn't even feel bad), just a lot of people and now, as I write this, the structure proposed by the Velvet Monkey Wrench has taken shape.

How to get from here to there is what this Segment is about. There is no intent to overthrow anything and substitute one ideology for another. The intent is to have a system in

221

which any ideology can flourish as long as it has a majority among a thousand people: to open our heads to an **inclusive way of thinking**.

The population of the continent of North America will soon be 340,000,000. The people in the United States and Canada speak English mostly, as they do in Jamaica and Belize. Canada has a large French speaking population, Haitians speak French and practically all other North Americans speak Spanish, except Icelandic in Iceland and Danish in Greenland where they also speak English. We can guess at a language split like 245 million English speakers, 100 million Spanish and about 12 million French. This adds up to more than 340 million because some people speak more than one language. The more languages a person speaks, the more adaptable. So, English, French and Spanish are the official languages of the RNA and this book will come in those three flavors.

Fortunately for our venture of trying to change all of North America into a boundariless space where we can all wander, work and live with permission needed from none, practically all of the countries claim to embrace the principle of voting for those who run the government. This means that an honest majority should be able to have the say about what *kind* of government it wants. People who read this book will either dig it or not. If over half of the voters dig it, we can go ahead and install the new system wriggling out of the old one like a snake sheds its skin. It doesn't skinlessly leave the old one behind, but waits until it has a new, shiny, though thin and tender one underneath.

Let's say more and more people do like these ideas and there are between 20 and 30 million books sold, the design sections have done their jobs: the Council boundaries are drawn, VMW, Inc., has actually built demonstration models of the Fact Finder and some of the computers. This would be the time to elect more members of all the Legislative Houses. In Mexico, the PRI would have to become convinced as members of this party are usually the only ones on the ballot and there are probably other little hookers. Canada might be a little conservative and the *strong men* or power groups that run some of the other North American countries might not want to give up their power right away. If countries like Iceland and Belize decide to join, it will be really easy for them because they come in as a Council and wouldn't need to do much changing. From here on out I will talk only about the United States. It is here that these ideas must have a firm hold as the geographical center of the RNA falls in this country and I think a majority might be easier to get here than elsewhere.

At the same time that people are trying to get on ballots, we can all start looking around our Neighborhoods, maybe even get some of our neighbors to meet and discuss what sorts of Rules of Order we'd come up with if given our choices. Write for the map of the Councils, see what kind of Council your Neighborhood would be in. Now is the time to object to any boundaries by writing Section 1 and stating your reasons. Every suggestion will be read and compared to one that came before to determine which makes the most sense. If a Neighborhood can get it together and decide it really wants to be a Neighborhood, draw your boundaries on the Council map. OK? Neighborhood boundaries will be determined by agreement within the Council.

One thing we might try to do is increase the number of representatives in the USA to about 1,000 so there would be one of them for every 200,000 people (does this figure suggest anything?). The Constitution of the USA clearly states that "the number of representatives shall not exceed one for every 30,000." The number of representatives was frozen at 435 for the entire country back in 1912 which makes for like 400,000 people to a representative...why? My guess is they didn't want to build a bigger building. With one representative for every 200,000 people we could try to get our Council boundaries accepted for the new apportionment and the changeover would be a breeze. But I'm going to assume we cannot change the number of representatives without a lot of hassle, so now what?

Step 1

Elect enough Representatives and Senators so people with these ideas have a majority in the U.S. Congress.

Step 2

Elect the President and Vice-President of the USA. The campaign is simple. If two brave, sharp people will volunteer for these jobs, their candidacy will be announced in the comic book and by other means so people will know who they are. Who they are will be obvious, though, if they never expose themselves, on TV even, much less shake a bunch of hands and kiss a bunch of babies. The rest of us who agree with these ideas go to the polls and vote for them and see if we are in the majority. I am assuming that everyone will act in a civilized manner and allow the majority of the voters to decide how they want to live their lives. If we don't have a majority the first time, four years later we can try again with the same or different candidates. After our candidates are inaugerated, we will divide the next four years into two parts: one year to set up the new foundations and the following three years to build the structure of the new system with money and protection furnished by the old umbrella.

Step 3

Security. From election day on, the new President, Vice-President and members of their families and their staffs will need a secure area in which to work and live. According to the Constitution, providing this protection is the task of the Treasury Department, the one that will exist the longest period of time as the new system causes old bureaus to fade out. Secret Service agents will first be given, then be taught to give, the short form FFTest, like one question: "Have you agreed with yourself or others to harm the President, Vice-President, etc.?" If the answer is negative and the machine doesn't buzz, that person can enter the secure area.

This circle of protection must be increased until the members of Congress, the Cabinet, the Media and the other people needed to do the work have room to move about. Security has to be as absolute as pollution control. When the cordon of protection includes all of the government parts of Washington, that's far enough.

Step 4

Call in the Joint Chiefs of Staff, give each a short FFTest at the perimeter and if one intends harm, tell that one to go home. Under no circumstances allow weapons in the area, anyway. At this meeting, tell them to gather all the army, navy, air force, marines inside the RNA boundaries described and divide themselves into three equal groups, one for each sector. Tell them to make plans to patrol their sectors and give them the Boundary Patrol design section's published recommendations. Ask them how long and how much it will take to get the required Psychiatric Care Center and Coventry areas going. They'll also need to present a plan for carrying cash from Washington to each Council.

Right here in Step 4 there could be a detour. The heads of the Army, etc., might decide we're all crazy and that it's up to them to save us from ourselves by taking over. They have the weapons and they may try. It has happened before in countries of our acquaintance and the military can make a mess of things like you wouldn't believe. If we don't see the face of our new President on telly every day, we might start shouting a bit, but do nothing.

Total action with inaction as its tool has proven to be The weapon against tyranny. Don't refuse to do anything, just require total supervision to do it. Get your money together and don't spend it. Don't wave any flags...that's Their game and one for which They made the rules. Above all, don't stand out, especially in groups. Feed yourselves but not them. Stall paying for anything that gives them revenue. By this time, remember, we have a true majority and the soldiers, etc., are 90% young and to keep bunches of People policed it takes a lot of soldiers...the reason I'm writing about this possibility at all is that if it should happen, we would all be prepared to do nothing except feed and keep ourselves warm and not freak.

There could be other forms of this detour, but sooner or later the President we want will be duly installed and we can proceed. If a detour such as this violated a bunch of people, our majority would probably be even greater when we hit the main road.

Step 5

Call a joint session of Congress and ask for the money to build Central according to the design section's plans. When this bread has been voted, the plans for
Central will be handed over to the military Corps of Engineers along with the
site location and they go off to work. They can hire whatever private contractors they need and pay them at cost plus ten percent. We have a year in which
to build Central: the plant, the computer buildings, the runways and equipment.
The Central computers and relay net components can now be ordered from the
lowest bidders. They will work all shifts to have Central computers ready to be
installed within the year. The military can be constructing their three sector
bases at Central at the same time. Some savvy reporters can stick around the
Central site to let the people know how it progresses.

Step 6

A most important one. At this point in time, the new President has done two
things (called the Joint Chiefs and the joint session of Congress) and it would be
silly to cause a lot of chaos by doing too much. Keep the thing together the way
it was. The system has wobbled along for many years and will continue to do
so during this period of change. The approved Cabinet members can take up
their jobs and run the bureaus the way they've been run. People are asked to
live as before and stay at their jobs as long as there's something to do. Make
sure everyone is warm and fed.

Income and other taxes will still need to be paid and the Internal Revenue
and tax payment enforcement agencies will continue to operate. We'll need this
bread so Congress can vote to keep things going as before, with some exceptions.
Any money being spent outside the RNA like foreign aid and CIA funds should
be cancelled along with Mars probes and holes through the earth but keep the
foreign services going awhile. The Department of Defense will need its money
to reorganize into the Boundary Patrol, set up their facilities at Central and establish Psychiatric Care Center and Coventry areas. The rule of thumb for
money voted by Congress is: If it heads in the RNA direction, fund it, if it
doesn't, don't. Like continue the farm programs that increase the production
and distribution of food and cancel those paying for nonproduction. Keep paying whatever money people have been receiving like government salaries, social
security, veterans payments and school and medical aid until the Councils can
take over. Keep the post office and transportation systems the way they are for
now. Remember: **mistakes *must* be made so we can learn from them.**

Don't worry about Business. They will have a copy of the book and will be
making changes right along, probably very efficiently. The market in bonds and
mortgages will undoubtedly head for the cellar but the stock market will prob-

ably be doing its regular thing as people try to convert what bonds and stuff they have to stock shares. Insurance, loan and mutual fund companies will probably be working to put their wealth into the hands of their individual policy and share holders, then shut down. Business will be creating a structure that will allow it to continue to make a profit in the new system. Congress can stop subsidizing any Business. A Business which needed to be subsidized in the old system sure as hell cannot last in the new one. Businesses which are eliminated by the new system will be laying off their people giving the new ones a tremendous labor pool to pick from. The telephone company, computer and FF manufacturers, for example, will be operating on all Shifts. Business will be busy changing its shift hours and cleaning up its pollution scene. The last microgram of mercury will be allowed to leave any plant on Change Day. Change Day is the day one year from the day we mail the letter in Step 7. If an industry cannot learn to sell everything that comes out of its plant by then, it will have to shut down. Changing will be hard but they'll be better off. Parties might be fewer but I bet the booze flows on.

Keep the perimeter around governmental functions secure and don't fuss too much about Business and the military. They'll both be reorganizing.

Row, but don't rock the boat. There's a year in which to get ready.

Step 7

The new President writes a letter, gets it approved by both Houses of Congress, phones the heads of the other RNA countries and invites them to a conference to find out where they're at about signing the letter. The letter is signed by the agreeing heads of RNA states, duplicated and mailed overseas to the rest of the world's countries. Like:

Dear Head of State:

With the advent of atomics, the computer and an enlightened electorate, we, the People of the United States, _____, _____, _____ and _____ and maybe _____ are preparing to change the definition of government. Please read the enclosed book. What we ask of you is tolerance and time while we set it up and get it running without any prime emergencies caused by you. We ask you to add up all the things we owe you (currency excepted) and the things you owe us, like lend lease and other loans, and Subtract. If we owe you, we'll pay you in gold and silver and if you owe us, it's OK, we'll call it even. Collect the currency you hold from the countries listed above and we'll buy it back using gold and silver.

In a year our Ambassadors and Consuls will be replaced by Speakers to keep communications open between us. These Speakers are direct representatives of the People and all questions put to them must be answered by the People, so word your questions in simple language that can be answered Yes or No.

We ask you to notify your People who wish to remain citizens of your country to leave the RNA before the end of the year except for foreign service and authorized media personnel. For the next three years our facilities for receiving ships, planes and people will be a mess while we are computerizing and making our Ports of Entry as efficient and automatic as possible. Expect no tourism or trade with us for the same three year period. We will try to handle emergencies but will need all our resources to make the change. At the end of the three years we will open our new facilities and begin trade with you once again—with a difference. We will not be able to withstand an imbalance of trade. Tourism, too, will begin after the three years and you will be welcomed. Your children under 19 years old will be able to come and tour practically free.

Our collective Armed Forces are being grouped together and renamed the Boundary Patrol and will remain within the boundaries outlined on the enclosed map. We are not claiming this ocean as territory, only the land and continental shelf areas. The ocean is free for all to use, but the Boundary Patrol will stop any garbage dumping, porpoise killing or other misuses of natural resources within the outlined boundary. We are going to learn about the ocean (and our land) so it can provide for the people forever rather than for a limited time and we expect you to respect what we are trying to do. To this end, we ask you to stay out of this area for the three year period while we evaluate and explore the possibilities of our undersea resources. We ask, but do not insist. If you feel a hardship is being imposed upon you by not entering the area, please apply to the Boundary Patrol Sector Commander for permission to enter before entering.

We promise that we will never by word or deed try to convince you that our system should be adopted or even adapted by others.

Sincerely and love,

_____for the People of the
United States

_____for the People of_____

Enclosures: map, copy of VMW   _____for the People of_____
                                                           etc.

Step 8

The following notice will be printed once a week in newspapers and posted in Embassies and Consulates; anywhere Citizens of RNA countries would be likely to see it:

ALL PASSPORT HOLDERS OF THE FOLLOWING UNDERSIGNED NORTH AMERICAN COUNTRIES SHOULD RETURN TO THE CONTINENT OF NORTH AMERICA IF THEY WISH TO BE CITIZENS OF THE RNA. Any person not within the boundaries of the RNA by _____, _____ (a year from the day the letter was mailed) will have to go through the immigration procedure to become a Citizen, but persons born in North America can always immigrate.

> (signed:)
> for the People of the U.S.A.
>
> for the People of _____
>
> for the People of _____
>
> etc.

Leave space at the bottom for adding countries.

All expatriots, please don't get shook. No one is going to force you to live in the RNA if you prefer Paris or Samarkand but you should return if you want to take care of your bread and your identification. Once you have your Card, you can split, if you have enough money to live in your Shangri-La. You will even receive your Share as soon as the system is installed and operating. However, if your income depends on our economy, stay and help us get swinging before you take off again. You get to decide.

Three years, eh? That's about the length of time I figure it will take to get our computers installed and running. At the same time as we're taking these three years, the other countries in the world will be adjusting themselves to the idea that we in the RNA are going to totally mind our own business and allow them to mind. theirs. This is a short time—really.

Step 9

Congress funds money for the Council computer configurations. Get the specifications and bids from the design sections, then ask Congress for the money to provide every Council in the RNA at this time with the following starter kit. This money will be paid back to Central by the Councils.

1. The Exchange, Small Business, Possession and Numbers Master computers.
2. 800 Exchange-Small Business-Direct (ESD) computer slaves: one for each Neighborhood Center, some for Council Center, the rest for shopping areas and industry.
3. Ten Exchange-Direct (ED) computer slaves for Council facilities.
4. Two Possession-Direct (PD) computer slaves for the Bank.
5. Two Exchange-Direct-Voting (EDV) computer slaves for each Neighborhood Center and three at Council Center.
6. About 2000 Exchange-Small Business-Credit (ES¢) slaves.
7. About 1000 radio operated ESR computer slaves and 1000 E¢R's.
8. One Numbers-Direct (ND) computer slave, 10 Card making machines, 10 ID machines and recorders.
9. Installation, connections and wiring provided by the Telephone Company plus an Exchange-Small Business-Telephone (EST) slave for every Neighborhood Order Office and one for all Council facilities. All new telephone hookups will use Exchange-Credit-Telephone (E¢T) instruments and these will eventually replace old telephones.

The first things we'll need are the Card making machines and ID recorders which are simple to make, but we will have needed ten shipped to each Council yesterday. As the other things are completed, they can be inspected and stored in a shed at the Central site at first and later shipped directly to the Councils.

Step 10

Establish provisional Council Centers. The people in each Council need to decide where their Center is to be. Where possible, vote by Neighborhoods: get your Neighborhood together and find the majority decision, then choose a person to meet with other people from the other Neighborhoods and talk it out. Use the newspapers and television stations to let People know what's happening. Remember, the location can be changed, just agree on a place for now.

What are needed are rooms for the ID equipment, the Card making machines, recording equipment and video tape storage. When this stuff comes, get it installed and working, registering people 24 hours a day. We'll also need right next door, cashiers' windows and facilities for paying Shares to People. These cashiers will be the very first Bank Tenders...people we can trust with cash.

With the three items installed and working, Congress, through the Treasury Department, will start to supply enough dollars to pay a weekly Citizen's Share to every Youth and Citizen plus two thirds of a Share per Child to Women with one or two Children registered in that Council. At the same time, the Federal Bureaus will stop other money headed to people in your Council, except Social Security and Veterans payments. This Share money will not be paid back by the Councils.

Registration is easy. It requires nothing but your existence—no papers, no passport, no birth certificate, just you—down at the provisional Council Center. Watch TV to find out when, probably different sun signs on different days. All you need to know is your sun sign and your birth year. Those who start all this will have as part of their E Numbers the Council of Registration number instead of their Council of birth number and the next four digits show the order in which you were registered in that Council under your sign in your birth year. OK?

There can be some cheating at this point with people registering in more than one Council or saying they are 12 when they are really 11. You'll get a Card with whatever information you supply on it. People are so used to the old system, they don't realize the new one can trip them up. In fact, the weekly Share will be really needed by some people who are out of work due to changes in Business, so if you are working, getting Social Security, Veterans money or dividends, just register—get your ID taken and your E Number on a Card—but don't bother to wait in line each week for your Share. Please note: there is no way this Share can be taken from you for old debts, old committments.

Just present your new Card to a Cashier at Council Center once a week and get paid. The Cashier will probably make a slip with your Card using photosensitive paper, have you put your thumbprint on the slip and give you cash. The Boundary Patrol will transport this cash to the Councils once a week and will help keep order. 200,000 possibles queed up waiting for their money could be something else. As soon as three-fourths of the Councils in any State or Province are set up, the Treasury will stop Federal aid to that State as an impetus to get the other Councils moving.

Step 11

Congress appropriates money for Fact Finders. You can see that many of these Steps are really taking place at the same time but it takes distances to write them out. Order enough FF's so each Council can have one for starters, then two, then more as they are finished and needed. Remember, we are still using the laws and enforcement procedures from the old system.

Step 12

Organization of Councils into Neighborhoods. This Step has already been going on, but now it's time to set up a provisional Order Office and choose a Representative, an Order Tender and an Education Tender. As less and less People are employed, they can volunteer to help keep Order. This is a good time to test which rules are easy to keep, which ones tough and which ones impossible. Fire prevention and putting out procedures will need to be thought about and set up. This time may be one of decision for a lot of people: "Is this where I really want to live right now?" The people in certain Neighborhoods may be too strict or too loose or too tough and you may want to wander around looking for a place where the people are more like you, so you can be part of the majority and thus be truly franchised.

The Education Tender won't have much to do as Children are still going to school. It's the law, remember.

Once the Representatives have been chosen, all the Councilors become members of the Bank and Lease Committee. There are still City, County and State agencies around with their particular axes to grind so Councilors keep their own counsel but elect one of themselves to be Senator.

Step 13

The Bank and Lease Committee assigns a number to each Neighborhood, then to each cohesive piece of land in the Council. Once a Neighborhood has a number, this Committee sets up in the temporary Order Office and asks each property owner in the Neighborhood to bring their deeds. The Committee needs a large, accurate aerial survey map with room to write seven digits on each parcel. (A three digit Neighborhood number and a four digit parcel number.) As the Committee assigns a number to a deed, it writes the number on the deed and on the map and assigns the lease to the deed holder. It also makes a note of the property taxes paid on the land and improvements and makes that figure the Land Lease Fee to be paid to the Council the following year and makes a note of any mortgages.

This Committee also assigns numbers to parcels held by Business, tells Business to fence its lease and guard it. Their Fees, too, will be the same as their property taxes were. In a Council with land owned by the Federal government, the parcel is assigned a number and held for lease to Central. State, County and City land will be given a number with no assigned lease for now. All deeds and ownership papers will be honored.

One of the things this Committee does is provide a lease on which each Neighborhood will have its Center. This land is probably State, County, City or Federal land at this time, so wait.

Step 14

Temporary voting channels are set up. The people of the RNA will have dozens of things to decide in the first weeks of operation. As soon as each Neighborhood has a Representative we can begin to vote using pieces of paper. Write the Bill number then Yes or No and drop it into the basket provided for that Bill number. These will have to be hand counted. The Representative will take the totals to provisional Council Center and drop the totals by Bill number into the baskets provided. After these are hand counted, the totals are phoned to Washington. Don't worry about People voting more than once. There will be so much voting and counting going on, we'll do well to vote once per Bill. Remember, Bills can be changed by another vote.

Step 15

Second Joint Chiefs Meeting. As soon as we receive a reply to our letter from a country, we will disconnect any ICBM's or other systems of attack aimed at it until, hopefully, they are all disarmed. We could disarm earlier, but I feel we'd get a lot of static from the *old guard*. Systems of defense must be explained to the People and to Congress so both can vote on which ones to keep.

The military clearly state their plans for patrolling the boundaries, money carrying and building Coventry and PCC areas. These plans must be approved by vote of the People (new system) and by Congress (old system). If the Coventry area location(s) as delineated by the design section are not yet part of the RNA, we can use smaller areas temporarily until they are.

Once their plans are approved, the Boundary Patrol can start to patrol the boundaries of the RNA as they exist at the moment as well as the future ocean boundaries. Any travel or trade restrictions made by North American countries which are not yet part of the RNA will be enforced by those countries. The Patrol's jobs along these borders are to be friendly and allow war materials to go in neither direction.

Military civilian personnel won't be needed any more and they can go home. Those who are in the military and wish to leave can do that and the Patrol can fill any gaps with regular enlistment procedures: no conscription desired or needed. Those people who make up the Boundary Patrol can start figuring their three years Service toward Membership the day the Bills are passed and there is a Boundary Patrol. They will be paid according to the old.scale and won't need their Shares until they have formed into Councils and have their computer set-ups. Actually, the Boundary Patrol might be a well fed, warm place to spend the next three years.

Step 16

Further Council organization. The first available Fact Finders go to the Councils which have their temporary Centers, are registering their people and contain a prison, mental hospital or institution of correction—anywhere there is a bunch of people behind bars for some reason or other. When the FF arrives, the Councilors will form a Justice Committee, hire a Head Justice Tender and post a notice at the Center, like: "The Fact Finder is here. Those interested in learning how to operate it, please come to _____." The Head Justice Tender will be trained to use the FF by the supplier, then choose people from among the volunteers as Trainees. These Trainees will ask permission from the authorities to give the inmates copies of this book so they can know what's happening. The inmates' cases will be the ones used by aspiring FFOperators to learn how. Trainees will go through the files, try to find the other Principal involved in the case and, using the FF, make a video tape right there in the institution. Failing to locate the other Principal, the Trainee will try to get another person familiar with the case (like the prosecuting attorney) to sit in the other chair. If no one can be found who knows anything about the case, the one Principal will have to tell the story. These tapes can be played to the people right away using time bought from the commercial TV Channels if the present state, county or whatever authorities are amenable. If these authorities won't cooperate, the tapes can be stored until the end of the year and shown to the People in the new Action-Consequence, no law society.

When a Council's cages are empty with the freed ones back in society or helping to build PCC and Coventry areas, we can all breathe the biggest sign of relief heard the world around—ever. We are never again going to force a human to live in a cage. Even a homicidal maniac will be given a key and thus the choice of staying locked in or of joining other homicidal maniacs wandering around the PCC.

During this year of preparation we have to start using the new system as much as possible even though it is overlaid by the old one. The amount the new system can be used will be different from Council to Council. It depends on how liberated the state and county is, how many People who agree with these ideas there are in the old government and in which branch. As soon as an FF is set up in a Council Center, start to use it using a cash register instead of a computer slave. Challenge whenever and wherever you can. All it costs is bread. Trainees can ask all Challengers and Challengees: "Did you register twice?" as one of the practice questions. The more experience Trainee FFOperators have, the better they'll serve Justice.

Step 17

Law enforcement agencies and fire departments. If you are a part of this type of public service and like what you're doing, you'll have to find a new way to operate. At the end of the year your public funding will stop and these services will become Businesses. It's possible that the Council will allow your new business to use the same buildings and equipment you've been using. Get the design section's recommendations. Don't you think *Rent-a-Cop* and *detective agency* sound better than *pig*?

Step 18

Banks. We are trying to make this change without anyone losing anything, money included. Banks shuffle enormous amounts of paper; paper that is mainly of two kinds: Business and Personal. The general idea is to split money into two categories: put taxable money (to be stored later in the E and P configurations) into one bank and tax free money into another (S and B configurations), so the Councils will have a source of income as soon as the old tax structure is dismantled.

Each Council will need a Personal bank and it can have branches. If a regular bank won't offer its facilities, a Council will use a building like a warehouse or something and make it secure until the Post Office-Bank is built. It will need to be big enough for about 100,000 accounts. The Bank and Lease Committee will choose the first Bank Tenders from among the people who agree with these ideas and are working in banks or as Cashiers.

When the Council Personal Bank is open for business everyone in the Council who is using banks will divide their financial paper into the two types and put their personal mortgages, loans, savings and checking accounts into the Personal bank and their business loans, mortgages, etc., into a Business bank. Personal Banks will be open A, B, C and D Shifts in order to handle all this work.

From Change Day on, Business banks will handle no cash, so when you want to deposit cash into your Business account, you'll have to do it at the Personal bank and they'll credit the cash to your account in a Business bank. When you're paid a salary, it will be by check on a Business Bank which you can cash at any Personal bank and pay your rate of tax on it right then. If you deposit the check, you pay your rate of tax every time one of your checks is cleared by the bank. Dividends will be cashed by Personal banks only. When you pay for articles to sell or materials used to make something for sale, you'd pay for them by check drawn on your account in a Business bank—no tax. We won't actually start to pay the Council taxes until Change Day.

Your tax rate between Change Day and computerization is up to you to figure out. Add your income for the past fifty weeks and divide by fifty, then look on the bulletin board in the Personal bank to find out your rate and tell a banker so it can be marked on your account. People living on their Shares only don't pay any taxes until the computers are installed and working.

This separating process may be slow at first but will accelerate as computerization approaches. It has to be complete before a Council's computers can be activated.

Step 19

Weekly Share payments move to the Neighborhood. When a Neighborhood has its temporary Order Office and voting setup working, its Representative can go to Council Center and tell the Head Cashier that the Neighborhood is ready to have Shares paid out of the Order Office. Each week thereafter until computerization, a Cashier will arrive with the cash (probably escorted by members of the Boundary Patrol) and pay the people their Shares. If you have a job, you are entitled to your Share, but you'll be asked not to take it unless you need it until your Council's computers are working.

Those who are 18 years old or more and have managed to hang on to a job with industry, government, farming, in a store or wherever, or are self-employed, will be considered to be Trainees by notifying their Order Tenders of their employment and after three years become Members. Those who do not have jobs or are not working on their own are potential Trainees. All they have to do to be a Trainee is ask for work once a week when they pick up their Shares at the Order Office, then do what they're asked to do. If the Representative or two Tenders have no work for a person to do, that person is still considered to be a Trainee working toward Membership just for asking for work.

When you have worked or asked for work for one year or for four three-month periods, you'll get a Service number digit and one third of a Citizen's Share dollar increase (or Credit increase, if the computers are installed and activated). At the end of the four years, there is no reason why everyone 21 years old or over should not be a Member. There will be no free rides to Membership. Even those over 65 and blind should ask for work once a week if they want to be Members. People confined in Vets Hospitals or otherwise disabled will become Members at the end of the third year of being registered which will be done as soon as we are organized to take the ID equipment to them or bring them to the ID equipment. All jobs with the new government will run on the new Shift hours. It's very important that we don't wear ourselves out making these changes—30 hours a week is enough.

Step 20

Council TV stations. As soon as a Council's Bank and Lease Committee sees that its jobs of parcel numbering and bank separating are well under way, the Councilors will split off another Committee: Education. This Committee heads off into the wilds of television land. With money from Federal programs like school aid, the Committee will hire the Head Education Tender who gets a UHF channel and begins with the news and video tapes of Challenges, then adds audio-visual courses with work books, according to the design section's plans. If there's no way to get a UHF channel, time can be bought from a regular commercial station for a while. If everyone in the Council kicks in a buck, this would probably be enough to pay for a UHF station using all tapes (no studios, cameras or all that expensive gear) and volunteer (Trainee) help.

Step 21

Preparing to pay our public debts. Since the first public bond issue, people have been brainwashed into accepting the idea that we can have whatever we want now; a waterworks, a school, a war and pay for them later. Who pays for them later? Someone in the future, that's who. It does seem that if we keep increasing the tax load of our grandchildren, they will at some point like maybe tomorrow, say, "Up yours," refuse to pay and flush any dreams of an orderly civilization down the drain. One of the biggest *earthquakes* we could have could result from everybody refusing to pay their bills and their taxes. As a continent, we can change from *have today, let someone else pay for it tomorrow* to *pay as we go* by paying the actual people who loan us the money, the people who buy Council annuities. Since these annuities retire upon the holder's death, the debt cannot continue. This idea takes care of future loans but we have the problem of past loans to deal with here. We must convert old public debts into annuities that can be paid off in one generation. Because of the variety of presently held debts the Finance design section will figure out how to handle each kind for an equitable program of repayment. Starting on Change Day, we can pass Central Bills according to this section's recommendations to determine interest rates, time to convert limits, etc. Thus the people will actually decide.

The basic idea is that we are going to exchange low interest rate, nontransferable Council life annuities which will pay the holder an income until death for public debts held by Members. This means that government bonds, for example, will have to be held by individuals. As corporations will no longer be considered to be individuals, those corporations holding bonds will have to get them into the hands of individuals before they can be converted to Council annuities. It seems to me that anyone who makes ₵1,000 a week from this conversion wouldn't be suffering.

From Change Day until the day you become a Member all you can do is fondle your certificates indicating public debt, then, on the day you become a Member, you can convert these certificates to low paying Council annuities in the manner and amounts determined by Central Bill and receive your weekly income from them in Credits. Your three years start as soon as you register and either work or ask for work.

Some proportion of our public debt will be owed to individuals, companies and corporations in countries outside of the RNA. This part of our debt would show up on the plus side for the country in which it's held when the Great Subtraction is made to determine whether we owe them or they owe us. If we owe them, we'll pay the government. The individual, company and/or corporation can apply to its government for payment. If the country ends up owing us, we won't ask for payment but that government will be responsible to pay its citizens who hold the debt. Our cash debts (currency and checks written against our banks) will have priority over other public debts. If our gold and silver reserves aren't enough to redeem all currency and pay all debts, we will mine gold and silver until they are.

Step 22

The corporate position. The year before Change Day is the last year corporations will have to pay taxes. After Change Day they can use this money to eliminate pollution made by their plants and to learn how to make a profit in an ecologically oriented society.

When the Central computers are installed, the buying and selling of shares will be transferred from the stock exchanges to the Market Central (MC) computer, but from Change Day until Members can transfer stock certificates into their Possession accounts, corporations will pay dividends, if any, by check which can be cashed or deposited at a Personal bank only. During these years corporations will be selling or transferring corporation held shares to individuals who can then store them in Possession Masters when they become Members.

Step 23

Social Security, Veteran, other government retirement funds. The thing here is to pay everyone what's due them by giving them enough high paying Council annuities to bridge the gap between what they were making from Federal payments and their weekly Shares. For example, if you are now being paid monthly from Social Security, from a Federal retirement program or for losing an arm or a leg in a war, you will receive this money until your Council's computers are hooked up, ready for action. When you go to open your Possession account, take your latest check with you, uncashed. A Bank Tender will put high paying Council annuities into your account to the percentage of your former check that has been approved by Central Bill. Councils with Veterans and mental hospitals will have to make sure that those who are so disabled they cannot manage for themselves are taken care of.

If, however, you have paid into Social Security (as most of us have in the USA and some other countries) but are not old enough to receive checks yet, write to Social Security and they will send you a card saying how much you've paid. When your accounts are computerized, take this card and you will be given high paying Council annuities based on some Central Bill approved percentage. People retire as far as Social Security is concerned when their Councils become computerized and they are Members. In the new system, retirement funds will be your choice. You can buy high paying Council annuities as you wish.

Step 24

Athletic Fields. Very important, especially during this changeover time. We must have places in which to run and play games and maybe even skip. There are such places in the now, but we'll need more of them in the then. Every open space in the Council and Neighborhood can be used. A City Neighborhood can block off a street or two to give kids and adults playing room. OK? This is the job of the Council Education Committee and the Neighborhoods.

Step 25

Councils get ready for Change Day. When the work of the Bank and Lease Committee is well started, Councilors can organize into their full ten Committees according to the type of Council. On Change Day, all Councils will need a Senator's Committee and a Tax Committee which hires a temporary Head Tax Tender to help Bank Tenders set rates and collect Council taxes until the computers are installed. The Maintenance Committee will need a Head Tender to start laying plans for Council Maintenance and Peripheral and Direct transportation which Councils will need right away. One of the first services needed in many Councils will be garbage and refuse collection. The plans for the ultimate system can be had from the design section but if a Council cannot implement this plan right away, it should provide some sort of temporary service so as not to be covered in its own dung. The Electrical Committee can hire a Head Tender who will start to get ready to provide free electrical power to the People so by the end of the next three years, the Council is the only entity receiving a bill for people's electricity. This Tender can also be thinking about the small atomic power plant (s) the Council will need. Port and Transcon Committees can be planning on how to get it together while City Administration will have its hands full.

These people cannot be paid as yet until the Tax Tenders are at work. The first thing we'll do with Council tax money is pay Tenders.

Step 26

Change Day. Look at where things are:

- A year ago the rest of the world was informed of what's happening.
- RNA citizens who want to come home have arrived and foreign citizens who didn't want to stay are gone, except for diplomats and their staffs.
- The Boundary Patrol has started to patrol and build its part of Central and the PCC and Coventry areas within the present RNA.
- The relay network at Central is finished and the other computers are being worked on.
- Congress has stopped funding any governmental organizations not needed in the RNA.
- Congress has ordered starter computer kits for every Council within the present RNA boundaries.
- Councils have temporary Council Centers where people are registering and receiving their Cards. This job is about complete.

- Congress has funded the weekly Share and most people are receiving theirs in their temporary Neighborhood Order Offices. Even if they are not, the Order Office is there to keep Order and voting is possible.
- Every Council has the use of one TV station.
- Everyone who even asks for work is a Trainee.
- Each Council has a Senator and a Senator's Committee.
- A lot of people have divided their financial paper into Personal and Business, but no Council tax collection has begun.
- Fact Finders are in general use and some people who were in cages are out and others are waiting for their Challenges.
- Federal tax collection agencies are busily at work and will be until all Federal taxes due prior to Change Day have been collected.
- Gold and silver reserves are being readied to ship overseas to buy our currency back.
- The day before Change Day, all of the people voted in their Neighborhoods on the Establishment Bill, something like:

  We, the People of North America, agree to form the RNA wherein government becomes the science and art of finding out what the people want, then helping them do it.

- The Council Senators gathered up the tallied votes.

On Change Day these Senators fly to Central to meet the President of the USA and the heads of the other governments in the RNA. During the morning the Senators have been filing past a digital computer punching in their total Yes and No votes. At 1200 Hours Central Standard Time people are in their Neighborhoods watching the last Senator punch in totals. The totals flash onto a board so all can see the Bill pass substantially.

The heads of states gather in the wind, maybe even in the rain or snow, TV cameras full blast, and hand over the responsibility for carrying out the People's will to the Senators who slog over to their trailer-offices to start the process of being responsible.

Step 27

The Senators elect a Head Senator and divide themselves into Committees which immediately go to work to hire the Head Tenders of the various Central Sections. The old heads of states return to their capitals and work themselves out of a job. Many old functions will remain intact until the Central and the Councils can pick them up, like Presidents, Cabinets, Commons, Deputies, Post Offices, Weights and Measures, Patents and Copyrights, Treasuries, Mints, medical and school aid, social security and some I've probably forgotten, but NOT the FBI.

The U.S. Treasury Department will continue to be the disbursement agency of the RNA until the Councils' tax and profit structures can support them. The currency situation may get tough if there's a lot of hoarding but the Mint still has the dies and can print dollars which will become the currency in general use in the RNA until computerization because the Shares in all Councils are paid in U.S. dollars. Of course, we'll use the currency we buy back from overseas and U.S. dollars can be printed for Canadian ones, Mexican pesos, etc., if they join before the computers come. The Treasury Department will pay for building or refurbishing Council Centers, for the bills that come in from the Council computer kits as well as for the contractors building Central.

Tax collection bureaus will continue to collect taxes owed for the last year by both Business and individuals. As soon as the Councils pick up tax collecting, the old collecting bureaus can fold up their books and split turning their open files over to Tax Tenders in the individual's or Business' *home* Council for collection there.

Federal governments turn over all the land they own including National Parks, Monuments and Forests to Central. Along with the land comes enough money to supervise and maintain the Parks, etc., so they can go on as they were for the next three years.

Step 28

Central organization. Since the Central Plant and housing facilities will be the last things finished at Central, Senators, Tenders, Boundary Patrol personnel and Trainees will probably be living in a giant trailer park along the new runways but Central will be alive and running.

The Senators have set up Committees and are busy hiring Head Tenders who hire the rest of the Tenders they need. Central Tenders and the Head Senator will be paid by their Councils of registration which will be given the money by the Treasury before computerization and by the Head Business Tender after computerization. Don't be surprised if these jobs change hands often in the beginning. One person doesn't need to run with the ball all the time.

Speakers and Media Tenders will be needed right away to let people in the RNA and foreign countries know how things are going. There'll be a lot of Bills coming up for vote and we have to keep information flowing about them to the People.

The Computer Sections can put in the order for Council computer kits B which include the Business Master, the SBDT and BDT slave computers, the loan and insurance vendors, the Banker's Memory, the computers needed for Tourists and the Possession-Direct (PD) slaves needed in Possession Rooms. This Section will be hiring and training computer experts to hook up and test Council computers. When the Councils and the computers are ready, there must be a group already familiar enough with the configurations to install them and to train Council Tax Tenders. This Section will also be checking and installing Central hardware as it comes from the manufacturers.

Step 29

Change Day and beyond in the Neighborhoods. Since Neighborhoods are the basic components, cells, of the new thing, they must be operating entities by Change Day. For the RNA to stand, the Neighborhoods must be firm. They must be able to express their decisions by voting and to take care of Order. Each Neighborhood will have to take a good hard look at where it is as far as food is concerned. A Neighborhood may, for some period of time, have to be ready to cooperatively feed its People: perhaps by sending people in cars and trucks to the country to buy and pick, then store and can food for 1000. Water is important; waste disposal and fire protection must be thought of.

Soon after Change Day, Education Tenders can begin Children's education using the morning hours audio-visually and setting up *learning to be with other people* sessions in the afternoons using Trainee help.

The sooner Neighborhoods can stand up as entities, the sooner old State, Province, County and City governments can collapse—GENTLY—upon the new structure. If a Neighborhood is part of a village, small city or town, the old structure will need to be held together to provide water and other services until the Council can work it out. So, towns survive longer than States, Provinces or Counties which can disappear from sight like slowly sinking ships as they are no longer needed.

Step 30

Councils from Change Day. Councils in which the split between Business and Personal banking is finished can now start collecting taxes at the time checks are cashed for personal use. Tax Tenders will help Bank Tenders collect taxes, but these people should know more about computers than tax collecting if they are to stay on. For people who have paid their taxes owing to old governments, the Council tax becomes the only one to pay. For Businesses which are paid up—that's it—no more taxes, ever. The Treasury Department will help Councils pay Shares for three more years and that's all.

Lease fees start to be paid to Councils on Change Day as well, but there will be no foreclosures for the next three years at least. States, Provinces, Territories, Counties and Cities will no longer be financed and these old institutions can start to clear up their books and disappear. Any funds they hold can go to the Council or Councils of their choice.   Not likely. Any property they hold goes to the Council in which the piece is located. When old schools, city halls, capitol buildings and such become Council Leases, the Bank and Lease Committee can make a map showing the land available for Neighborhood and Council Centers.

Councils, then, pass Bills to locate a more permanent Council Center site and voluntary Trainees can begin building the Post Office-Bank (POB), the Computer Security and ID Rooms first, with the other rooms following. Trainees can be housed in tents, trailers, buses, empty buildings like schools or wherever is practical until Trainee Housing and Council Houses are built. Neighborhoods, too, can decide on Centers and begin building or redoing an old building according to their chosen design section plan. Councils will provide the materials, but labor will come from voluntary Trainees.

Step 31

Computerization. As the first Council computer kits are made they are sent to Central where teams of experts hook up a complete kit. They make audiovisual tapes for installation teams on how to set up the configurations and check them out.

The first Council to be computerized will be the one Central is in. This Council can be compared to the spot where a pebble is dropped into a still pond. Computerization will follow the wave pattern until a megapolis Relay Station is reached. Here another pebble is dropped and computerization will follow its wave pattern. Right?

The installation team needed will consist of an expert in each of the configurations plus assistants, telephone company installers, Business Tenders and Trainees. These teams are trained at Central and one member of each team will stay behind to replace the temporary Head Tax Tender for the Council. These Council installations then become training grounds along with Central and the installation teams expand like a giant chain letter. Out of the first installation group comes enough groups to install the surrounding Councils until at peak there will be like 250 teams operating with problems being relayed by facsimile to Central for solution by the team coordinators. If it takes three months to install a Council's computers, about 200 Councils could be computerized the first year, 600 the second year and the rest the third year. As phase one kits are done, the teams will return to connect phase two: the Business Masters, etc.

The general procedure is:

1. The Masters are mounted on the prepared foundations.
2. The voting and other cross connections are installed.
3. The slaves in Neighborhood and Council Centers are tied in.
4. The system is tested under every conceivable mode of operation and power supply.
5. Council Tax Tenders are instructed in use, maintenance and repair of all equipment and the installation team nurses the Council through one voting day, then moves into the next Councils having picked up more trained experts from Central and leaving behind the new Head Tax Tender and the Business Tenders.

Tax Tenders will begin by transferring recorded ID and E Numbers from the tapes to the Numbers Master using the Numbers-Direct slave.

Now starts the Big Parade. Every individual is urged to see where the Master computers live and what they look like. People do this by going to the ID Room and registering their A Numbers, their vehicle numbers and land lease numbers to be crossfiled when the Library Central is working. They are then escorted through the Security Room to watch their E and A Numbers registered into the Exchange Master. This parade will last three months when cash disbursement of Shares stops. From here on out Share Credits will appear in everyone's account automatically once a week, Cards will be used to spend Credits and Council tax will be paid on Credits spent from accounts in E Master computers.

To begin with, the tax rate will be the one we have been paying at the Personal bank. The weekly income represented by this rate of tax will be punched into the EM 50 times. The next week our actual income will be added and one of those 50 weeks will be subtracted.

During these three months, there'll be a lot of Audio-Visual going on so everyone can learn how to use the Card. People will go to the Personal bank with their cash and, with a Bank Tender's and Business Tender's help, they will transfer this cash plus the assets they have in the bank into Credits in their Exchange and Possession accounts, remembering that anything put into the Possession Master cannot be reached until they become Members. Those in Business will then head over to the Business bank to pick up a check for assets they wish to transfer to the Small Business Master—from there to the new POB to rent a slave computer and get a B Number—a quick walk to the ID Room for a Card with the B Number on it and back to the POB where Bank Tenders and Business Tenders will help transfer the check into Credits in the Small Business Master. The only person who can change cash or bank deposits into Credits is a Central Business Tender.

To register a vehicle, give the Trainee in the ID Room the kind of vehicle, the manufacturer, the model and year and the month in which you bought it (guess, if you can't remember) and the Trainee will complete the number. Now, you can make your own license plates (two) as the license plate makers have quit. Vehicle manufacturers will start assigning numbers and stamping them on as soon as they gain confidence in the system.

Six months have passed since the computer installation team arrived in the Council. They installed for three months and people were starting to use the installations for the next three months. This second three month period might be confusing while some people use old currency and some, Credits, but with everyone receiving a Share in cash, it will work out. Remember all Council facilities are open 24 hours a day, every day. The big day arrives and whirrr hummm , you'll never have to count money or figure tax again, unless you go visiting.

Personal and Business banks will still be needed, so don't go away just yet. Personal banks and other banks taken over by the Council will receive Council Bank Shares for their bank shares held by stockholders of record as of Change Day based on the bank's condition. These Shares are worthless right now but wait. As people in a Council become Members, Personal bank personnel will be kept on the Council payroll to process people's public debt claims into low paying Council annuities; Social Security, government retirement and veterans payments into high paying annuities; and help with corporation stock shares, lease liens and other loans. These things will be put into accounts in the Possession Master. When a Personal bank has reduced its pile of paper to the uncollectables and untransferables, it can quietly disappear. Business banks that are retained by Business, i.e., not taken over by the Council, are none of our business. They become Business business.

What happens when computerization has begun and there are a few lone Councils in the center of North America using Credits while throughout the rest of the RNA people are using old currency? Central Business Tenders will stay in a Council about 30 days after computerization is complete to make tardy changes, then they go to the periphery which could still be in that Council. A money barrier is set up at the periphery with Credits on the inside and dollars on the outside. Remember, people get their Shares in dollars no matter where they live until their money is computerized. To cross the barrier, Central Business Tenders will be on hand to transfer cash into Credits and vice versa. Card making machines and Tourist Tenders will also be on hand to make like a Tourist Card, the same kind they'll make later for visitors to the RNA.

Step 32

Financing Central. The Senators at Central might become a little anxious to start their projects before the three years are up and there is a Central Budget Bill. As soon as about 100 Councils have been computerized, these Councils can begin to pay Central for their computers, FF machines and their Council Centers by selling high paying Council annuities. This money can be deposited into Central's account in that Council's Business Master computer giving the Central some bread to start things like surveying ocean and other natural resources. There may even be enough to lend Councils so they can order small atomic power plants.

On the day the last of the Councils that approved the Establishment Bill on Change Day is computerized, Central Business Tenders will stop giving the currency they've been collecting back to the Treasury Department to disburse. The Treasury Department will transfer over to the Head Business Tender and will stand ready to pay out Shares and loans in dollars until the last Council in North America is part of the RNA. This Treasury function of the Central Business Section will retain enough dollars to accomplish this purpose. It will also pay late joiners' foreign debts in gold and silver. Old currencies (most dollars included) will be destroyed or kept until the whole RNA is computerized to sell to numismatists.

It's time for the first Central Budget Bill and a Bill to determine the actual number of Credits that will be in circulation to be voted on. We're ready to open up the Ports of Entry and resume trading and touristing. The old Federal governments involved in the RNA have dephased themselves and shut down leaving Museums and Libraries behind.

Step 33

OK, what's next? With computerization completed and Central fully operating, the North American countries which haven't joined the RNA can watch the gain in time and efficiency computerization gives us: the time and freedom to live. They can either join or not as they wish and when they wish. I don't feel that any country which, given the option to join, would stay out very long after watching it work.

When we are gathered in Neighborhoods of People who like each other and have the same sorts of living patterns; when the place is starting to look clean and beautiful with flowers and kids are playing in the streets where cars used to rush by; when cities smell better and people are healthier...a little poorer in money maybe, but richer in life, we got it on.

When the Councils and Central are pulling together to make the same basic standard of living possible for all with more for those who want to stretch a bit, it's a gas.

When everyone seems to have more time to live and Be, that's us...BLOSSOMING.

When the Fact Finders begin to rust from lack of use because what's the use of lying or teaching kids to, we got it on.

When people actually begin to FEEL they have a say about what's happening, they walk tall.

When the automatic machines pull our pollution-free economy back up to the level we deserve as creative people of this planet and the People's Share is enough to allow everyone their time in the sun, who's suffering?

When People can learn anything they want to and have found out that each is different from the other and it's fun, we got it on.

When all these things are done and many more that are available to a free, creative and loving people, throw the book away and go from there. OK? We can wander the earth together on diverse paths each understanding that the other is busy and a smile is sufficient.

HUMANKIND WILL LEARN TO PROGRESS WITHOUT CONTENTION

AND LIVE IN COOPERATION

AFTERWORD

John Muir died in November 1977—at home surrounded by friends/family, somewhat prepared to go on what he called "the greatest journey of them all."

I'd like to share with new readers some of his thoughts about *The Velvet Monkey Wrench*. He really appreciated people who could see how funny it is. And, in a new edition, he wanted to emphasize the size and type of atomic power plants. "They're still into huge and dirty," he said, "don't seem to be able to change their *bomb* mentality."

He suggested that someone might design and build a small box that could run a household or a car for many years. When it was exhausted, we'd take it to the Council Recharging Center for immediate servicing. Each of us with a tiny piece of the sun in a box—a birthright.

"I suppose," he pulled on his long-haired eyebrows, "if you have power over people it's impossible to give it up. Greed is hard to change."

"If people behaved in the way nations do they would all be put in straitjackets." —Tennessee Williams, American dramatist (1911-1983)

We've traveled in time to a new century, the 21st—at least by the Western calendar—and I, for one, cannot see where we've learned a whole lot in the last 100 years. Maybe during these next 100 years we can agree to change the things that aren't working for most of us. We have all the data from the botched experiments in the 20th as what not to do. (*Fact:* each day, the world produces enough grain to adequately feed every man, woman and child. *Fact:* each day, sixty-thousand people die from hunger and related diseases.)

It amazes and amuses me how far ahead John could project, like envisioning electronic money, trial by TV, housing for juveniles (although this housing is still used as punishment rather than as loving living). We're playing with the speed limit concept and have allowed states to enact their own, but we still don't drive by our individual speed limits.

John did not foresee the web in cyberspace, except as way out there sci-fi as written by Robert Heinlein. He would have adored it, however, because it seems to be a means of communication that, so far at least, is fairly uncontrollable. We mice are getting out from under the cat's thumbs. We'll have to watch and see how much control the honchos in China can muster.

He also did not foresee that the multinational corporations would become even larger and more powerful, exploiting people and environments as they please, by law not answerable to any except their stockholders, most of whom seem to be into making money no matter what. Maybe in the 21st century stockholders will learn to be more environmentally and humanistically aware. Like, not allowing their chosen corporations to continue to poison us.

More than once John and I fought heartily over the words:

MANKIND MUST LEARN TO PROGRESS WITHOUT CONTENTION.

I wanted:

HUMANKIND MUST LEARN TO PROGRESS WITHOUT CONTENTION

because "man" made me feel left out. He kept saying that mankind included all humans and enough women agreed with him that my case went down the drain. In the end, however, by lasting longer, I win.

It probably is time that we humans learn to progress without contention, then continue with cooperation, and eventually maybe...with love.

"There is a Law that man should love his neighbor as himself.
In a few hundred years it should be as natural to mankind as breathing or
the upright gait; but if he does not learn it he must perish."
—Alfred Adler, Austrian psychoanalyst (1870-1937)

Eve Muir
New Orleans, 1999

"If man has conquered the air merely to fill it with bombs and illiteracy,
we might as well discount this civilization and try a new one."
—Robertson Davies, Canadian author (1913-1995)

"Government is actually the worst failure of civilized man. There has
never been a really good one, and even those that are most tolerable are
arbitrary, cruel, grasping, and unintelligent."
—H.L. Menken, American journalist, critic and essayist (1880-1956)

"It was naive of the 19th century optimists to expect paradise from technology
—and it is equally naive of the 20th century pessimists to make technology
the scapegoat for such old shortcomings as man's blindness, cruelty,
immaturity, greed and sinful pride."
—Peter F. Drucker, management philosopher (1909-)

ORDER BLANKS

IF YOUR DEALER CANNOT SUPPLY YOU, ORDER DIRECT FROM US!

Please send ____ copies of *The Velvet Monkey Wrench*
@ $20 each (postage paid) to:

Name _____

Address _____

City & State _____ Zip _____

OCEAN TREE BOOKS, PO Box 1295, Santa Fe NM 87504

Please send ____ copies of *The Velvet Monkey Wrench*
@ $20 each (postage paid) to:

Name _____

Address _____

City & State _____ Zip _____

OCEAN TREE BOOKS, PO Box 1295, Santa Fe NM 87504

"The Cut-Away City" (frontispiece), 25" x 34" poster,
$18 each (postage paid), *signed by Peter Aschwanden
and mailed to you in a tube:*

Name _____

Address _____

City & State _____ Zip _____

FLATHEAD GRAPHIX, PO Box 45, Coyote, NM 87012

Foreign orders: Payment must be in US$ (PMO or check drawn on a U.S. bank)